10,000
GERMAN
WORDS

Also available

The Oxford Paperback German Dictionary
German Grammar
10,000 German Words

The Oxford Paperback French Dictionary
French Grammar
French Verbs
10,000 French Words

The Oxford Paperback Italian Dictionary
The Oxford Paperback Spanish Dictionary

10,000
GERMAN
WORDS

William Rowlinson

Oxford   New York

OXFORD UNIVERSITY PRESS

1994

Oxford University Press, Walton Street, Oxford OX2 6DP

Oxford New York Toronto
Delhi Bombay Calcutta Madras Karachi
Kuala Lumpur Singapore Hong Kong Tokyo
Nairobi Dar es Salaam Cape Town
Melbourne Auckland Madrid

and associated companies in
Berlin Ibadan

Oxford is a trade mark of Oxford University Press

British Library Cataloguing in Publication Data
Data available

Library of Congress Cataloging in Publication Data
Data available
ISBN 019 283095 3

1 3 5 7 9 10 8 6 4 2

Typeset by Pentacor PLC, *High Wycombe, Bucks*
Printed in Great Britain by
Clays Ltd.
Bungay Suffolk

CONTENTS

INTRODUCTION

This book contains more than 10,000 German words, phrases, and structures arranged by topic and function. They are collected under fifty-six headings ordered alphabetically, and are then further split into appropriate sub-areas.

The aim has been to make the vocabulary of a topic easily accessible and to provide the most comprehensive information possible about it. So most sub-areas are themselves divided into noun, verb, adjective, and structure sections, with items arranged alphabetically within each section. For many items, closely associated words are given in round brackets immediately after the headword.

- Genders of all head-nouns are indicated by **der/ die/das**, bracketed where the noun is usually used without its article. The gender of an element in a noun phrase is shown by *m* or *f*.
- Irregular genitive singulars and all plurals of nouns that commonly take a plural are given, in square brackets after the noun.
- Feminine forms of masculine nouns (e.g. professions, occupations) are given, where they exist.
- Cases taken by prepositions are given in all prepositional constructions.
- Irregular verbs are asterisked, separable prefixes are marked off by |, inseparable ones by '.
- Main sections end with a comprehensive set of cross-references to related topics.

ABBREVIATIONS

abb	abbreviation
A	accusative
adj	adjective
adj n	adjective used as noun
colloq	colloquial
D	dative
jm	**jemandem** (somebody, *dative*)
jn	**jemanden** (somebody, *accusative*)
et	**etwas** (something)
f	feminine
G	genitive
inf	infinitive
inv	invariable
m	masculine
n	neuter
℗	proprietary term
pl	plural
sb	somebody
sing	singular
sth	something

PLURALS

If a diphthong is umlauted in the plural, the umlaut goes on the first of the two vowels (**Baum, Bäume**).

Final **ß** changes to **ss** when a plural ending is added, unless the previous vowel is long (**Biß, Bisse**; **Fuß, Füße**). A change in the plural from **ß** to **ss** is indicated thus: **Biß [-sse]**.

1. Accidents Unfälle

der Aufprall [-e] impact
die Explosion [-en] explosion
der Flugzeugabsturz [ˑe]; **das Flugzeugunglück** [-e] aircraft crash
die Gehirnerschütterung concussion
das Mißgeschick [-e] mishap
das Pech bad luck (**Pech *haben bei/mit** + D have bad luck with;
  vom Pech verfolgt *sein be dogged by bad luck)
die Rücksichtslosigkeit heedlessness
der Schaden [ˑ] *often pl* damage (**der Schaden(s)ersatz**
  compensation; **Schaden(s)ersatz leisten für** + A compensate for)
der Schock [-s] shock
die Seenot distress at sea (**jn aus Seenot retten** rescue sb in
  distress)
der/die Tote *adj n* dead person
der Unfall [ˑe] accident (**der Arbeits-/Verkehrsunfall** industrial/
  traffic accident)
die Verbrennung [-en] burn
die Vergeßlichkeit forgetfulness
die Verletzung [-en] injury (**der/die Verletzte** *adj n* injured
  person)
der Zeuge [-n]/**die Zeugin** [-nen] witness (**der Augenzeuge/die
  Augenzeugin** eye-witness; **der Augenzeugenbericht** [-e] eye-
  witness report)
der Zufall [ˑe] chance; coincidence
der Zusammenstoß [ˑe]; **der Zusammenprall** [-e] collision

be'schädigen damage
das Bewußtsein *ver'lieren lose consciousness
*davon|kommen (**mit** + D) escape (with)
demolieren demolish
er'sticken suffocate
explodieren explode
kaputt|machen destroy

*sterben die (**seinen Verletzungen** *f* D *pl* ***er'liegen** die of one's injuries)
töten; ***um|bringen** kill
*um|kommen get killed
ums Leben *kommen lose one's life
*ver'gessen forget
*ver'lieren lose
ver'ursachen cause
*zer'brechen break
zer'stören smash up; destroy
*zusammen|stoßen; **zusammen|prallen** collide

betrunken drunk
eingeschlossen [person]; **eingeklemmt** [part of body] trapped
gedankenlos thoughtless
leichtsinnig reckless
sicher und wohlbehalten safe and sound
tot dead
unaufmerksam inattentive
ungeschickt clumsy
unversehrt unscathed
unvorsichtig careless
verletzt injured (**leicht** slightly; **schwer** seriously)
zerstreut absent-minded

Verkehrsunfälle und Eisenbahnunglücke
Road and rail accidents

Alkohol *m* **am Steuer** drunken driving (**das Steuer** [-] steering-wheel; **unter Alkoholeinfluß** *m* under the influence of alcohol; **die Alkoholkontrolle** [-n] breath test; **der Führerscheinentzug** [ᵉe] disqualification; driving ban)
das Eisenbahnunglück [-e] rail accident
die Entgleisung [-en] derailment
die Geldstrafe [-n] fine
das Glatteis black ice

die Massenkarambolage [-n] pile-up
die Müdigkeit fatigue (***leiden an** + D suffer from)
der Nebel fog (**die schlechte Sicht** poor visibility)
der Prellblock [railway] buffers
das Rasen speeding (**die Geschwindigkeitsüberschreitung** [-en] [legal term] (case of) speeding)
die Reifenpanne [-n]; **der Platte** *adj n* puncture
der Straßenzustand state of the road
der Totalschaden write off (**Totalshaden *ent'steht an** + D . . . is a write-off)
das Überholen overtaking (**beim Überholen** when overtaking)
der Verkehrsrowdy [-s] road-hog
der Verkehrsunfall [⁼e] traffic accident
das Versagen failure (**die Bremsen ver'sagen** the brakes fail)
der Zusammenstoß [⁼e] crash (**der Frontalzusammenstoß** head-on crash)

be'schleunigen accelerate
ent'gleisen be derailed
*fahren gegen + A run into
die Kontrolle *ver'lieren lose control
die näheren Umstände *auf|schreiben take the particulars
platzen burst
riskieren risk (**sein Leben in Gefahr *bringen** risk one's life)
das Rotlicht [-er]/**das Signal** [-e] ***über'fahren** go through the red light/signal
schlittern; [more serious] **schleudern** skid (**ins Schleudern *ge'raten** go into a skid)
*über'fahren run over
über'holen overtake (**in der Kurve** on the bend)
sich *über'schlagen turn over
die Vorfahrt nicht be'achten ignore priority; not give way

Unfälle auf See Accidents at sea

das Ertrinken drowning
der/die Ertrunkene *adj n* drowned person

4 ACCIDENTS

die Kollision [-en] collision [between ships] **(auf Kollisionskurs** *m*
on a collision course)
die Mannschaft [-en] crew
das Rettungsboot [-e] lifeboat **(das Rettungsfloß [ⁿe]** life-raft;
der Rettungsring [-e] lifebelt)
der Schiffbruch shipwreck **(Schiffbruch *er'leiden** be ship-
wrecked)
die Schwimmweste [-n] life-jacket

*er'trinken drown
gegen einen Felsen/eine Mine/einen Eisberg *laufen hit a rock/
mine/iceberg
kollidieren collide [of ships]
retten rescue
*schwimmen to swim **(schwimmen *können** be able to swim)
*sinken sink
unter der Wasserlinie leckgeschlagen *sein be holed under the
waterline

Flugzeugunglücke Aircraft accidents

der Absturz [ⁿe] crash
die Bruchlandung [-en] crash-landing
der Fallschirm [-e] parachute
der Irrtum [ⁿer] des Piloten pilot error
das Luftloch [ⁿer] air pocket
die Metallermüdung metal fatigue
der Motorschaden engine trouble
der Notausgang [ⁿe] emergency exit
die Notlandung [-en] forced landing
der Steward [-s] steward **(die Stewardeß [-ssen]** stewardess)
die Turbulenz turbulence

aus|setzen fail [engine]
bruch|landen *inf and past part. only* crash-land
landen land **(im Bach landen** *colloq* ditch)
notlanden *inf and past part.*(**notgelandet**) *only* do an emergency
landing

Unfälle im Haushalt Accidents in the home

das Feuer [-] fire (**der Rauchmelder** [-] smoke alarm; **die
Feuertreppe** [-n] fire-escape)
der Stromschlag [ːe] electric shock (**einen Stromschlag
*be'kommen** get an electric shock; **durch Stromschlag getötet
*werden** be electrocuted)
der Sturz [ːe] (**aus/von** + D) fall (from)

*fallen fall (***fallen|lassen** drop)
sich [D] **den Knöchel** [etc.] **ver'stauchen/*brechen** sprain/break
one's ankle [etc.]
sich *schneiden an + D cut oneself on (**sich** [D or A] **in den
Finger** [etc.] **schneiden** cut one's finger [etc.])
*um|stoßen knock over
sich *ver'brennen burn oneself
sich ver'brühen scald oneself
ver'schütten spill

Die Notdienste Emergency services

der Abschleppwagen [-] breakdown truck (**der Abbschleppdienst**
recovery service)
der Arzt [ːe]/**die Ärztin** [-nen] doctor
die Erste Hilfe first aid
der Feuerlöscher [-] fire extinguisher
die Feuerwehr fire brigade (**der Feuerwehrmann** [*pl* ːer or **-leute**]
fireman; **die Leiter** [-n] ladder; **der Schlauch** [ːe] hose)
die Hilfe help
der Krankenwagen [-] ambulance
die Mund-zu-Mund-Beatmung kiss of life (**der Mund** [ːer] mouth)
der Notfall [ːe] emergency
der Pannendienst breakdown service
die Polizei police
der Rettungsdienst ambulance service (**der Seerettungsdienst**
lifeboat service)
der/die Sanitäter/in [-/-nen] ambulance man/woman

6 ACCIDENTS

die Trage [-n] stretcher
der Verbandskasten [≑]; die Erste-Hilfe-Ausrüstung first-aid kit
die Versicherung [-en] insurance

ab|schleppen tow away
Bereitschaftsdienst *m* *haben be on call
einen Bericht er'statten make a report
einen Krankenwagen kommen *lassen call an ambulance
die Polizei *an|rufen call the police (110 [eins eins null] wählen
  dial 999)

SEE ALSO: **Birth, Marriage, and Death; Disasters; Health and Sickness; The Human Body**

2. Adornment Verschönerung

Make-up Make-up

der Augenbrauenstift [-e] eyebrow pencil (**die Augenbraue [-n]** eyebrow)

der Entferner [-] remover

der Eyeliner [-] eye-liner

die Feuchtigkeitscreme [-s] moisturizer

die Gesichtscreme [-s] face cream (**das Gesicht [-er]** face)

der Gesichtspuder face-powder (**die Puderdose [-n]** compact; **die Puderquaste [-n]** powder-puff)

die Grundierungscreme [-s] foundation cream

der Körperpuder talcum powder (**der Körper [-]** body)

die Kosmetik beauty culture

der Lidschatten eye-shadow (**das Lid [-er]** eyelid)

die Lippenpomade [-n] lipsalve

der Lippenstift [-e] lipstick (**die Lippe [-n]** lip)

der Lockenwickler [-] curler

das Make-up make-up

das Mascara; die Wimperntusche mascara

die Nagelfeile [-n] nail-file (**der Nagel [=]** nail; **die Sandpapierfeile** emery board)

der Nagellack nail varnish (**der Nagellackentferner** nail-varnish remover)

die Nagelschere [-n] (pair of) nail scissors

die Nagelzange [-n] (pair of) nail clippers

das Papiertuch [=er] paper tissue

die Pinzette [-n] (pair of) tweezers

das Rouge blusher

die Schönheit beauty (**der Schönheits-/Kosmetiksalon [-s]** beauty salon; **die Schönheitsprodukte** *n pl*; **die Kosmetika** *n pl* cosmetics)

der Spiegel [-] mirror

sich ab|schminken take off one's make-up
***auf|tragen auf** + A put on [lipstick etc.]
sich [D] die Fingernägel lackieren varnish one's nails
sich schminken make up (one's face)
sich zurecht|machen put on one's make-up

Schmuck Jewellery

der Anhänger [-] pendant
die Anstecknadel [-n] pin
das Armband [ːer] bracelet (**das Glieder-/Amulettarmband** chain/
  charm bracelet)
die Armbanduhr [-en] (wrist-)watch
der Armreif(en) [-e/-] bangle
die Brosche [-n] brooch
das Diadem [-e] tiara
das Halsband [ːer] choker
das/der Juwel [-en]; [more valuable] **der Edelstein [-e]** jewel
  [= precious stone] (**das Schmuckstück [-e]** jewel [= ornament];
  der Halbedelstein semi-precious stone; **künstlich; Kunst-**
  imitation)
die Kette/Halskette [-n]; **das Kollier [-s]** necklace
das Kettchen [-] (neck-)chain; chain-bracelet
der Klipp [-s]/der Clip [-s] clip (**der Ohr(en)klipp** ear-clip)
der Krawattenhalter [-] tie-clip
die Krawattennadel [-n] tie-pin
das Kreuz [-e] cross
die Krone [-n] crown
der Manschettenknopf [ːe] cuff-link
der Ohrring [-e] ear-ring (**das Ohrgehänge [-]** drop ear-ring)
der Ring [-e] ring (**der Trau-/Ehering** wedding-ring; **der**
  Verlobungs-/Siegelring engagement/signet ring)
der Schmuck jewellery (**der Modeschmuck** costume jewellery)
der Schmuckkasten [ː] jewel box
die Tiara [*pl* Tiaren] tiara
die Uhr [-en] watch (**die Quarz/Digitaluhr** quartz/digital watch)

Edelsteine und Metalle Jewels and Metals

der **Amethyst** [-e] amethyst
der **Bernstein** amber
das **Chrom** chromium (**verchromt** chrome-plated)
der **Diamant** [-en] diamond
das **Elfenbein** [substance] ivory (**eine Elfenbeinschnitzerei** [-en] an
  ivory [object]; **elfenbeinern** ivory *adj*)
die **Emaille/das Email** enamel (**emailliert** enamel *adj*)
das **Gold** gold (**golden** gold(en); **vergoldet** gold-plated; gilt)
der/die **Jade** jade
die **Koralle** [-n] coral (**korallen** coral *adj*)
das **Kristall** crystal [glass] (**der Kristall** [-e] crystal [formation])
das **Kupfer** copper (**kupfern** copper *adj*)
der **Onyx** [-e] onyx
die **Perle** [-n] pearl; bead (**die Perlenkette** [-n] pearl necklace;
  string of beads)
der **Pewter** pewter
das **Platin** platinum
der **Rubin** [-e] ruby
der **Saphir** [-e] sapphire
das **Silber** silver (**silbern** silver *adj*; **versilbert** silver- plated)
der **Smaragd** [-e] emerald
der **Stahl** steel (**rostfrei** stainless; **der Edelstahl** stainless steel)
der **Straß** [-sse]; der **Similistein** [-e] imitation gem
der **Topas** [-e] topaz
der **Türkis** [-e] turquoise
das **Zinn** tin; pewter

Parfüm Perfume

das **Badesalz** bath salts (**das Schaumbad** bubble bath)
das **Deodorant** [*pl* -s or -e] deodorant
das **Eau de Cologne**; das **Kölnisch Wasser** eau-de-Cologne
das **Parfüm/Parfum** [-s] perfume; scent
das/der **Spray** [-s] spray (**das/der Deospray** deodorant spray)

10 ADORNMENT

das Toilettenwasser; das Eau de Toilette toilet water

sich parfümieren put on perfume
*riechen; [pleasanter] **duften nach** + D smell of

SEE ALSO: **Clothing; Describing People; Hair; The Human Body**

3. Animals Tiere

die **Amphibie** [-n] amphibian
das **Beuteltier** [-e] marsupial
der **Fisch** [-e] fish
das **Insekt** [-en] insect
das **Reptil** [-ien] reptile
das **Säugetier** [-e] mammal
das **Tier** [-e] animal (**das Haustier** pet)
der **Vogel** [⸗] bird (**der Raubvogel** bird of prey; **das Geflügel** poultry)
das **Weichtier** [-e]; die **Molluske** [-n] mollusc
das **Wirbeltier** [-e] vertebrate (**der Evertebrat** [-en] invertebrate)
der **Wurm** [⸗er] worm

Säugetiere Mammals

der **Affe** [-n] monkey
die **Antilope** [-n] antelope
der **Bär** [-en] bear (**der Eisbär** polar bear)
der **Biber** [-] beaver
der **Bock** [⸗e] buck; ram; billy-goat
der **Büffel** [-] buffalo
der **Dachs** [-e] badger (**der Bau** [-e] sett)
der **Delphin** [-e] dolphin
das **Eichhörnchen** [-] squirrel
der **Elefant** [-en] elephant
der **Esel** [-] donkey
die **Feld-/Wühlmaus** [⸗e] vole
die **Fledermaus** [⸗e] bat
das **Frettchen** [-] ferret
der **Fuchs** [⸗e] fox (**die Füchsin** [-nen] vixen)
die **Gazelle** [-n] gazelle
die **Gemse** [-n] chamois
die **Giraffe** [-n] giraffe

der Gorilla [-s] gorilla

der Hamster [-] hamster

der Hase [-n] hare (**die Häsin** [-nen] doe-hare)

der Hirsch [-e] deer; stag

der Hund [-e] dog (**die Hündin** [-nen] bitch; **der junge Hund** puppy; **der Schäfer-/Windhund** Alsatian/greyhound; **die Hundehütte** [-n] kennel; **wau, wau!** bow-wow!)

die Hyäne [-n] hyena

der Igel [-] hedgehog

der Iltis [-se] polecat

das Kamel [-e] camel (**das Dromedar** [-e] dromedary)

das Kaninchen [-] rabbit (**der Stall** [⸗e] hutch)

die Katze [-n] cat (**der Kater** [-] tom-cat; **das Kätzchen** [-] kitten; **miau!** miaow!)

die Kuh [⸗e] cow (**der Stier** [-e]; **der Bulle** [-n] bull; **das Kalb** [⸗er] calf; **das Rind** [-er] cow/bull; *pl* cattle; **das Vieh** cattle; **der Kuhstall** [⸗e] cowshed; **muh!** moo!)

der Leopard [-en] leopard

der Löwe [-n] lion (**die Löwin** [-nen] lioness)

der Luchs [-e] lynx

das Maultier [-e] mule

der Maulwurf [⸗e] mole

die Maus [⸗e] mouse (**die Brand-/Haselmaus** field-mouse/dormouse)

das Meerschweinchen [-] guinea-pig

das Nashorn [⸗er] rhinoceros

das Nil-/Flußpferd [-e] hippopotamus

der Ochse [-n] ox

der Otter/Fischotter [-] otter

der Panther [-] panther

das Pferd [-e] horse (**die Stute** [-n] mare; **das Fohlen** [-] foal; **das Hengstfohlen** [-] colt; **das Arbeitspferd** cart-horse; **das Pony** [-s] pony; **der Pferdestall** [⸗e] stable)

der Pudel [-] poodle

die Ratte [-n] rat

das Reh [-e] roe-deer (**das (Reh)kitz** [-e] fawn)

das Renntier [-e] reindeer

die Robbe [-n]; **der Seehund** [-e] seal
das Schaf [-e] sheep (**das Mutterschaf** ewe; **der Schafbock** [ᵘe];
  der Widder [-] ram; **das Lamm** [ᵘer] lamb; **der Schafstall** [ᵘe]
  sheep-fold; **mäh!**; **bäh!** baa!)
das Schwein [-e] pig (**die Sau** [ᵘe] sow; **der Eber** [-] boar; **das
  Wildschwein** [-e] wild boar; **das Ferkel** [-] piglet; **der
  Schweinestall** [ᵘe] pigsty)
der Schweinswal [-e] porpoise
der Seelöwe [-n] sea-lion
das Stachelschwein [-e] porcupine
der Tiger [-] tiger (**die Tigerin** [-nen] tigress)
der Wal [-e]; **der Walfisch** [-e] whale
das Wiesel [-] weasel
der Wolf [ᵘe] wolf (**die Wölfin** [-nen] she-wolf)
das Zebra [-s] zebra
die Ziege [-n] goat (**der Ziegenbock** [ᵘe] billy-goat; **die Zicke** [-n]
  nanny-goat; **das Kitz** [-e]; **das Zicklein** [-] kid)

Vögel Birds

der Adler [-] eagle (**der Horst** [-e] eyrie)
der Alk [G -s *pl* -en] auk
die Amsel [-n] blackbird
der Beo [-s] mynah bird
der Buchfink [-en] chaffinch
der Bussard [-e] buzzard
die Dohle [-n] jackdaw
die Drossel [-n] thrush
der Eisvogel [ᵘ] kingfisher
die Elster [-n] magpie
die Ente [-n] duck (**der Enterich** [-e]; **der Erpel** [-] drake; **das
  Entenküken** [-] duckling)
die Eule [-n] owl (**der Uhu** [-s] eagle owl; **die Schleiereule** barn
  owl)
der Falke [-n] falcon
der Fink [-en] finch
der Flamingo [-s] flamingo

die Gans [ºe] goose (**der Gänserich** [-e] gander; **das Gänseküken**
  gosling)
der Geier [-] vulture
der Gimpel [-] bullfinch
der Habicht [-e] hawk
das Huhn [ºer] chicken; hen (**der Hahn** [ºe] cock; **die Henne** [-n]
  hen; **das Küken** [-] chick; **der Hühnerstall** [ºe] hen-house;
  kikeriki! cock-a-doodle-doo!)
der Ibis [-se] ibis
der Kakadu [-s] cockatoo
der Kanarienvogel [º] canary
der Kiebitz [-e] lapwing
der Kormoran [-e] cormorant
die Krähe [-n] crow
der Kuckuck [-e] cuckoo
die Lerche [-n] lark
der Mauersegler [-] swift
die Meise [-n] tit (**die Blaumeise** blue tit)
die Möwe [-n] gull
die Nachtigall [-en] nightingale
der Papagei [G -en or -s *pl* -e(n)] parrot
der Papageientaucher [-] puffin
der Pelikan [-e] pelican
der Pfau [-en] peacock (**die Pfauhenne** [-n] peahen)
der Pinguin [-e] penguin
der Rabe [-n] raven
der Raubvogel [º] bird of prey
das Rauhfußhuhn [ºer] grouse
der Reiher [-] heron
das Rotkehlchen [-] robin
die Saatkrähe [-n] rook
die Schwalbe [-n] swallow
der Schwan [ºe] swan
der Sittich [-e] parakeet (**der Wellensittich** budgerigar)
der Spatz [-en]; **der Sperling** [-e] sparrow
der Specht [-e] woodpecker
der Star [-e] starling

der **Stieglitz** [-e]; der **Distelfink** [-en] goldfinch
der **Storch** [ِe] stork
der **Strauß** [-e] ostrich
die **Taube** [-n] dove; pigeon (die **Ringel-/Turteltaube** wood-
    pigeon/turtle-dove)
das **Teichhuhn** [ِer] moorhen
der **Truthahn** [ِe]/die **Truthenne** [-n]; [especially food] der **Puter**
    [-]/die **Pute** [-n]/turkey(-cock)/turkey-hen

Fische und Weichtiere Fish and molluscs

der **Goldfisch** [-e] goldfish (das **Goldfischglas** [ِer] goldfish-bowl)
der **Hai** [-e]; der **Haifisch** [-e] shark
der **Krake** [-n] octopus
die **Qualle** [-n] jellyfish
der **Seeigel** [-] sea-urchin
das **Seepferdchen** [-] sea-horse
der **Tintenfisch** cuttlefish; octopus; squid

FOR EDIBLE FISH SEE: **Food**

Insekten Insects

die **Ameise** [-n] ant
die **Biene** [-n] bee (die **Hummel** [-n] bumble-bee; der **Bienenstock**
    [ِe] beehive; der **Bienenstich** [-e] bee-sting)
der **Falter** [-] moth; butterfly (der **Nachtfalter** moth; die **Motte**
    [-n] clothes moth; der **Schmetterling** [-e] butterfly; die **Raupe** [-n]
    caterpillar; die **Puppe** [-n] chrysalis)
die **Fliege** [-n] fly (die **Stuben-/Schmeißfliege** house-fly/blue-
    bottle)
der **Floh** [ِe] flea
die **Grille** [-n] cricket
die **Heuschrecke** [-n] grasshopper (die **Wanderheuschrecke**
    locust)
die **Hornisse** [-n] hornet
der **Käfer** [-] beetle

die **Schabe/Küchenschabe** [-n]; der **Kakerlak** [-en] cockroach
die **Larve** [-n] grub
die **Laus** [-̈e] louse
die **Libelle** [-n] dragon-fly
die **Made** [-n] maggot
der **Maikäfer** [-] cockchafer
der **Marienkäfer** [-] ladybird
der **Moskito** [-s] mosquito
die **Mücke/Stechmücke** [-n] midge; gnat; mosquito
die **Pferdebremse** [-n] horse-fly
die **Schnake** [-n]; der **Weberknecht** [-e] daddy-long-legs
die **Spinne** [-n] spider (das **Spinnennetz** [-e] spider's web)
die **Wanze** [-n] bug
die **Wespe** [-n] wasp
die **Zikade** [-n] cicada

Reptilien, Amphibien und Würmer
Reptiles, amphibians, and worms

der **Alligator** [G -s *pl* -en] alligator
die **Blindschleiche** [-n] slow-worm; blindworm
die **Boa** [-s] boa
der **Egel/Blutegel** [-] leech
die **Eidechse** [-n] lizard
der **Frosch** [-̈e] frog (die **Kaulquappe** [-n] tadpole)
die **Kobra** [-s] cobra
das **Krokodil** [-e] crocodile
die **Kröte** [-n] toad
die **Meeres-/Wasserschildkröte** [-n] turtle
die **Pythonschlange** [-n] python
die **Ringelnatter** [-n] grass snake
die **Schildkröte** [-n] tortoise
die **Schlange** [-n] snake (die **Klapperschlange** rattlesnake)
die **Seidenraupe** [-n] silkworm
die **Viper** [-n]; die **(Kreuz)otter** [-n] viper; adder
der **Wurm** [-̈er] worm (der **Regenwurm** earthworm)

Beuteltiere Marsupials

das Känguruh [-s] kangaroo
der Koala [-s] koala

Ihre Körper Their bodies

das Bein [-e] leg
der Beutel [-] pouch [of marsupial] (**der Kehlsack [ˌe]** pouch [of pelican])
die Feder [-n] feather
das Fell [-e] coat; fur (**der Pelz [-e]** skin; fur [when dead])
der Flecken [-] spot
die Flosse [-n] fin
der Flügel [-] wing
das Geweih [-e] (set of) antlers
das Haar [-e] hair
das Haus [ˌer] shell [of snail]
der Höcker [-] hump
das Horn [ˌer] horn
der Huf [-e] hoof (**das Hufeisen [-]** horseshoe)
die Kieme [-n] *sing rare* gill
die Kralle [-n]; die Klaue [-n] claw; talon
die Mähne [-n] mane
das Maul [ˌer] mouth
der Panzer [-] shell [of tortoise, turtle]
die Pfote [-n]; die Tatze [-n] paw (**die Pranke [-n]** paw [of lion, tiger, bear])
der Rüssel [-] trunk; proboscis; snout [of pig]
der Schnabel [ˌ] beak; bill
die Schnauze [-n] muzzle; snout [of mouse]
die Schuppe [-n] scale
der Schwanz [ˌe] tail
der Stachel [-n] spine
der Stoßzahn [ˌe] tusk
der Streifen [-] stripe

das Vlies [-e]; das Schaffell [-e] fleece
das Vorderbein [-e] front leg (**das Hinterbein** back leg)

Ihre Rufe Their calls

bellen bark
blöken bleat; low
brüllen bellow; roar
brummen growl [bear]; buzz [insect]
gackern; glucken cluck
grunzen grunt
gurren coo
iahen bray
kläffen yap
kollern gobble
knurren growl
krähen caw; crow
meckern bleat
miauen miaow; mew
muhen moo
piepsen cheep
quaken quack
quiek(s)en squeal
schnattern cackle; chatter
schnurren purr
*schreien howl; bray; screech; hoot
*singen sing
trompeten trumpet
tschilpen [sparrow]; **zirpen** [cricket] chirp
wiehern whinny; neigh
zischen hiss
zwitschern twitter

Was sie tun What they do

der Biß [-sse] bite
der Stich [-e] sting; bite [mosquito]
die Verbrennung [-en] sting [jellyfish]

auf|richten; spitzen prick up [ears]
*beißen bite (**Vorsicht, bissiger Hund!** beware of the dog!)
blecken bare [teeth]
einen Buckel machen arch its back
Eier *n pl* **legen** lay eggs
flattern flutter
*fliegen fly
*fressen eat (**das Hunde-/Katzenfutter** dog/cat food)
sich häuten cast its skin
hüpfen; [hare] **hoppeln** hop
*kriechen crawl
*laufen run
ein Nest [-er] bauen build a nest
einen Satz machen/*tun leap
sich schlängeln wriggle
*schleichen slink; creep
schwärmen swarm
schweben hover
*schwimmen swim
segeln soar
*springen jump
*stechen sting
*trompeten trumpet
sich ver'wandeln in + A change into
wedeln (mit dem Schwanz *m***)** wag (tail)

Was wir ihnen antun What we do to them

der Blinden(führ)hund [-e] guide-dog
die Jagd [-en] hunting (**die Fuchs-/Hirschjagd** fox/stag-hunting;
  jagen hunt)
der Käfig [-e] cage
das Pferderennen [-] horse-race (**der Pferderennsport** horse-
  racing)
das Reiten (horse-)riding (**der Ritt [-e]** ride; **der Zügel [-]** rein; **der
  Sattel [=]** saddle)

der Stierkampf [ˀe] bullfight
der Wachhund [-e] guard dog (**be'wachen** guard)

eine Falle legen / (auf|)stellen set a trap (**in einer Falle *fangen**
 trap)
***frei|lassen** set free (**der/die Tierrechtler/in** [-/-nen] animal-rights
 activist)
gehorsam/zahm *sein be obedient/tame
Männchen machen sit up and beg
***melken** milk
Nester *n pl* ***aus|nehmen** rob birds' nests
Pfötchen *geben shake hands; put out a paw
***reiten** ride (**zu Pferd** on horseback)
***scheren** shear
streicheln stroke

nieder!; leg dich! down!
sitz!; Platz! sit!

SEE ALSO: **Food; Nature**

4. Arguments For and Against
Argumente für und gegen

---

das Argument [-e] argument
die Debatte [-n] debate
der Dialog [-e] dialogue
die Diskussion [-en] discussion
der Einwand (gegen + A) criticism (of); objection (to)
die Erklärung [-en] statement
das Gespräch [-e]; die Unterhaltung [-en] conversation
die Idee [-n] idea
die Kritik [-en] (an + D) criticism (of)
die Meinung [-en]; die Ansicht [-en] opinion
das Mißverständnis [-se] misunderstanding
der Standpunkt [-e] point of view
der Streit *no pl* argument (**immer Streit *haben** be always arguing)

Argumente für Arguments for

be'einflussen influence
be'tonen emphasize
er'klären state; declare
er'wähnen mention
hinzu|fügen add
informieren inform
recht *haben be right
ver'teidigen defend
*voraus|sehen predict
wahr *sein be true/right
wieder'holen repeat
zu|stimmen agree

als Beispiel by way of example
auf alle Fälle in any case

auf den ersten Blick at first sight
aus gutem Grund with good reason
das hat zur Folgen, daß the consequence of that is
das sind nackte Tatsachen these are hard facts
den Standpunkt vertreten, daß take the view that
den Tatsachen ins Auge sehen face the facts
einfach weil for the simple reason that
ein Grund mehr, zu . . . all the more reason to . . .
es besteht kein Zweifel, daß there's no question that
es geht nur darum, zu . . . it's only a question of . . . ing
es geht um + A it concerns
es hängt davon ab, ob it depends on whether
es ist genau wie it's just the same as
es ist so viel leichter, zu . . . it's so much easier to . . . .
es wäre viel besser, wenn it would be much better if
ganz abgesehen davon, daß quite apart from the fact that
große Fortschritte machen make great strides
ich gebe gern zu, daß I'm ready to admit that
im allgemeinen in general
immer besser better and better
in diesem Fall in that case
in diesem Moment at this moment in time
in erster Linie geht es darum, daß/zu the first priority is to
infolgedessen as a result (of this)
laut Meinungsumfragen according to opinion polls
man darf nicht vergesssen, daß one must not forget that
man muß auch damit rechnen, daß one must also take into
  account the fact that
meinerseits; von mir aus for my part; as far as I'm concerned
meines Erachtens; meiner Meinung/Ansicht nach in my view
natürlich; selbstverständlich of course
nicht nur . . . sondern auch not only . . . but also
offen gesagt to be frank
sicher ist, daß what is certain, is that
sowohl . . . als auch both . . . and
sozusagen so to speak; as it were
Tatsache ist, daß the fact is that

um so mehr, weil all the more so because
und außerdem moreover
Ursache davon ist vor allem that is due above all to
von + D ganz zu schweigen not to mention
vor allem above all
was auffällt, ist what strikes one is
was . . . betrifft as far as . . . is concerned
wenn nötig if necessary
wir können es als gegeben annehmen, daß we can take it for
  granted that
zunächst einmal first and foremost
zweifellos undoubtedly

Argumente gegen Arguments against

ab|lehnen decline; reject
antworten answer (**be'antworten** answer sth)
be'haupten claim
*be'streiten contest; deny (**sich *streiten** argue)
be'zweifeln doubt
*ein|wenden object
ent'gegnen (+ D) reply (to); retort
falsch *sein be wrong [fact] (**unrecht *haben** be wrong [person])
kritisieren criticize
täuschen deceive
*über'treiben exaggerate
ver'leumden slander
vor|täuschen pretend; feign
wider'legen refute
*wider'sprechen contradict

aber; jedoch however
andererseits on the other hand
angenommen, (daß) assuming that
auf alle Fälle in any case
auf keinen Fall on no account
aus keinem ersichtlichen Grund for no obvious reason

dagegen läßt sich vieles einwenden there's a lot to be said against that

da liegt das Problem nicht that's not where the problem lies

das glauben Sie selbst nicht you can't be serious

das ist doch kaum zu glauben that's incredible

das ist ein sehr negativer Standpunkt that's a very negative point of view

das ist etwas ganz anderes that's something else again

das ist zu nichts nütze that serves no useful purpose

das wäre der allerschlimmste Ausgang that would be the worst possible outcome

das will nicht sagen, daß that doesn't mean that

eine schwache Stelle in der Argumentation a weak point in the argument

es hat nichts damit zu tun it has nothing to do with that

es ist eigentlich schade, denn it's rather a pity, because

es ist nicht der Fall it isn't the case

es wäre besser, wenn it would be better if

es wird sicher nicht genug sein, zu it certainly won't be enough to

ganz im Gegenteil quite the reverse

ich bin nicht ganz einverstanden (mit + D) I'm not entirely in agreement (with sb/sth)

ich frage mich, ob I wonder whether

im besten Fall at best

immerhin all the same

in gleicher Weise equally; in the same way

in Wirklichkeit in reality

man könnte genausogut sagen one might just as well say

nicht so sehr not as much as all that

ohne . . . zu erwähnen not counting . . .

sicher, aber certainly, but

Sie stellen mich vor vollendete Tatsachen you're presenting me with a *fait accompli*

Sie werden doch zugeben müssen, daß you must admit that

was noch merkwürdiger ist what is even more extraordinary

weit entfernt far from it

wie die Frage, so die Antwort ask a silly question and you'll get a silly answer
wir neigen zu sehr dazu, zu . . . we tend too much to . . .

Zu einem Schluß kommen
Drawing a conclusion

sich auf|regen (über + A) get worked up (about)
kapieren *colloq* understand; follow
über'reden persuade
über'zeugen convince
*ver'stehen understand (**zu verstehen *geben** give to understand)

auf jeden Fall at all events
das wird keine Probleme aufwerfen that will pose no problems
deshalb therefore
deswegen for that reason; that's why
einerseits . . . andererseits; auf der einen Seite . . . auf der anderen Seite on the one hand . . . on the other hand
ein für allemal once and for all
fest steht jedenfalls: this much is certain:
ich jedenfalls I for one
im allgemeinen in general
im schlimmsten Fall; schlimmstenfalls if the worst comes to the worst
in höherem/geringerem Maße to a greater/lesser extent
klar ist, daß what is clear, is
kurz gesagt in short
letztendlich in the end
letzten Endes in the event
mit anderen Worten in other words
mit einem Wort in a word
mit einer einzigen Ausnahme with a single exception
ohne weiteres (Aufhebens) without more ado
schließlich ultimately
sich grundsätzlich einigen come to a general agreement
stimmt! I agree!

teilweise partly
überzeugt convinced (**überzeugend** convincing)
was ist denn zu tun? what then is to be done?
wenn es nicht anders geht if there's no other way
wir können nur darin übereinstimmen, daß wir nicht übereinstimmen we can only agree to differ
wir sind uns darüber einig we're in agreement about it
wir wollen klare Verhältnisse schaffen we must set things straight
zusammenfassend möchte ich sagen in summing up, I should like to say

SEE ALSO: **Liking, Dislike, Comparing**

5. Art and Architecture
Kunst und Architektur

Kunst Art

der Abdruck [≞e] cast (**der Gipsabdruck** plaster cast)

der Akt [-e] nude [male or female]

das Aquarell [-e] [painting]; **die Wasserfarbe** [-n] [paint] water-colour

das Atelier [-s] studio

die Ausstellung [-en] exhibition

das Bild [-er] picture

der Bildhauer [-] sculptor (**die Bildhauerin** [-nen] sculptress)

die Bildhauerei; **die Plastik** sculpture [the art] (**eine Plastik** [-en]; **eine Skulptur** [-en] a sculpture [the product])

der Bildteppich [-e]; **die Tapisserie** [-n] tapestry

die Büste [-n] bust

die Farbe [-n] colour; paint (**die Ölfarben** oils)

der Firnis [-se] (picture) varnish

das Fresko [*pl* **Fresken**] fresco

das Gemälde [-] picture; painting

die Gemäldegalerie [-n] picture-gallery

die Glasmalerei [-en] glass-staining; stained glass

die Holzschnitzerei [-en] wood-carving [art and object]

die Karikatur [-en] caricature; cartoon

der Katalog [-e] catalogue

die Keramik [-en]; **die Töpferware** [-n] ceramic(s); pottery

die Kohle charcoal

die Kunst [≞e] art (**die schönen Künste** fine arts; **die bildenden Künste** the plastic arts; **das Kunstwerk** [-e] work of art)

die Kunstgalerie [-n] art gallery

der/die Künstler/in [-/-nen] artist

der Kupferstich [-e]; [the art] **die Gravierung** engraving

die Landschaft [-en] landscape (**die Landschaftsmalerei** land-scape painting)

der/die Maler/in [-/-nen] painter
die Malerei painting
die Miniatur [-en] miniature
das Modell [-e] model (**Modell *stehen/*sitzen** + D model for)
das Mosaik [G -s *pl* -en or -e] mosaic (**der Mosaikboden** [⸚]
  mosaic [floor])
das Museum [*pl* **Museen**] museum
die Palette [-n] palette (**das Palettenmesser** [-] palette-knife)
die Pastellkreide [-n] pastel (**die Pastellzeichnung** [-en] pastel
  [drawing])
der Pinsel [-] brush
das Porträt [*pl* -s or -e]/**das Portrait** [-s]; **das Bildnis** [-se] portrait
der Rahmen [-] frame
die Sammlung [-en] collection (**die Kunstsammlung** art collection)
die Skizze [-n] sketch
der Sockel [-] plinth
die Staffelei [-en] easel
die Statue [-n] statue
das Stilleben [-] still-life
der Ton [-e] clay
das Zeichnen [the activity]; **die Zeichnung** [-en] [the product]
  drawing

be'arbeiten (**zu** + D) shape (into)
formen (**aus** + D) mould (from)
gravieren engrave
malen paint (**in Öl** in oils)
meißeln [stone]; **schnitzen** [wood] carve
posieren pose
*schaffen; kreieren create
skizzieren sketch
zeichnen draw (**nach dem Leben** *n* from life)

künstlerisch artistic
künstlich artificial
kunstvoll ornate

Architektur Architecture

der/die Architekt/in [-en/-nen] architect (**das Architektenbüro [-s]**
firm of architects)
die Architektur [-en] architecture; edifice
der Baustil [-e] architectural style
der Bogen [≃] arch
der Dom [-e] cathedral
das Gebäude [-]; der Bau [*pl* Bauten] building [edifice] (**der Bau**
no pl building [the act]; **im Bau** under construction; **bauen**
build)
das Gewölbe [-] vault
das Kapitell [-e] capital
die Kuppel [-n] cupola; dome
die Mauerstrebe [-n] buttress (**der Schwibbogen [≃]** flying
buttress)
der Pfeiler [-] pillar
die Säule [-n] column
der Säulenvorbau [*pl* -bauten] portico
das Schmücken [act]; der Schmuck [object] decoration

architektonisch architectural
barock baroque (**das Barock** baroque *noun*)
gothisch Gothic (**die Backstein-/Neogothik** Brick Gothic/Gothic
Revival)
klassisch classical
romanisch Romanesque (**die Romanik** the Romanesque)

SEE ALSO: **Cinema and Photography; Colours; Materials**

6. Birth, Marriage, and Death
Geburt, Ehe und Tod

Geburt Birth

das Baby [-s] baby (**die Babynahrung** baby food)

der/die Babysitter/in [-/-nen] baby-sitter (**das Babysitting** baby-sitting; **babysitten** *inf only* baby-sit)

die Empfängnis conception

der Fötus [-se]/der Fetus [pl -se or Feten] foetus

die Geburt [-en] birth (**feiern** celebrate; **die Geburtsanzeige [-n]** birth announcement)

das Geburtsdatum [pl -daten] date of birth

der Geburtstag [-e] birthday (**Geburtstag feiern** celebrate one's birthday; **das Geburtstagsgeschenk [-e]** birthday present)

der Hochstuhl [̈e] high chair

das Kinderbett [-en] cot

der Kinderwagen [-] pram

die Mutter [̈] mother

der Namenstag [-e] saint's day

der Pate/Taufpate [-n]; der Patenonkel [-] godfather (**die Patin/Taufpatin [-nen]; die Patentante [-n]** godmother; **das Patenkind [-er]** godchild; **der Patensohn [̈e]** godson; **die Patentochter [̈]** goddaughter)

die Saugflasche [-n]; das Fläschen [-] feeding-bottle

der Säugling [-e] baby; infant

der Schnuller [-] dummy

die Schwangerschaft [-en] pregnancy

der Sportwagen [-] push-chair

die Taufe [-n] christening; baptism

der Vater [̈] father

die Windel [-n] nappy (**die Wegwerfwindel** disposable nappy)

ab|stillen wean

füttern (mit + D) feed (with)

*gebären bear; give birth to (**geboren *sein** be/have been born)
stillen breast-feed
trocken|legen change [a baby]

Ehe Marriage

die Aussteuer dowry
die Braut [ӟe] bride (**der Bräutigam** [-e] bridegroom; **das
Brautpaar** [-e] bridal couple; **die Brautjungfer** [-n] bridesmaid;
das Brautkleid [-er] wedding dress)
die Ehe [-n] marriage (**die Vernunftsehe** marriage of convenience; **die (Ehe)frau** [-en] wife; **der (Ehe)gatte** [-n]/**die
(Ehe)gattin** [-nen] spouse; **der (Ehe)mann** [ӟer] husband; **das
Ehepaar** [-e] married couple; **der Ehe-/Trauring** [-e] wedding-
ring; **das Ehevermittlungsinstitut** [-e] marriage bureau)
der Ehebruch adultery
der Ex-Mann [ӟer] ex-husband (**die Ex-Frau** [-en] ex-wife; **mein
Verflossener/meine Verflossene** *adj n, colloq* my ex)
der Familienstand marital status
der Freund [-e] boy-friend (**die Freundin** [-nen] girl-friend)
die Heirat [-en] marriage (**die Liebesheirat** love match)
der Heiratsantrag [ӟe] proposal (**jm einen Heiratsantrag machen**
propose to sb; ***an|nehmen** accept; ***ab|weisen** refuse)
die Hochzeit [-en] wedding (**die silberne/goldene Hochzeit** silver/
golden wedding)
die Hochzeitseinladung [-en] wedding invitation
das Hochzeitsessen [-] wedding breakfast
das Hochzeitsgeschenk [-e] wedding present
der Hochzeitskuchen [-] wedding-cake
die Hochzeitsnacht [ӟe] wedding-night
die Hochzeitsreise [-n] honeymoon [trip] (**die Flitterwochen** *f pl*
honeymoon [period])
der Hochzeitstag [-e] wedding day; wedding anniversary
der Junggeselle [-n] bachelor (**die Junggesellin** [-nen] single girl;
die alte Jungfer [-n] old maid; **der eingefleischte Junggeselle**
confirmed bachelor)
die Jungverheirateten *adj n, pl* newly-weds

die Kirche [-n] church
das Konfetti confetti
die Scheidung [-en] divorce
das Standesamt [ˬer] registry office (**sich standesamtlich trauen
  *lassen** be married in a registry office)
der Trauschein [-e] marriage certificate
der Trauzeuge [-n]/**die Trauzeugin** [-nen] witness
die Trennung separation
der/die Verlobte *adj n* fiancé/fiancée
die Verlobung [-en] engagement (**der Verlobungsring** [-e]
  engagement ring; **die Verlobung auf|lösen** break the engage-
  ment)
die Zeremonie [-n] ceremony

gratulieren (**zu** + D) congratulate (on) (**ich gratuliere!** congratulations!)
heiraten + A; **sich ver'heiraten mit** + D marry (**wieder heiraten**
  remarry)
sich scheiden *lassen (**von** + D) divorce (sb)
sich trennen separate; split up
sich ver'loben get engaged

geschieden divorced
getrennt separated (**getrennt leben** be separated)
ledig single
verheiratet/unverheiratet married/unmarried
verlobt engaged

Tod Death

die Asche *sing* ashes
die Beerdigung [-en]; [more formal] **die Bestattung** [-en] funeral;
  burial
das Bestattungsunternehmen [-] funeral firm (**der/die Bestattungs-
  unternehmer/in** [-/-nen]; **der/die Leichenbestatter/in** [-/-nen]
  undertaker)
die Einäscherung [-en] cremation
der Erbe [-n] heir (**die Erbin** [-nen] heiress)

die Erbschaft [-en]; **das Erbe** *no pl* inheritance
der Friedhof [⸚e] cemetery; churchyard
der/die Gestorbene *adj n* the deceased
das Grab [⸚er] grave (**das Grabmal** [⸚er] monument; **der
  Grabspruch** [⸚e] epitaph; **der Grabstein** [-e] gravestone)
der Kranz [⸚e] wreath
das Krematorium [*pl* **Krematorien**] crematorium
das Legat [-e] (**an** + A) bequest (to)
die Leiche [-n] corpse (**das Leichentuch** [⸚er] shroud; **der
  Leichenwagen** [-] hearse)
der Mord [-e] murder (**der Selbstmord** suicide; **Selbstmord
  *be'gehen** commit suicide)
der Nachlaß estate
der Sarg [⸚e] coffin
der Scheiterhaufen [-] funeral pyre
das Testament [-e] will
der Tod death
der/die Tote *adj n* dead person (**das Toten-/Sterbebett** deathbed;
  der Totengräber [-] grave-digger; **der Totenschein** [-e] death
  certificate)
die Trauer mourning (**in Trauer *sein**; **Trauer *tragen** be in
  mourning)
der Traurerakt [-e]; **die Trauerfeier** [-n] funeral ceremony
der Trauerfall [⸚e] bereavement
der Trauerzug [⸚e] funeral procession
die Urne [-n] urn
die Waise [-n] *always f*; **das Waisenkind** [-er] orphan (**er ist Waise**
  he's an orphan; **verwaist** orphaned)
die Witwe [-n] widow (**der Witwer** [-] widower; **verwitwet**
  widowed)

be'erdigen bury
ein|äschern cremate
ent'erben disinherit
erben inherit
***er'trinken** drown
***hinter'lassen** leave [in will]

*sterben die (**eines natürlichen/gewaltsamen Todes sterben** die a natural/violent death)
töten; *um|bringen kill
trauern mourn
*um|kommen perish
ver'machen bequeath

SEE ALSO: **Accidents; Disasters; Health and Sickness; Identity; Relationships; War, Peace, and the Armed Services**

7. Cinema and Photography
Kino und Fotografie

Kino Cinema

die Anzeige [-n] advert
die Aufführung [-en]; **die Vorstellung** [-en] showing; performance
die Dekoration [-en] set
das Drehbuch [¨er] film script
der Dokumentarfilm [-e] documentary
der Film [-e]; *colloq* **der Streifen** [-] film (**der Schwarzweiß-/Farb-/Stumm-/Kurzfilm** black-and-white/colour/silent/short film; **der Spiel-/Hauptfilm** feature film)
der Filmausschnitt [-e] film clip
die Filmkamera [-s] cine-camera
der Filmschauspieler [-] film actor (**die Filmschauspielerin** [-nen] film actress)
der Horrorfilm [-e] horror film
das Kamerateam [-s] film crew
die Karte [-n] ticket (**die Eintrittskarte** [-n] entrance ticket)
die Kasse [-n] box-office (**der Kassenerfolg** [-e] box-office success)
das Kino [-s] cinema
die Kopie [-n] print
der Kriminalfilm [-e]; **der Krimi** [*pl* -s or -] thriller; crime film
die Leinwand [¨e] screen
das Parkett *sing* stalls
die Pause [-n] interval
der Platz [¨e] seat (**die Platzanweiserin** [-nen] usherette)
das Programm [-e] programme
der Projektor [G *-s pl* -en] projector
das Publikum spectators
der Rang [¨e] circle
der/die Regisseur/in [-e/-nen] director
der Saal [*pl* Säle] cinema [the building]

der Science-fiction-Film [-e] science-fiction film (**die Science-fiction** science fiction)
der Star [-s] star [male or female]
der Trickfilm/Zeichentrickfilm [-e] cartoon (film)
der Untertitel [-] subtitle (**OmU** [= **Originalfassung mit Untertiteln**] subtitled)
das Video [-s] video [the medium or the object] (**der Videofilm** [-e] video film)
die Videoaufzeichnung [-en] video recording
das Videoband [¨er] videotape
der Videoclip [-s] videoclip
die Videokamera [-s] camcorder
die Videokassette [-n] video cassette
der Videorecorder [-] video recorder
der Western [-] western
die Zeitlupe slow motion (**in Zeitlupe** in slow-motion)

drehen shoot; make [film]
filmen film
*laufen be running/showing
synchronisieren dub
unter'titeln subtitle
ver'filmen film [a book]
vor|be'stellen; reservieren *lassen book (in advance)
zum Kino/Film *gehen go into films (**ins Kino gehen** go to the cinema)

Fotografie Photography

der Abzug [¨e] print (**der Glanz-/Mattabzug** glossy/matt print)
das Album [*pl* **Alben**] album
die Batterie [-n] battery
die Belichtung; [shot] **die Aufnahme** [-n] exposure (**der Belichtungsmesser** [-] exposure meter)
das Blitzlicht flash (**mit Blitzlicht fotografieren** use flash; **die Blitzlichtaufnahme** [-n] flash photo; **das Blitzbirnchen** [-] flash bulb; **der Blitzwürfel** [-] flash-cube)

das Dia [-s]; **das Diapositiv** [-e] slide/transparency (**der Dia(positiv)projektor** [G -s *pl* -en] slide projector)
die Dunkelkammer [-n] dark-room
der Entfernungsmesser [-] range-finder
die Entwicklung development
der Film [-e] film (**der Rollfilm** roll film; **die Filmkassette** [-n] cassette/cartridge; **der Filmtransport** [-e] film winder)
der Filter [-] filter
das Foto [-s] photo (**das Schwarzweiß-/Farbfoto** black-and-white/ colour photo)
der Fotoapparat [-e]; **die Kamera** [-s] camera
der/die Fotograf/in [-en/-nen] photographer
die Fotografie [-n] photography; photograph
die Kameratasche [-n] camera case
das Negativ [-e] negative
das Objektiv [-e] lens (**der Objektivdeckel** [-] lens cap; **das Weitwinkel-/Teleobjektiv** wide-angle/telephoto lens)
das Paßbild [-er] passport photo
der Rahmen [-] frame
die Scharfeinstellung focus (**die Schärfentiefe** depth of focus)
der Schnappschuß [÷sse] snapshot
das Stativ [-e] tripod
der Sucher [-] viewfinder
die Vergrößerung [-en] enlargement
der Verschluß [÷sse] shutter (**die Verschlußzeit** [-en] shutter speed/ setting; **der Auslöser** [-] shutter release)

*ab|ziehen print
be'lichten expose (**zu kurz belichten** underexpose)
ein|legen (in + A) load (into)
ein|rahmen frame
ein|stellen (auf + A) focus (on)
ent'wickeln develop
klemmen; sich ver'klemmen be stuck; jam
machen; *schießen take [photo]
retuschieren retouch
ver'größern enlarge

automatisch automatic
Feinkorn- fine grain
hochempfindlich fast [film]
scharf/unscharf in focus/out of focus

SEE ALSO: **Art and Architecture; Leisure and Hobbies; The Media; Theatre**

8. Clothing Kleidung

Was man auf dem Kopf trägt . . .
What you wear on your head . . .

die Baskenmütze [-n] beret
die Haube [-n] bonnet
der Hut [≃e] hat (**die Krempe** [-n] brim)
das Kopftuch [≃er] headscarf
die Melone [-n] bowler
die Mütze [-n] cap (**die Badekappe** [-n] bathing-cap)
der Schleier [-] veil
der Sonnenhut [≃e] sun-hat
der Strohhut [≃e] straw hat

. . . und an den Füßen . . . on your feet

der Freizeitschuh [-e] casual shoe
der Hausschuh [-e] slipper
der Holzschuh [-e]; [fashionable] **der Clog** [-s] clog
der Mokassin [-s] moccasin
der Pantoffel [-n] (backless) slipper; mule
die Sandale [-n] sandal
der Schuh [-e] shoe (**das Paar** [-e] pair; **der Wander-/Strandschuh**
 walking-/beach shoe; **die Schuhcreme** shoe polish)
die Socke [-n] sock
der Stiefel [-] boot (**der Gummistiefel** wellington boot)
der Strumpf [≃e] stocking; long sock (**der Kniestrumpf** knee sock;
 die Strumpfhose [-n] (pair of) tights)
der Trainingsschuh [-e] trainer
der Turnschuh [-e] gym shoe; trainer
der Überstrumpf [≃e]; **der Legwarmer** [-s] leg-warmer

... und am Körper ... on your body

die Abendkleidung *no pl* evening dress (**das Abendkleid [-er]**
  [woman's] evening dress; **der Gesellschaftsanzug [≟e]** [man's]
  dress-suit)

der Anorak [-s] anorak

der Anzug [≟e] suit (**der Straßen-/Büro-/Maßanzug** lounge/office/
  made-to-measure suit)

der Arbeitsanzug [≟e] (set of) working clothes

der Badeanzug [≟e] swim-suit

die Badehose [-n] (pair of) swimming-trunks

der Bademantel [≟]; [woman's] **der Morgenrock [≟e]** dressing-
  gown

der Bikini [-s] bikini (**im Bikini** in a bikini)

das/der Blouson [-s] blouson; bomber jacket

die Bluse [-n] blouse

das Braut-/Hochzeitskleid [-er] wedding dress

die Brille [-n] (pair of) spectacles (**die Sonnenbrille** sun-glasses)

der Büstenhalter [-]/der BH [*pl* - or -s] bra

das Dinnerjacket [-s]; **der Smoking [-s]** dinner-jacket

der Dufflecoat [-s] duffle-coat

der Fausthandschuh [-e] mitten

der Frack [≟e] tailcoat (**im Frack** in tails)

die Freizeitkleidung *no pl* casuals; casual clothes

der Gehrock [≟e] frock-coat

der Gürtel [-] belt

der Handschuh [-e] glove

die Handtasche [-n] handbag (**die Umhängetasche** shoulder-bag)

das Hemd [-en] shirt (**das Sporthemd** sports shirt)

das Höschen [-] (pair of) panties (**heiße Höschen** *n pl* hotpants)

die Hose [-n] (pair of) trousers (**die Hosenträger** *m pl* braces)

der Hosenanzug [≟e] trouser-suit

der Hosenrock [≟e] (pair of) culottes

der Hüfthalter [-] girdle

die Jacke [-n]; [of suit] **das Jackett [-s]** jacket (**der/das Sakko [-s]**
  (sports) jacket)

die Jeans [-] *sing or pl*; **die Jeanshose** [-n] (pair of) jeans
der Jumper [-] jumper
das Kleid [-er] dress (**die Kleider** *pl* dresses; clothes; **tief
ausgeschnitten** low-necked; **hochgeschlossen** high-necked)
die Kleidung *sing* clothing; clothes (**die Konfektionskleidung**
ready-mades; **die Gesellschaftskleidung** formal dress)
die Kniehose [-n] (pair of) knee-breeches
das Kostüm [-e] [woman's] suit (**das Schneiderkostüm** tailored
suit)
die Latzhose [-n] (pair of) dungarees
die Lederhose [-n] (pair of) lederhosen/leather shorts
die Lumpen *m pl* rags
der Mantel [⸚] (over)coat (**der Pelzmantel** fur coat)
der Muff [-e] muff
das Nachthemd [-en] night-dress; night-shirt
der Overall [-s] (pair of) overalls
der Pullover [-]/**der Pulli** [-s] pullover; sweater (**mit V-Ausschnitt**
V-necked)
der Pullunder [-] slip-over
der Regenmantel [⸚] raincoat
der Regenschirm [-e] umbrella (**der Sonnenschirm** parasol)
der Rock [⸚e] skirt (**der Minirock** mini-skirt)
der Rollkragenpulli [-s]/**der Rolli** [-s] polo-neck sweater
der Schal [*pl* -s or -e] scarf
der Schlafanzug [⸚e]; **der Pyjama** [-s] (pair of) pyjamas
der Schlips [-e]; **die Krawatte** [-n] tie (**die Fliege** [-n] bow-tie)
der Schlüpfer [-] (pair of) panties
die Schürze [-n] apron
die Shorts *pl* shorts
die Skihose [-n] (pair of) ski pants
der Slip [-s] (pair of) briefs
der Spazierstock [⸚e] walking-stick
die Stola [*pl* Stolen] stole; shawl
der Stresemann [man's] morning dress (**der Cut(away)** [-s]
morning coat)
die Strickjacke [-n] cardigan

die Strumpfbänder *n pl*; **die Strumpfhalter** *m pl* suspenders (**der Strumpfbandgürtel** [-] suspender belt; **die Sockenhalter** *m pl* sock-suspenders)

das Sweatshirt [-s] sweat-shirt

das Taschentuch [≃er] handkerchief

die Tracht [-en] costume; uniform (**die Nationaltracht** national costume)

der Trainingsanzug [≃e] tracksuit

das T-Shirt [-s] T-shirt

das Umschlagtuch [≃er] shawl

die Uniform [-en] uniform

das Unterhemd [-en] vest

die Unterhose [-n] (pair of) (under)pants

der Unterrock [≃e] petticoat; underskirt

die Wäsche/die Unterwäsche underwear (**die Damenunterwäsche** lingerie)

die Weste [-n] waistcoat

der Zweireiher [-] double-breasted jacket

Teile eines Kleidungsstücks
Parts of a piece of clothing

der Absatz [≃e] heel (**der Stöckelabsatz** stiletto heel; **der Stöckelschuh** [-e] stiletto-heeled shoe; **hochhackig** high-heeled; **flach** low-heeled)

der Ärmel [-] sleeve (**hoch|krempeln** roll up; **in Hemdsärmeln** in shirt-sleeves; **ärmellos** sleeveless)

der Aufschlag [≃e] turn-up

das Band [≃er] ribbon

der Druckknopf [≃e] press-stud

die Falte [-n] pleat

das Futter *no pl*; **die Fütterung** [-en] lining

der Gürtel [-] belt (**das Koppel** [-] uniform belt)

der Haken [-] hook

der Knopf [≃e] button (**das Knopfloch** [≃er] buttonhole)

der Kragen [-] collar (**der Rollkragen** polo neck; **der Kragenknopf**
[¨e] collar-stud)
die Manschette [-n] cuff (**der Manschettenknopf** [¨e] cuff-link)
die Naht [¨e] seam
der Reißverschluß [¨sse] zip
der Saum [¨e] hem
die Schnalle [-n] buckle
der Schnürsenkel [-] shoe-lace
die Sohle [-n] sole (**die Leder-/Gummi-/Krepp-/Plateausohle**
leather/rubber/crêpe/platform sole; **der Plateauschuh** [-e] platform shoe; **die Einlegesohle** insole)
die Tasche [-n] pocket
die Verzierung [-en] trimming (**der Spitzenbesatz** lace trimmings)

Wie Kleider aussehen What clothes are like

abgetragen threadbare; worn out
altmodisch old-fashioned
auffällig flashy
bauschig bouffant
bedruckt print(ed)
bequem geschnitten loose-fitting
bestickt embroidered
bügelfrei non-iron; drip-dry
dekolletiert low-cut
einfach plain; simple
einreihig single-breasted (**zweireihig** double-breasted)
elegant elegant
eng tight
enganliegend close-fitting
farbecht colour-fast
die Figur betonend figure-hugging
formell formal
geblümt flowered
gefältelt pleated
gepunktet spotted
geschmackvoll in good taste (**geschmacklos** in bad taste)

gestreift striped
in *colloq*; **in Mode** in; in fashion
kariert check
knallig loud; gaudy
knitterfrei crease resistant
kurzärm(e)lig short-sleeved (**langärm(e)lig** long-sleeved)
lässig casual
maßgeschneidert made to measure
modisch fashionable
nagelneu brand-new
passend (zu + D) matching
proper trim; neat
rauh rough
schäbig shabby
schick smart
schlampig slovenly; sloppy
schlicht sober
sportlich casually smart
steif stiff
synthetisch synthetic
uni *inv* plain
von der Stange off the peg
zerknittert crumpled
zerrissen torn

Was man damit tut What you do with them

*ab|laufen [shoes]; ***auf|tragen** [clothes] wear out
*ab|nehmen take off [from head]
ändern alter
*an|haben [on body]; ***auf|haben** [on head] have on
an|nähen sew on
an|probieren try on
sich *an|ziehen get dressed (**anziehen** put on [clothes])
auf|knöpfen unbutton
auf|setzen put on [on head]
aus|bessern mend

sich *aus|ziehen get undressed (**ausziehen** take off [clothes])
be'setzen mit + D trim with
be'sohlen sole
*binden tie (*auf|binden untie)
bügeln iron (**der Hosenbügler** [-] trouser-press)
*ein|laufen shrink
fälteln pleat
flicken patch
knittern crease
kürzer/länger machen shorten/lengthen
öffnen unfasten
passen (+ D) fit (sb) (**passen zu** + D go well with)
säumen hem
schlüpfen in + A slip into
schnallen buckle
schneidern make; tailor (**schneidern *lassen** have made)
*sitzen fit; be straight
*stehen (+ D) suit (sb)
stopfen darn
stricken knit
*tragen wear
sich *um|ziehen get changed (**die Umkleidekabine** [-n] changing-cubicle)
*waschen wash (**in der Waschmaschine waschen** machine-wash; **in die Handwäsche *kommen** be washed by hand)
zu|knöpfen button up
zu|machen fasten

Textilien Textiles

das Acryl acrylic
der Batist cambric
die Baumwolle cotton (**der Baumwollsamt** velveteen)
der Chiffon chiffon
der Cord cord (**der Cordsamt** corduroy; cord velvet)
der Denim®; der Jeansstoff denim
der Drillich drill

der Filz felt
der Flanell flannel
das/der Frottee terry
der Gabardine gabardine
das/der Gummi rubber (**das/der Kreppgummi** crêpe)
der Jersey jersey
der Kambrik cambric
das Kamelhaar camel-hair
das Kammgarn worsted
der Kaschmir cashmere
der Krepp crêpe
der Kunststoff [-e] synthetic material; plastic (**die Kunstfaser [-n]** man-made fibre)
das Leder leather (**ledern** leather *adj*)
das Leinen linen
die Leinwand canvas
der Manchester [heavy] corduroy
das Nylon® nylon
der Pelz [-e]; das Fell [-e] fur
der Polyester polyester
der Popelin(e) poplin
der Samt velvet (**samten** velvet *adj*; **samtig**; **samtweich** velvety)
der Satin satin
die Seide silk (**seiden** silk *adj*; **die Kunstseide** artificial silk; rayon)
die Spitze lace (**Spitzen-** lace *adj*)
der Stoff [-e] cloth; fabric
das Stroh straw
der Tweed tweed
das Wachstuch oilcloth
das Wildleder; [finer] das Veloursleder suede
die Wolle wool (**die Schurwolle** new wool; **wollen** woollen)

Mode Fashion

der Dressman [*pl* -men] male model
die Haute Couture *haute couture*
die Kollektion [-en] (fashion) collection

die Konfektion off-the-peg clothes; the clothing industry (**die Damen-/Herrenkonfektion** ladies'/men's fashions)

das Mannequin [-s]; das Modell [-e] (fashion) model

die Mode [-n] fashion (**die Damen-/Herrenmode** ladies'/men's fashions; **große Mode** all the rage; **in Mode** in fashion)

der Modeartikel [-] fashion accessory

die Modebranche rag trade

das Modegeschäft [-e] fashion boutique

das Modellkleid [-er] model dress

die Modenschau [-en] fashion show

der/die Modeschöpfer/in [-/-nen] fashion designer (**modellieren** design [clothes])

das Muster [-] pattern

die Schattierung [-en] shade

die Schneiderei tailoring; dressmaking

der/die Schneider/in [-/-nen] tailor; dressmaker

die Stange [-n] (clothes) rail (**von der Stange** off the peg)

SEE ALSO: **Adornment; Colours; The Human Body; Numbers and Quantities**

9. Colours
Farben

Welche Farbe hat es? What colour is it?

es ist . . . it is . . .
  beige beige
  blau blue (**himmel-/königs-/marineblau** sky/royal/navy blue; **ein blaues Auge** a black eye)
  blond blonde
  braun brown (**kastanienbraun** chestnut; maroon)
  creme *inv*; **cremefarben** cream
  fleischfarben flesh-coloured
  gelb yellow
  gelbbraun buff; tawny [hair]
  golden gold(en)
  grau grey
  grün green (**grün und blau** black and blue)
  hazelnußbraun hazel
  indigoblau indigo (blue)
  infrarot infra-red
  karminrot carmine
  lavendel *inv*; **lavendelblau** lavender
  lila *inv* mauve (**dunkellila** purple)
  mehr-/vielfarbig multicoloured
  orange *inv*; **orangefarben** orange
  purpurn; purpurrot crimson
  rehfarben fawn
  rosa *inv*; **rosafarben**; **rosafarbig** pink (**rosarot** deep pink)
  rot red
  scharlachrot scarlet
  schwarz black (**schwarzweiß** black and white [film etc.]; **schwarz auf weiß** in black and white)
  silbern silver
  türkis *inv*; **türkisfarben** turquoise

ultraviolett ultraviolet
violett violet; purple
weiß white (schneeweiß white as snow)
zitronengelb lemon

dunkel- dark
hell- light; pale
leuchtend; knall- bright

blaßrosa *inv* pinkish
bläulich bluish
bräunlich brownish
gelblich yellowish; sallow
gräulich greyish
grünlich greenish
rötlich reddish (rötlich-braun reddish brown)
schwärzlich blackish
weißlich whitish

bräunen brown (an|bräunen brown [food])
grünen turn green
sich röten redden (er'röten blush)
schwärzen blacken
ver'gilben (turn) yellow
ver'golden gild
ver'silbern silver
weißen whiten [shoes, wall]

SEE ALSO: **Adornment; Clothing; Hair; Materials; The Senses**

10. Cooking and Eating
Kochen und Essen

Küchenausstattung Kitchen equipment

das Besteck cutlery
das Brotbrett [-er] breadboard
der Brotkasten [¨] bread-bin
die Brotmaschine [-n] bread-slicer
die Butterdose [-n] butter-dish
die Dose [-n]; die Büchse [-n] can; tin (**der Dosenöffner [-]** can-opener)
der Durchschlag [¨e] colander
der Eierbecher [-] egg-cup
die Flasche [-n] bottle (**der Flaschenöffner [-]** bottle-opener)
die Friteuse [-n] deep fryer
die Gabel [-n] fork
das Gedeck [-e] place-setting (**ein Gedeck auf|legen** lay a place)
das Geschirr dishes; crockery; kitchenware (**feuerfestes Geschirr** ovenware)
das Glas [¨er] glass; (glass) jar (**das Weinglas** wine-glass; **der Sprung [¨e]** crack)
der Herd [-e] stove; cooker (**der Elektro-/Gasherd** electric/gas cooker; **der Ofen [¨]** oven)
die Kaffeemaschine [-n] coffee-maker (**der Kaffeefilter [-]** coffee-filter; filter-paper; **die Kaffeemühle [-n]** coffee-grinder)
die Kanne [-n] pot; jug (**die Kaffee-/Teekanne** coffee-/teapot; **die Milchkanne**; [smaller] **das Milchkännchen [-]** milk jug)
die Karaffe [-n] carafe
die Kasserolle/Stielkasserolle [-n] saucepan (**der Stiel [-e]** long handle
die Kelle/Schöpfkelle [-n] ladle
der Kessel/Wasserkessel [-] kettle
die Klarsichtfolie cling-film
die Knoblauchpresse [-n] garlic press

das Kochbuch [≃er] cookery book (**das Rezept** [-e] recipe)
der Kochtopf [≃e]; **die Kasserolle** [-n] saucepan
der Korb [≃e] basket
der Korken [-] cork (**der Korkenzieher** [-] corkscrew)
der Krug [≃e] jug (**der Milchkrug** milk jug)
die Küchenmaschine [-n] food processor
der Löffel [-] spoon (**der Eß-/Servier-/Kaffee-/Teelöffel** soup- or dessert-/table/coffee-/teaspoon)
das Messer [-] knife (**das Küchen-/Brotmesser** kitchen-/bread knife; **das Schälmesser** potato peeler)
die Metallfolie foil
der Mixer [-] mixer; blender
die Pfanne/Bratpfanne [-n] frying-pan
die Pfeffermühle [-n] pepper-mill
die Platte [-n] (flat) dish
die Reibe [-n]; [coarser] **die Raspel** [-n] grater
der Salz-/Pfefferstreuer [-] salt-cellar/pepper-pot
die Sauciere [-n] sauce-boat
die Schale [-n] bowl (**die Zuckerschale** sugar-bowl)
die Schere [-n] (pair of) scissors
der Schneebesen [-] whisk
der Schnellkochtopf [≃e] pressure-cooker
die Schnur [≃e] (length of) string; (electric) lead
die Schüssel [-n] (large) bowl; basin
die Serviette [-n] table napkin
das/der Set [-s] place-mat
das Sieb [-e] sieve; strainer
das Streichholz [≃er] match
der Strohhalm [-e] drinking-straw
das Tablett [*pl* -s or -e] tray
die Tasse [-n] cup (**die Suppen-/Kaffeetasse** soup-bowl/coffee-cup)
die Teigrolle [-n]; **das Nudelholz** [≃er] rolling-pin
der Teller [-] plate (**der Suppenteller** soup-plate)
die Terrine [-n] tureen
das Tischtuch [≃er] tablecloth
die Thermosflasche [-n] flask; thermos ℗

der Toaster [-] toaster
der Topf [≃e] pot [cooking or container]; jar; casserole; saucepan
 (**der Topfhandschuh** [-e] oven glove)
die Untertasse [-n] saucer
die Waage [-n] (pair of/set of) scales
die Zuckerdose [-n] sugar-bowl

Gewürze Seasonings

der Anis aniseed
das Aroma [*pl* **Aromen**] flavouring
das Basilikum basil
der Brüh-/Suppenwürfel [-] stock-cube
der Dill dill
der Essig vinegar
der Estragon tarragon
das Gewürz [-e] spice; herb; seasoning (**das Gewürzkraut** [≃er]
 herb)
die Nelke/Gewürznelke[-n] clove
der Honig honey
der Ingwer ginger
die Kaper [-n] *usually pl* capers
der Kerbel chervil
der Knoblauch garlic (**die Knoblauchzehe** [-n] clove of garlic; **die**
 Knoblauchzwiebel [-n] head of garlic)
das Kraut [≃er] herb
der Kümmel caraway (**der Kreuzkümmel** cumin)
das Lorbeerblatt [≃er] bay-leaf
der Majoran marjoram
der Mazis; die Muskatblüte mace
die Minze mint (**die Pfefferminze** peppermint)
die Muskatnuß [≃sse]; **der Muskat** [-e] nutmeg
der Oregano/der Origano oregano
der Paprika paprika
die Paprikaschote [-n] pepper [capsicum]
die Petersilie parsley
der Pfeffer pepper

der/das Piment; der Nelkenpfeffer pimento
der Rosmarin rosemary
der Safran saffron
der/die Salbei sage
das Salz salt
der Schnittlauch chives
der Senf [-e] mustard
der Süßstoff (artificial) sweetener
der Thymian thyme
die Vanille vanilla
der Wacholder juniper
die Würze [-n] seasoning
der Zimt cinnamon
der Zucker sugar (**das Stück [-e]** lump; **die Raffinade** granulated
sugar)

Fette Fats

die Butter butter
die Margarine [-n] margarine
das Öl [-e] oil (**das Oliven-/Erdnuß-/Sonnenblumenöl** olive/
ground-nut/sunflower oil)
das Schweineschmalz lard

Zubereitung Preparation

*ab|gießen drain
*an|braten brown
auf|tauen thaw
aus|beinen [meat]; **ent'gräten** [fish] bone
aus|pressen crush
*backen bake
*be'gießen baste
be'reiten prepare [food, drink]
*braten fry; roast (**am Spieß** *m* on a spit/skewer; **durchgebraten**
well done [meat]; **halb durchgebraten** medium rare; **englisch
gebraten**; **blutig** rare)

dämpfen; **dünsten** steam
ein|tauchen soak
füllen stuff
garnieren garnish
grillen grill; barbecue
hacken chop; dice
klein|hacken mince
kochen cook; boil (**es kocht** it's boiling)
marinieren marinate
panieren bread [meat]
pochieren poach
räuchern smoke
*reiben; [coarser] **raspeln** grate
rösten roast [coffee]; toast [bread])
rühren; **um'rühren** stir (**rühren in** + A mix into)
schälen peel; shell (**ent'hülsen** shell [peas])
*schlagen beat
schmoren braise
*schneiden cut (**in Scheiben schneiden** slice; **dünn** thinly)
toasten toast [bread]
*über'backen gratiné; top with cheese and brown
ver'dünnen dilute
ver'kneten knead
würzen season
*zer'lassen melt
ziehen *lassen simmer
zu|be'reiten prepare

Mahlzeiten Meals

das Abendbrot supper
das Abendessen [evening] dinner; supper
das Bankett [-e] banquet
das Festessen [-] feast
das Frühstück breakfast (**frühstücken** have breakfast)
der Imbiß [-sse]; **die Zwischenmahlzeit** [-en] snack
die Mahlzeit [-en] [the occasion]; **das Essen** [the food] meal

das Mittagessen lunch (**zu Mittag *essen** eat lunch; **zum Mittagessen** for lunch)
das Picknick [*pl* -s or -e] picnic

Essen Eating

der Appetit [-e] appetite (**guten Appetit!** enjoy your meal!; **den Appetit *ver'derben** spoil one's appetite)
der Geschmack [ˮe] taste
die Portion [-en] portion; helping

***an|bieten** offer
be'dienen serve (**sich be'dienen** serve oneself; **die Selbstbedienung** self-service)
***bitten um** + A ask for
***essen** eat (**et gern essen** like [eating] sth; **zu Mittag/zu Abend essen** have lunch/dinner)
Hunger *m* ***haben**; **hungrig *sein** be hungry
leben von + D live on
***mögen** like
***nach|geben** offer a second helping of (**die zweite Portion** [-en] second helping)
reichen pass (**herum|reichen** pass round)
schlucken swallow
schmecken taste (**es schmeckt gut** it tastes good; **schmeckt es?** do you like it?; **kosten; probieren** taste [= try])
***schneiden** cut
***ver'schlingen** devour
tranchieren; *auf|schneiden carve

es ist . . .
 altbacken stale
 angebrannt burnt
 angegangen high [meat, game]
 appetitlich appetizing
 bitter bitter
 eßbar; genießbar edible
 fade tasteless; insipid

gar cooked
geräuchert smoked
halbgar underdone; half-done
knusprig crisp
nahrhaft nourishing
pikant savoury; well-seasoned
ranzig rancid
reichhaltig ample
roh raw
salzig salty
sauer sour
scharf hot
stark strong
süß sweet
trocken dry (**getrocknet; Trocken-** dried)
ungenießbar inedible
verdaulich/unverdaulich digestible/indigestible
verkocht overcooked
würzig spicy
zäh tough
zart tender

Essen gehen Eating out

der Aschenbecher [-] ashtray
die Bedienung service (**einschließlich/inklusive Bedienung** service charge included)
die Beilage [-n] side-dish; side-salad; accompanying vegetables
die Bestellung [-en] order (**nur auf Bestellung** to order only)
die Bierhalle [-n] beer hall
das Café [-s] café (**die Café-Konditorei [-en]** pastry shop with café attached)
die Eisdiele [-n] ice-cream parlour
der Gasthof [ˆe]; das Gasthaus [ˆer] inn
der Gesamtbetrag [ˆe] total (**insgesamt** in total)
die Grillstube [-n] steak-house
die Imbißbude [-n] snack-stall; hot-dog stand

die Karte/Speisekarte [-n] menu (**die Weinkarte** wine list; **das Menü** [-s]; **das Gedeck** [-e] set meal; **das Tagesmenü** meal of the day)

der Kellner [-] waiter (**die Kellnerin** [-nen] waitress; **Herr Ober!/ Fräulein!** waiter!/waitress!; **der/die Weinkellner/in** wine waiter)

der Oberkellner [-] head waiter

die Pizzeria [*pl* -s or **Pizzerien**] pizzeria

die Raststätte [-n] motorway service restaurant

die Rechnung [-en] bill

das Restaurant [-s]; [less formal] **die Gaststätte** [-n] restaurant (**das Restaurant mit Straßenverkauf** take-away; **das Essen zum Mitnehmen** take-away food; **et zum Mitnehmen** a take-away)

der Ruhetag [-e] closing day (**dienstags Ruhetag** closed Tuesdays)

der Schnellimbiß [-sse] snack-bar (**der Imbiß** snack)

das Schnellrestaurant [-s] fast-food restaurant (**das Fast food** fast food)

die Serviette [-n] napkin

die Spezialität [-en] (**des Hauses**) speciality (of the house) (**hausgemacht** home-made)

der Stammtisch [-e] regulars' table

das Trinkgeld [-er] tip

die Weinstube [-n] wine bar

das Wirtshaus [̈er]; **die Bierstube** [-n]; **das Lokal** [-e]; *colloq* **die Kneipe** [-n] pub

der Zahnstocher [-] toothpick

der Zuschlag [̈e] supplement

aus|suchen choose

be'stellen order

*emp'fehlen recommend

*essen eat (**beim Chinesen/Griechen/Italiener essen** eat Chinese/ Greek/Italian)

falsch/zu viel *heraus|geben give the wrong/too much change

ins Café/Restaurant *gehen go to a café/restaurant

reservieren *lassen book

stimmen be correct (**es stimmt so** keep the change)

sich ver'rechnen make an error
zahlen pay (**getrennt zahlen** pay separately).

SEE ALSO: **Drinks; Food; The Senses; Tobacco and Drugs**

11. Crimes and Criminals
Verbrechen und Verbrecher

Verbrechen Crimes

die Alarmanlage [-n] burglar alarm

der Angriff [-e] attack

das Attentat [-e]; der Mordanschlag [≃e] attempt on sb's life
(**ver'üben** make [attempt on life])

die Bestechung bribery (**das Bestechungsgeld [-er]** bribe)

der Betrug fraud

die Beute loot

die Brandstiftung arson (**in Brand** *m* **setzen** set fire to)

der Diebstahl [≃e] theft

der Drogenhandel drug-trafficking

der Einbruch [≃e] burglary; break-in

die Entführung [-en] hijack; abduction

die Erpressung [-en] blackmail

die Fälschung [-en] forgery

der Faustschlag [≃e] punch (**an den Kopf** to the head)

der Fußtritt [-e] kick

die Gaunerei [-en] swindle; swindling

die Geiselnahme hostage-taking (**die Geisel [-n]** [male or female]
hostage; **als Geisel *nehmen/*fest|halten** take/hold sb hostage)

die Handgreiflichkeiten *f pl* scuffle (**handgreiflich *werden** come
to blows; **es kam zu Handgreiflichkeiten** a scuffle broke out)

der Hausfriedensbruch; das unbefugte Betreten trespass

das Kidnapping [-s] kidnapping (**das Lösegeld [-er]** ransom)

die Kuppelei procuring

der Ladendiebstahl [≃e] shop-lifting; shop theft

die Landstreicherei; [in cities] die Stadtstreicherei vagrancy

der Meineid perjury

der Mord [-e] murder

die Prostitution prostitution

der Raub [*pl* **Raubüberfälle**] robbery (**der bewaffnete Raubüberfall** robbery with violence)
das Rauschgift narcotics
die Schlägerei [-en]; **die Rauferei** [-en] fight; brawl
der Schmuggel smuggling
der Schuß [﹦sse] shot
der Schwindel *no pl* fraud; confidence trick
die Spionage espionage
der Straßendiebstahl highway robbery
der Taschendiebstahl [﹦e] pocket-picking
der Totschlag manslaughter; homicide
der Überfall [﹦e] hold-up; attack
die Unterschlagung embezzlement
das Verbrechen [-] (**an** + D; **gegen** + A) crime (against)
die Vergewaltigung [-en] rape
die Vergiftung poisoning (**das Gift** [-e] poison)
der Verrat treason (**der Hochverrat** high treason)
die Waffe [-n] weapon (**bewaffnet** armed)

Verbrecher Criminals

die Bande [-n]; **die Gang** [-s] gang
der Bandit [-en] bandit
der/die Brandstifter/in [-/-nen] arsonist
der/die Dieb/in [-e/-nen] thief
der/die Drogenhändler/in [-/-nen] drug dealer
der/die Einbrecher/in [-/-nen] burglar
der/die Entführer/in [-/-nen]; **der/die Hijacker/in** [-/-nen] hijacker
der/die Erpresser/in [-/-nen] blackmailer
der/die Erst-/Rückfalltäter/in [-/-nen] first/persistent offender
der Gangster [-] gangster (**die Gangsterbraut** [﹦e] gangster's moll)
der Gauner [-] crook
der/die Geiselnehmer/in [-/-nen] hostage-taker
der/die Hehler/in [-/-nen] receiver
der/die Kidnapper/in [-/-nen] kidnapper
der Komplize [-n]/**die Komplizin** [-nen] accomplice
der/die Kriminelle *adj n* criminal

der/die **Landstreicher/in** [-/-nen]; [in cities] **der/die Stadt-
streicher/in** [-/-nen] vagrant
der/die **Meineidige** *adj n* perjurer
der/die **Mörder/in** [-/-nen] murderer
der/die **Räuber/in** [-/-nen] robber; kidnapper
der **Rowdy** [-s] hooligan; yob
der/die **Schmuggler/in** [-/-nen] smuggler
der/die **Spion/in** [-e/-nen] spy
der/die **Taschendieb/in** [-e/-nen] pickpocket
der/die **Terrorist/in** [-en/-nen] terrorist
der/die **Übeltäter/in** [-/-nen] wrong-doer
der/die **Verbrecher/in** [-/-nen] criminal
der **Verräter** [-] traitor (**die Verräterin** traitress)
der **Wilderer** [-]; der **Wilddieb** [-e] poacher
der **Zuhälter** [-] pimp

Was sie tun What they do

*an|greifen attack
*auf|brechen break into [car]
aus|rauben rob [bank, safe, etc.] (be'rauben rob [person])
be'drohen threaten
*be'gehen; ver'üben commit
be'lästigen importune
*be'stechen bribe
*be'stehlen um + A rob (sb) of
betroffen *sein von + D be implicated in
*be'trügen swindle
durch'suchen (nach + D) search (for)
*ein|brechen in + A break into; burgle
ent'führen hijack; abduct
*ent'kommen escape
er'morden murder
*er'schießen shoot dead (*schießen auf + A shoot at; das
Gewehr [-e] gun; der Revolver [-] revolver; die Pistole [-n] pistol)
*er'stechen stab to death (das Messer [-] knife; der Dolch [-e]
dagger)

er'würgen strangle
gaunern swindle
kämpfen mit + D fight with
kidnappen kidnap
plündern loot
sich prostituieren prostitute oneself
sich raufen um + A fight over
rücksichtslos/unter Alkoholeinfluß *fahren drive recklessly/under
  the influence of alcohol (**Alkohol** *m* **am Steuer** drink-driving)
*schießen auf + A shoot at
spionieren spy
sprengen; in die Luft sprengen blow up
*stehlen steal (**klauen** *colloq* pinch)
täuschen deceive
töten; *um|bringen kill
*über'fallen attack; hold-up; mug
*unter'schlagen embezzle
ver'gewaltigen rape
ver'giften poison
*zwingen; [break open] *auf|brechen force

Ausrufe Cries

es brennt! fire!
haltet den Dieb! stop thief!
Hände hoch! hands up!
hau ab! clear off!
Hilfe! help!
hör auf! stop it!
laß mich los! let go!
Mord! murder!
Vorsicht! look out!

SEE ALSO: **Describing People; Justice and Law**

12. Describing People
Beschreibungen von Menschen

---

das Alter [-] age
das Aussehen appearance (**dem Aussehen nach** to judge by
  appearances)
das Benehmen; das Verhalten behaviour (**D + gegenüber**
  towards; **das Betragen** behaviour [of child])
die Beschreibung; die Schilderung description
der Charakter character
die Eigenschaft [-en] quality
die Entschuldigung [-en] excuse
der Fehler [-] fault
das Gewissen conscience (**rein** clear; **schlecht** bad)
die Gewohnheit [-en] habit
der Instinkt [-e] instinct
das Laster [-] vice
die Laune [-n]; **die Stimmung** [-en] mood (**guter/schlechter Laune**
  in a good/bad mood)
die Moral *sing* morals
die Natur; das Wesen nature (**von Natur aus** by nature)
die Schwäche [-n] weakness; demerit
die Tugend [-en] virtue
der Vorzug [¨e] merit

sich *be'nehmen; sich *ver'halten behave
***be'schreiben** describe
***scheinen** seem; appear
zeigen show

Das Äußere External appearance

die Ähnlichkeit (mit + D) resemblance (to)
der Ausdruck [¨e] expression
das Doppelkinn double chin

die **Falte** [-n] wrinkle
der **Gang** gait
die **Gesichtsfarbe** [-n]; der **Teint** [-s] complexion
der **Gesichtszug** [ːe] feature
die **Geste** [-n] gesture
das **Gewicht** weight
die **Größe** height
das **Grübchen** [-] dimple
die **Haltung** bearing
der **Körperbau** build
der **Leberfleck** [-e] mole
die **Miene** [-n] (facial) expression
die **Narbe** [-n] scar
der **Pickel** [-] spot
die **Reinlichkeit**; die **Sauberkeit** cleanliness
die **Schmutzigkeit** dirtiness
der **Schönheitsfleck** [-e] beauty spot
die **Sommersprosse** [-n] freckle

ähnlich sein (+ D) be like (sb)
*aus|sehen **(wie)** look (like)
sich *be'nehmen behave
. . . **Meter groß** *sein be . . . metres tall
*scheinen seem
*wiegen weigh

wie ist er/sie? what's he/she like?
 adrett smart
 aktiv active
 alt old
 auffallend striking
 bärtig bearded
 blaß pale
 blaßgelb sallow
 blind blind
 braungebrannt tanned
 bucklig hunchbacked
 dick fat

doof daft
dünn thin
eigenartig odd
einsam lonely
elegant; smart smart
ernst serious
faltig wrinkled
fett obese
fleckig blotchy
gebrechlich frail
glatt rasiert clean-shaven
groß big; tall (**der Riese [-n]/die Riesin [-nen]** giant/giantess)
gutaussehend good-looking
häßlich ugly
hellhäutig fair-skinned
hübsch pretty
jung young
kahl bald (**eine Glatze** a bald head)
klein small (**der/die Zwerg/in [-e/-nen]** dwarf)
komisch funny; odd
kräftig strong
kurzsichtig short-sighted
lächerlich ridiculous
lahm lame
lang long
mager thin
mittelgroß; mittlerer Größe medium-sized; of medium height
müde tired
muskulös muscular
nett nice
niedlich cute
oval oval [face]
pick(e)lig pimply; spotty
proper trim
rechtshändig right-handed (**linkshändig** left-handed)
reizend charming
rund round

sauber clean
schlank slim
schön beautiful; handsome
schmächtig weedy
schmutzig dirty
schwer heavy
seltsam; sonderbar strange
sinnlich sensual; sensuous
sonnengebräunt sun-tanned
spitz pointed [face, nose]
stumm dumb
süß sweet
taub deaf
traurig sad
weitsichtig long-sighted
winzig tiny
zart delicate
zierlich slight
zornig angry

Gute Eigenschaften Good qualities

der Adel nobility   **edel** noble
die Anständigkeit decency   **anständig** decent
die Aufrichtigkeit sincerity   **aufrichtig** sincere
die Bescheidenheit modesty   **bescheiden** modest
der Charme charm   **charmant** charming
die Dankbarkeit gratitude   **dankbar** grateful
die Demut humility   **demütig** humble
die Ehre honour (**das Ehrenwort** word of honour)   **ehrenwert;**
  ehrenhaft honourable
der Ehrgeiz ambition   **ehrgeizig** ambitious
die Ehrlichkeit honesty   **ehrlich** honest
der Eifer zeal   **eifrig** zealous
die Einfachheit simplicity   **einfach** simple
die Einsicht understanding   **einsichtig** understanding
der Ernst seriousness   **ernst; ernsthaft** serious

die Exaktheit precision   **exakt** exact; precise
der Fleiß industry   **fleißig** industrious
die Freigebigkeit generosity   **freigebig** generous
die Freude joy   **freudig** joyful
die Freundlichkeit friendliness   **freundlich** friendly
die Fröhlichkeit cheerfulness   **froh; fröhlich** cheerful
die Furchtlosigkeit fearlessness   **furchtlos** fearless
die Geduld patience   **geduldig** patient
der Gehorsam obedience   **gehorsam** obedient
der Geist wit   **geistreich** witty
die Gerechtigkeit justice   **gerecht** just
die Geschicklichkeit; die Geschicktheit skilfulness (**das Geschick**
 [**-e**] skill)   **geschickt** skilful; clever
das Gewissen conscience   **gewissenhaft** conscientious
die Gnade mercy   **gnädig** merciful
die Großherzigkeit magnanimity   **großherzig** magnanimous
die Großzügigkeit generosity   **großzügig** generous
die Güte goodness; kindness   **gut** good; **gütig** kindly
die Gutmütigkeit good nature   **gutmütig** good-natured
die Herzlichkeit cordiality   **herzlich** cordial
die Höflichkeit politeness; courtesy   **höflich** polite; courteous
der Humor humour (**der Sinn für Humor** sense of humour)
 humorvoll humorous [person]
die Intelligenz intelligence   **intelligent** intelligent
die Klugheit cleverness   **klug** clever
die Kraft [⁼e] strength; power; energy   **kräftig** strong; powerful
die Liebe love   **liebevoll** loving
die Liebenswürdigkeit kindness   **liebenswürdig** kind
die Mäßigkeit moderation   **mäßig** moderate
die Menschlichkeit; die Humanität humanity   **menschlich**
 human; **human** humane
die Milde benevolence   **mild** benevolent
das Mitgefühl compassion   **mitfühlend** compassionate
das Mitleid pity   **mitleidig** pitying; sympathetic
der Mut bravery   **mutig** brave; courageous
die Natürlichkeit naturalness   **natürlich** natural
die Nettigkeit kindness   **nett** nice; kind

die Offenheit candour; openness   **offen** candid; open
der Optimismus optimism   **optimistisch** optimistic
die Reinheit purity   **rein** pure
der Respekt (vor + D) respect (for)   **respektvoll** respectful
die Rücksichtnahme consideration   **rücksichtsvoll** considerate
die Ruhe calmness   **ruhig** calm
die Sanftmütigkeit gentleness   **sanftmütig** gentle
der Scharfsinn astuteness   **scharfsinnig** astute
die Schlichtheit unpretentiousness   **schlicht** unpretentious
der Schneid guts   **schneidig** gutsy; daring
die Selbstsicherheit self-reliance   **selbstsicher** self-reliant
die Sensibilität sensitivity   **sensibel** sensitive
die Sorgfalt care (**die Sorgfältigkeit** carefulness)   **sorgfältig**
  careful
die Stärke strength   **stark** strong
der Stolz pride   **stolz (auf + A)** proud (of)
der Takt tact   **taktvoll** tactful
die Tapferkeit gallantry   **tapfer** gallant
die Toleranz tolerance   **tolerant** tolerant
die Treue loyalty; fidelity   **treu** loyal; faithful
die Umsicht circumspection   **umsichtig** circumspect
die Unschuld innocence   **unschuldig** innocent
die Vernunft reason; common sense   **vernünftig** sensible
die Verschwiegenheit discretion   **verschwiegen** discreet
das Vertrauen trust   **vertrauensvoll** trustful
die Voraussicht foresight   **vorausschauend** foresighted
die Vorsicht care; caution   **vorsichtig** careful; cautious
die Weisheit wisdom   **weise** wise
die Wohltätigkeit; die Nächstenliebe charity   **wohltätig**
  charitable
die Zartheit delicacy   **zart** delicate
die Zärtlichkeit tenderness   **zärtlich** tender; loving
die Zufriedenheit contentment   **zufrieden** content
die Zurückhaltung reserve   **zurückhaltend** reserved

billigen approve
be'lohnen reward

danken (+ D) thank (sb)
loben praise
miteinander *aus|kommen get along together
ruhig *bleiben; die Ruhe be'wahren keep cool
sich *zusammen|nehmen pull oneself together

Fehler Faults

die Affektiertheit affectation   **affektiert** affected
die Angeberei showing-off   **angeberisch** pretentious
die Ängstlichkeit timidity   **ängstlich** timid; anxious
der Ärger annoyance; anger   **ärgerlich (über + A)** annoyed
 (at)
die Arroganz arrogance   **arrogant** arrogant
die Beiläufigkeit casualness; off-handedness   **beiläufig** casual;
 offhanded
die Blödheit stupidity   **blöd** stupid
die Boshaftigkeit; die Bösartigkeit maliciousness   **boshaft;
 bösartig** malicious
die Bosheit malice   **böse** wicked; malicious [also cross]
die Doofheit *colloq* daftness   **doof** *colloq* daft
die Dummheit stupidity   **dumm** stupid
die Eifersucht jealousy   **eifersüchtig (auf + A)** jealous (of)
die Eitelkeit vanity   **eitel** vain
die Falschheit deceitfulness   **falsch** deceitful
die Faulheit laziness (**der/die Faulenzer/in** [-/-nen] lazybones)
 faul lazy
die Feigheit cowardice   **feig(e)** cowardly
die Feindseligkeit hostility   **feindlich; feindselig** hostile
die Frechheit cheek(iness)   **frech** cheeky
die Gedankenlosigkeit thoughtlessness   **gedankenlos** thoughtless
die Gefräßigkeit gluttony   **gefräßig** gluttonous
die Gehässigkeit spite(fulness)   **gehässig** spiteful
die Gerissenheit; die Schläue cunning   **gerissen; schlau** cunning
die Gier greed   **gierig** greedy
die Gleichgültigkeit indifference   **gleichgültig** indifferent

die Grausamkeit cruelty   **grausam** cruel
die Grobheit coarseness   **grob** coarse
die Großspurigkeit boastfulness   **großspurig** boastful
die Hartnäckigkeit obstinacy   **hartnäckig** obstinate
die Hinterhältigkeit underhandedness   **hinterhältig** under-
   handed
der Hochmut arrogance   **hochmütig** arrogant
die Impulsivität impulsiveness   **impulsiv** impulsive
die Intoleranz intolerance   **intolerant** intolerant
die Langweiligkeit boringness (**die Langeweile** boredom)   **langweilig** boring
die Launenhaftigkeit moodiness   **launenhaft; launisch** moody
das Mißtrauen mistrust   **mißtrauisch** mistrustful
die Nachlässigkeit carelessness   **nachlässig** careless
die Naivität naïvety   **naiv** naïve
der Neid envy   **neidisch (auf + A)** envious (of)
die Neugier(de) inquisitiveness   **neugierig** inquisitive
der Pessimismus pessimism   **pessimistisch** pessimistic
die Prahlerei boasting   **prahlerisch** boastful
die Primitivität coarseness   **primitiv** coarse
die Rücksichtslosigkeit recklessness   **rücksichtslos** reckless
die Schäbigkeit meanness   **schäbig** mean
die Scheinheiligkeit hypocrisy   **scheinheilig** hypocritical
die Schlampigkeit slovenliness   **schlampig** slovenly
die Schlauheit craftiness   **schlau** crafty
die Schlechtigkeit badness   **schlecht** bad
die Schmeichelei flattery   **schmeichlerisch** flattering
die Schüchternheit shyness   **schüchtern** shy
die Schwäche [-n]; die Schwachheit [-en] weakness   **schwach**
   weak; **schwächlich** frail
die Selbstgefälligkeit; der Egotismus egotism   **selbstgefällig**
   egotistical
die Selbstzufriedenheit complacency   **selbstzufrieden** compla-
   cent
die Strenge strictness; severity   **streng** strict
die Taktlosigkeit tactlessness   **taktlos** tactless

die **Treulosigkeit** disloyalty **treulos** disloyal
die **Unartigkeit** naughtiness **unartig** naughty
die **Undankbarkeit** ingratitude **undankbar** ungrateful
die **Unehrlichkeit** dishonesty **unehrlich** dishonest
die **Unfreundlichkeit** unfriendliness **unfreundlich** unfriendly
die **Ungeduld** impatience **ungeduldig** impatient
der **Ungehorsam** disobedience **ungehorsam** disobedient
die **Ungeschicklichkeit; die Ungeschicktheit; das Ungeschick**
  clumsiness **ungeschickt** clumsy
die **Ungeselligkeit** unsociability **ungesellig** unsociable
die **Ungezogenheit** naughtiness; insolence **ungezogen** naughty;
  cheeky
die **Unhöflichkeit** rudeness **unhöflich** rude; impolite
die **Unordentlichkeit** untidyness **unordentlich** untidy
die **Unsittlichkeit** immorality **unsittlich** immoral
die **Unverschämtheit** impudence **unverschämt** impudent
die **Unzugänglichkeit** unapproachability **unzugänglich** unap-
  proachable
die **Verachtung** disdain **verachtungsvoll** disdainful
die **Verdrießlichkeit** sullenness **verdrießlich; mürrisch** sullen
die **Verlegenheit** embarrassment **verlegen** embarrassed
die **Verlogenheit** lying; mendacity **verlogen** mendacious
die **Verrücktheit** madness **verrückt** mad; crazy
die **Vulgarität** vulgarity **vulgär** vulgar
die **Wut** rage; fury (**in Wut *ge'raten** get in a rage) **wütend**
  furious
die **Zerstreutheit** absent-mindedness **zerstreut** absent-minded
der **Zorn** anger **zornig** angry

ärgern annoy (**sich ärgern** get angry)
sich auf|regen über + A get worked up about
aus|schimpfen tell off
be'dauern regret
be'leidigen insult
be'reuen + A repent of
be'strafen punish [person or deed]
sich ent'schuldigen apologize (**bei** + D to; **für** + A for)

grollen (+ D); **einen Groll *haben** (**auf** + A) hold a grudge
(against sb)
kränken offend
kritteln an + D find fault with
*lügen lie
miß'billigen [thing]; **ab|lehnen** [person] disapprove of
sich schämen (**für** + A/**wegen** + G) be ashamed (of)
(sich) täuschen deceive (oneself)
ver'ärgern vex
*ver'geben forgive

SEE ALSO: **Clothing; Education; Hair; Health and Sickness; The
Human Body; Identity; Jobs; Places, People, and Languages;
Relationships**

13. Directions Auskünfte

Was man fragt What you ask

bin ich hier richtig bei Xs? is this the Xs' house?
ist es sehr weit? is it very far?
wie komme ich zu + D, bitte? how do I get to . . . ?
wo liegt die X-Straße, bitte? where is X street?

Wo es ist Where it is

am Ende *n* at the end (**am anderen Ende** at the other end)
am Verkehrskreis(el) *m* at the roundabout
an der Ecke at the corner
an der Kreuzung at the crossroads
auf der anderen/dieser (Straßen)seite on the other/this side
auf der Straße/dem Platz *m* in the street/square
bei + D at X's [= at the house/shop of X]
beinah(e); fast almost
dort; [less precise] **da** there (**dort drüben** over there; **dort unten/
oben** down/up there)
draußen outside (**drinnen** inside; indoors)
entlang + D [or preceding A] along
etwa [+ time/distance] **von hier aus** about [+ time/distance] from
here
gegen + A against
gegenüber [+ preceding D] opposite
gerade just
geradeaus straight on
hinten im Garten at the bottom of the garden
hinter + D behind; beyond
im ersten [etc.] **Stock** on the first [etc.] floor
im Nachbarhaus next door
im Norden/Süden/Osten/Westen to the north/south/east/west (**im
Nordwesten** to the north-west)

in der entgegengesetzten/dieser Richtung in the opposite/this
  direction (**in Richtung Stadt/Bahnhof** towards town/the station)
in der Mitte (+ G/**von** + D) in the middle (of)
in der Nähe von + D near (**in unmittelbarer Nähe** right next to)
irgendwo somewhere (**nirgendwo** nowhere)
links (**von** + D) on the left (of) (**nach links** to the left)
mitten in + D in the middle of
nach + D after
neben + D beside
nördlich/südlich/östlich/westlich von + D north/south/east/west
  of
oben (**auf** + D) at the top (of); on top (of)
rechts (**von** + D) on the right (of) (**nach rechts** to the right)
über + D above
überall everywhere
unter + D under; among (**unten** underneath)
unterwegs nach + D on the way to
von + D **bis** + A from . . . to
vor + D in front of; before (**kurz vor** just before)
weit von + D (**entfernt**) far from
zwanzig Meter entfernt twenty metres away
zwischen + D **und** + D between . . . and

Was man tut What you do

*ab|biegen turn off (**rechts/links abbiegen** turn left/right)
*biegen turn (**um die Ecke biegen** turn/take the corner)
deuten/hin|deuten auf + A; ***hin|weisen auf** + A point to
*fahren [in vehicle]; ***gehen** [on foot] go (**entlang|gehen;**
  entlang|fahren go along; **hinunter|gehen; hinunter|fahren** go
  down; **hinauf|gehen; hinauf|fahren** go up; **vorbei|gehen; vor-**
  bei|fahren an + D go past; **vorwärts|gehen; vorwärts|fahren** go
  forwards; **rückwärts|gehen; rückwärts|fahren** go backwards;
  weiter|gehen; weiter|fahren (**bis**) keep going (until); **zur-**
  ück|gehen; zurück|fahren go back)
folgen + D follow
fragen ask

*nehmen take
*sehen see
suchen look for (***finden** find)
zeigen show
zurück|setzen reverse; back (**wenden** turn around)

SEE ALSO: **Holidays; Places, People, and Languages; Shops and Shopping; Towns; Transport**

14. Disasters Katastrophen

Was sie sind What they are

der **Blitzschlag** [ːe] thunderbolt
die **Dürre** [-n] drought
die **Epidemie** [-n] epidemic
das **Erdbeben** [-] earthquake (der **Erdrutsch** [-e] landslide)
das **Feuer** [-]; der **Brand** [ːe] fire
die **Flutwelle** [-n] tidal wave
die **Hungersnot** *no pl*; die **Knappheit** [-en] famine
die **Lawine** [-n] avalanche
der **Notfall** [ːe] emergency (der **Ausnahmezustand** [ːe] state of
  emergency)
der **Orkan** [-e]; [tropical storm] der **Hurrikan** [-s] hurricane
die **Pest** *no pl* plague
der **Sturm** [ːe] gale; tempest (der **Wirbelsturm** cyclone)
der **Taifun** [-e] typhoon
der **Tornado** [-s] tornado
die **Überschwemmung** [-en] flood
das **Unwetter** [-] storm (das **Gewitter** [-] thunderstorm)
der **Vulkanausbruch** [ːe] volcanic eruption (der **Vulkan** [-e]
  volcano; die **Lava** lava)

Was sie veranlassen What they cause

***ab|schneiden** cut off (**durch den Schnee/durch die Flut** by snow/
  flood; **von der Außenwelt** from the outside world)
***aus|brechen** erupt
beben tremble; shake
be'schädigen damage
***ein|brechen; ein|stürzen** cave in; collapse
ent'wurzeln uproot
er'sticken (an + D) suffocate (on)
explodieren explode

*fallen fall
herunter|strömen flow down [lava]
in Schutt und Asche *liegen lie in ashes (**der Schutt** rubble)
*nieder|brennen burn down
platzen burst
rutschen slide
*schlagen/ein|schlagen in + A strike [lightning]
*sinken sink
töten kill
*über|laufen overflow (**über die Ufer** *n pl* ***treten** overflow its
  banks; **über'fluten** flood)
ver'nichten; kaputt|machen destroy
*zer'brechen smash
zer'stören demolish

Ihre Folgen Their results

der/die Ertrunkene *adj n* drowned person
die Explosion [-en] explosion
das Koma [*pl* -s or **Komata**] coma (**im Koma *liegen** be in a
  coma)
die Lebensgefahr danger of death
der Mangel an + D lack of
das Opfer [-] victim (**der/die Tote** *adj n* dead person; **der/die
  Überlebende** *adj n* survivor; **der/die Verwundete** *adj n* casualty;
  injured person)
die Panik panic
der Schaden [⸚] *often pl* damage
der Schock [-s] shock
der Sturz [⸚e] fall
die Unterernährung malnutrition
die Verbrennung [-en] burn
die Verletzung [-en] injury
die Vernichtung destruction
die Wunde [-n]; wound
die Zerstörung demolition

sich [D] das Bein [etc.] *brechen break one's leg [etc.]
das Bewußtsein *ver'lieren lose consciousness (wieder zu
Bewußtsein *kommen regain consciousness)
bluten bleed (Blut *n* *ver'lieren lose blood)
eingeklemmt *sein be trapped
sich *er'brechen vomit; be sick
*er'trinken drown
*leiden an + D suffer from
schwer verletzt *sein be seriously injured
*sterben die (an Hunger/Durst/seinen Verletzungen of hunger/
thirst/one's injuries)
*ver'schwinden disappear

Hilfe! Help!

der Arzt [⁼e]/die Ärztin [-nen] doctor
die Bergwacht; der Bergrettungsdienst mountain rescue service
die Erste Hilfe first aid (die Sanitätswache [-n] first-aid post)
die Feuerwehr fire brigade (der Feuerwehrmann [*pl* ⁼er or -leute]
fireman; das Löschfahrzeug [-e] fire-engine; der Schlauch [⁼e]
hose; der Feuermelder [-] fire-alarm)
der/die Freiwillige *adj n* volunteer
die Hilfe help (die Hilfsorganisation [-en] relief organization)
der Hubschrauber [-] helicopter
der Krankenwagen [-] ambulance (der/die Sanitäter/in [-/-nen]
ambulance man/woman; die Trage [-n] stretcher)
die künstliche Beatmung artificial respiration (die Mund-zu-
Mund-Beatmung kiss of life; der Mund [⁼er] mouth)
die Leiter [-n] ladder
der Notfall [⁼e] emergency (der Notausgang [⁼e] emergency exit;
die Nothilfe emergency assistance)
die Rettung rescue; rescuing (die Rettungsaktion [-en] rescue
(operation); der Rettungs-/Seerettungsdienst ambulance/life-
boat service; der Seenotrettungseinsatz air-sea rescue)
der/die Rettungs-/Katastrophenhelfer/in [-/-nen] relief worker
das Rote Kreuz Red Cross (der Rote Halbmond Red Crescent)
das SOS SOS (SOS funken send an SOS)

Alarm *schlagen raise the alarm
jm zu Hilfe *kommen come to sb's aid
löschen put out [fire]
retten rescue

SEE ALSO: **Accidents; Crimes and Criminals; Health and Sickness;
War, Peace, and the Armed Services; The Weather**

15. Drinks Getränke

das Getränk [∺e]; der Drink [-s] drink
zwei Glas Wein two glasses of wine (**zwei Flaschen Bier** two
  bottles of beer [only f containers pluralize])
zwei Kaffee; zweimal Kaffee two coffees

Alkoholfreie Getränke Non-alcoholic drinks

das Coke [-s]; das/die Cola [-s] coke®
der Espresso [*pl* -s or **Espressi]** espresso coffee
das Fruchtsaftgetränk [∺e] squash
der Kaffee coffee (**Kaffee kochen** make coffee; **die Kaffeesahne**
  coffee cream; **mit/ohne Sahne** white/black; **koffeinfrei** decaf-
  feinated; **der Instant-/Pulverkaffee** instant coffee; **der Filter-
  kaffee** filter coffee; **der Mokka** strong black coffee)
der Kakao cocoa
die Limonade [-n] fizzy drink (**die Zitronenlimonade** lemonade)
die Milch milk (**entrahmt** skimmed; **das Milchmixgetränk [∺e]**
  milk shake)
die Orangeade orangeade
der Saft [∺e] (fruit) juice (**der Frucht-/Apfel-/Orangen-/Zitronen-/
  Tomaten-/Grapefruit-/Traubensaft** fruit/apple/orange/lemon/
  tomato/grapefruit/grape juice; **frisch ausgepreßt** freshly
  squeezed)
die Schokolade chocolate
das Soda(wasser) soda
der Tee tea (**mit Zitrone/Milch** with lemon/milk; **der Kräuter-/
  Eistee** herb/iced tea)
das Tonic tonic (water)
das Wasser water (**das Mineralwasser** mineral water; **mit/ohne
  Kohlensäure** sparkling/still)

Alkoholische Getränke Alcoholic drinks

der Aperitif [-s] aperitif

der Apfelwein [-e] cider (**der Cidre** [-s] Normandy/Brittany cider;
der Apfelschnaps apple brandy)

das Bier [-e] beer (**das Pils** [-] Pils(ner); **das Malzbier** malt beer;
das Faßbier/Bier vom Faß draught beer; **das Faß** [=sser] barrel;
das Flaschenbier bottled beer; **dunkel** dark; **hell** light)

der Branntwein [-e] spirit(s)

der Burgunder burgundy

der Champagner champagne℗ (**der Sekt** [-e] [quality] sparkling
wine)

der Gin gin (**Gin (und) Tonic** *n* gin and tonic)

der Glühwein mulled wine

der Kirsch; **das Kirschwasser** kirsch; white cherry brandy

der Korn corn schnapps

der Kümmel caraway brandy

der Likör [-e] liqueur (**der Eierlikör** egg-flip)

der Portwein port

die Radlermaß; **der Radler**; **das Alsterwasser** shandy

der Rum rum

der Schaumwein [-e] sparkling wine

der Schnaps [-e] spirits; schnapps

der Schoppenwein [-e] wine by the glass; draught wine (**der
Schoppen** [-] large glass of wine/beer)

die Schorle spritzer

der Sherry sherry

der Wein [-e] wine (**der Weiß-/Rotwein** white/red wine; **der Rosé**
[-s] rosé wine; **die Spät-/Auslese** late vintage)

der Weinbrand [=e]; **der Kognak** [-s] brandy (**der Cognac** [-s]
cognac℗)

der Wermut vermouth

der Whisky [-s] (Scotch) whisky (**der Whiskey** [-s] (American/
Irish) whiskey)

der Wodka vodka

Ihre Behälter Their containers

eine Dose Bier a can of beer
eine Flasche Wein a bottle of wine
ein Glas *n* **Limonade** a glass of lemonade
eine Kanne/[smaller] ein Kännchen Kaffee a pot of coffee
ein Krug *m*/**eine Kanne Wasser** a jug of water
eine Tasse Tee a cup of tea
eine Tüte Milch a carton of milk

Wie man sie lieber trinkt How you prefer them

der/die/das Halbe half (litre of beer)
die halbe Flasche [-n] half bottle
der Viertelliter quarter-litre

auf Zimmertemperatur *f* at room temperature
berauschend heady [wine]
frisch crisp
fruchtig fruity
halbtrocken medium-dry
herb very dry [wine]
mild light [wine]; smooth [brandy]
mit Blume *f* with a head [beer]
mit Wasser *n*/**Eis** *n* with water/ice (**der Eiswürfel** [-] ice-cube)
pur neat
schäumend; sprudelnd bubbly
schaumig frothy
süß; lieblich sweet
trocken [wine] dry
vollmundig full-bodied [wine]
würzig full-flavoured [beer, wine]

Was man tut What you do

betrunken *sein/*werden (von + D) be/get drunk (on) (**sich
*be'trinken** get [intentionally] drunk; **der/die Trinker/in [-/-nen]/**
[more derogatory] **der/die Säufer/in [-/-nen]** drunk; drunkard)
Durst *m* ***haben; durstig *sein** be thirsty
seinen Durst löschen/stillen quench one's thirst
ein|schenken pour (out)
herunter|kippen swig down
nippen (an + D) sip (from)
nüchtern *sein/*werden be/get sober
eine Runde kaufen buy a round [of drinks]
schlucken swallow
einen Schuß *geben in + A lace [drink]
*trinken (auf + A) drink (to) (**einen Schluck Wasser trinken**
have a drink of water; **einen trinken** have a drink; **jn unter den
Tisch trinken** drink sb under the table)
die Weinkarte ver'langen ask for the wine-list

Was man sagt What you say

auf dein/Ihr Wohl! good health!
das ist aber gut für dich! but it's good for you!
das schmeckt gut! that tastes good!
das tut gut! that does you good!
köstlich delicious
trinkbar/nicht trinkbar drinkable/not drinkable
ungenießbar undrinkable
was trinken Sie? what will you have?
zum Wohl!; [less formal] **pros(i)t!** cheers!

SEE ALSO: **Cooking and Eating; Food; The Senses; Tobacco and
Drugs**

16. Education Erziehung

Anstalten Institutions

die Berufsschule [-n] vocational school
die Fachhochschule [-n] specialist tertiary college
die Fachschule [-n] technical college (**die kaufmännische
Fachschule** business school)
die Gesamtschule [-n] comprehensive school
die Grundschule [-n] primary school
das Gymnasium [*pl* Gymnasien] academic secondary school
(= grammar school)
die Handelsschule [-n] commercial college
die Hauptschule [-n] non-academic secondary school
das Internat [-e] boarding-school
der Kindergarten [≐] kindergarten; nursery school
die Mittel-/Realschule [-n] practical secondary school
die pädagogische Hochschule [-n] teacher-training college
die Privatschule [-n] private school
die Schule [-n] school (**zur/in die Schule *gehen** go to school; **die
höhere Schule** secondary school; **die Schule *ver'lassen** leave
school)
die Universität [-en]; die Hochschule [-n]; *colloq* **die Uni [-s]**
university (**die technische Hochschule** technical college/univer-
sity)

Wer man ist Who people are

der/die Direktor/in [G -s/- *pl* -en/-nen] head/principal
der/die Grundschullehrer/in [-/-nen] primary-school teacher
der/die Gymnasiast/in [-en/-nen] grammar-school boy/girl
der/die Hauptschüler/in [-/-nen] secondary (modern)-school boy/
girl
der/die Hochschüler/in [-/-nen] college/university student
der/die Internatschüler/in [-/-nen] boarder (**der/die externe
Schüler/in [-/-nen]** day-boy/-girl)

der/die Klassenkamerad/in [-en/-nen] class-mate
der/die Klassensprecher/in [-/-nen] class representative
der/die Lehrbeauftragte *adj n* university teacher; lecturer (**der/die Dozent/in** [-en/-nen] senior lecturer)
der/die Lehrer/in [-/-nen] teacher (**der Lehrkörper** staff; **der/die Deutschlehrer/in** German teacher)
der/die Mitschüler/in [-/-nen] fellow pupil
die Null [-en] dunce
der/die Professor/in [G -s/- *pl* -en/-nen] (**für** + A) professor (of)
der/die Prüfer/in [-/-nen] examiner
der/die Rektor/in [G -s/- *pl* -en/-nen] [school] head; [university] = vice-chancellor
der/die Schulabgänger/in [-/-nen] school-leaver
der/die Schulanfänger/in [-/-nen] child starting school
der/die Schüler/in [-/-nen] pupil
der/die Schulfreund/in [-e/-nen] schoolfriend
der Schuljunge [-n] schoolboy (**das Schulmädchen** [-] schoolgirl; **das Schulkind** schoolchild)
der/die Schulkamerad/in [-en/-nen] schoolfriend
der/die Schulleiter/in [-/-nen] head
der Schulrat [⁼e]/**die Schulrätin** [-nen] schools inspector
der/die Schulschwänzer/in [-/-nen] truant
der/die Schulsprecher/in [-/-nen] pupils' representative
der/die Student/in [-en/-nen] student
der/die Studienassessor/in [G -s/- *pl* -en/-nen]; **der/die Studienreferendar/in** [-e/-nen] probationary teacher
der Studienrat [⁼e]/**die Studienrätin** [-nen] post-probationary secondary teacher

Was man tut What they do

*ab|schreiben (**bei** + D) copy (from sb)
antworten answer
anwesend/abwesend *sein be present/absent
arbeiten work
*auf|haben have as homework
auf|passen pay attention

be'antworten; antworten auf + A answer
be'fragen über + A question on
begabt/unbegabt *sein be talented/untalented
sich *be'nehmen; brav *sein behave (well) (**sich schlecht benehmen** behave badly)
be'strafen punish
buchstabieren spell (aloud) (**wie schreibst du das?** how do you spell that?)
*durch|sehen read through
ein|sammeln collect in
faul/fleißig/gewissenhaft *sein be lazy/hard-working/conscientious
faulenzen idle (about)
fragen ask (**Fragen** *f pl* **stellen** ask questions)
*geben teach [a subject]
gut *können be good at
klingeln ring (**es hat schon geklingelt** the bell's gone)
lehren; unter'richten teach [a person or a subject]
lernen learn (**auswendig lernen** learn by heart)
*lesen read
loben praise
sich melden put one's hand up
*nach|sitzen be in detention (**nachsitzen *lassen** put in detention)
prüfen test; examine
*schreiben write (**eine Arbeit schreiben** do a test)
die Schule *ver'lassen leave school
schwänzen truant (**eine Stunde schwänzen** cut a lesson)
*sitzen|bleiben repeat a year
studieren be at university; study
ver'bessern; korrigieren correct
*ver'weisen expel
wieder'holen revise
*wissen know [facts]
zur Schule *gehen attend/be at school

Was man lehrt und lernt
What they teach and learn

die **Algebra** algebra

die **Arithmetik**; das **Rechnen** arithmetic (**das Kopfrechnen** mental
  arithmetic)

die **Biologie** biology

die **Chemie** chemistry

die **Computerwissenschaft** computer science

das **Deutsch** German

die **Dichtung** poetry

die **Elektronik** electronics

das **Englisch** English

die **Erdkunde**; die **Geographie** geography

das **Fach** [⸚er] subject (**das Pflichtfach** compulsory subject; das
  Wahlfach option)

das **Französisch** French

die **Fremdsprache** [-n] foreign language

die **Geometrie** geometry

der **Gesang(s)unterricht** singing

die **Geschichte** history

die **Grammatik** grammar

das **Handarbeiten** needlework

die **Hauswirtschaftslehre** domestic science

die **Kunst** art

das **Latein** Latin

das **Lesen** reading

die **Literatur** literature

die **Mathematik**; *colloq* die **Mathe** *both sing* maths

die **Medizin** medicine

die **Musik** music

die **Pharmazie** pharmacy

die **Philosophie** philosophy

die **Physik** physics

die **Psychologie** psychology

die **Rechtschreibung** spelling

die **Rechtswissenschaft** law
die **Religion; der Religionsunterricht** religious education
das **Schreiben** writing
der **Schulunterricht** *no pl* lessons (**der Unterricht** teaching)
das **Spanisch** Spanish
die **Sprache** [-n] language (**neuere Sprachen** modern languages)
die **Technik** technology
das **Turnen; der Sportunterricht** physical education
das **Werken** craft
der **Werkunterricht** woodwork and metalwork
die **Wirtschaftslehre** business studies
die **Wissenschaft** [-en]/die **Naturwissenschaft** *usually pl* science
  (**rein** pure; **angewandt** applied; die **Sozialwissenschaften** *pl*
  social science; die **exakten Naturwissenschaften** *pl* physical
  science)
der **Zeichenunterricht** drawing

Die Umgebung Things around them

die **Aufgabe** [-n] exercise
der **Aufsatz** [ǂe] essay
die **Aula** [*pl* -s or **Aulen**] (assembly) hall
die **Bibliothek** [-en] library
der **Bleistift** [-e] pencil (der **Spitzer** [-] pencil-sharpener)
das **Buch** [ǂer] book (das **Schulbuch** school-book)
der **Computer** [-] computer
die **Disziplin** discipline
der **Entwurf** [ǂe]; das **Konzept** [-e] rough copy
die **Erziehung** education
das **Feder-/Schreibmäppchen** [-] pencil-case
der **Filzstift** [-e] felt pen
die **Frage** [-n] question (die **Antwort** [-en] answer; **stellen** ask;
  be'antworten answer)
der **Füllhalter** [-]; der **Füller** [-]; der **Federhalter** [-] fountain-pen
  (die **Feder** [-n] nib; quill-pen)
der **Gang** [ǂe] corridor
die **Garderobe** [-n] cloakroom

der Gummi/Radiergummi [-s] rubber; eraser

die Hausaufgabe [-n] (piece of) homework (**machen** do)

das Heft [-e] exercise book

der Hof/Schulhof [ˉe] playground

die Kantine [-n]; **das Kasino** [-s] canteen

das/der Katheder [-]; **das Pult** [-e] (lecturer's) lectern

die Klasse [-n]; **der Kurs** [-e] class

das Klassenbuch [ˉer] class register (and work record)

das Klassenzimmer [-] class-room

die Klingel [-n] bell

die Kreide [-n] chalk

der Kugelschreiber [-]; **der Kuli** [-s] ball-point

das Laboratorium [*pl* **Laboratorien**]; **das Labor** [*pl* -s or -e]
lab(oratory) (**das Sprachlabor** language laboratory)

das Lehrerzimmer [-] staff room

das Lexikon [*pl* **Lexika** or **Lexiken**] encyclopaedia

das Lineal [-e] ruler

die Mappe [-n] briefcase (**die Schulmappe; die (Schul)tasche** [-n];
der (Schul)ranzen [-] schoolbag; satchel)

die Nachhilfe coaching (**die Nachhilfestunde** [-n] private lesson)

das Nachsitzen detention (**eine Stunde /nachsitzen *müssen** have
an hour's detention)

das Notizbuch [ˉer] notebook

das Papier paper (**das Blatt** [ˉer] sheet)

die Pause break (**klein** short; **groß** long)

die Preisverleihung prize-giving

die Prügelstrafe corporal punishment

der Rechner [-] calculator (**der Taschenrechner** pocket calculator)

die Reinschrift [-en] fair copy (**ins reine *schreiben** make a fair
copy of)

das Schließfach [ˉer] locker

der Schrank [ˉe] cupboard

der Schreibblock [*pl* -s or ˉe] pad

die Schulaufgabe [-n]; **die Schularbeit** [-en] (item of) homework

der Schüleraustausch [-e] school exchange

der Schulfunk schools broadcasting

das Schulgelände school grounds

der/die Schulleiter/in [-/-nen] head

die Schulordnung *sing* school rules

die Schultüte [-n] cone of sweets [given to child on first day at school]

der Schwamm [ːe] sponge; duster

der Speisesaal [*pl* -säle] dining-hall

das Staubtuch [ːer] duster

die Strafe [-n] punishment (**zur Strafe** as a punishment; **die Strafarbeit** [-en] imposition)

das Studentenheim [-e] hall of residence

das Studium [*pl* **Studien**] study

die Stunde [-en] lesson (**die Lektion** [-en] lesson [in book]; **der Stundenplan** [ːe] timetable)

die Tafel [-n] blackboard (**an die Tafel *schreiben** write on the board)

die Tinte [-n] ink (**der Klecks** [-e] blot)

der Tisch [-e] [school] desk (**der Lehrertisch** teacher's desk)

das Tonbandgerät [-e] tape recorder

die Turnhalle [-n] gymnasium (**das Seil** [-e] rope; **das Reck** [*pl* -e or -s] horizontal bar; **der Barren** [-] (set of) parallel bars; **das (Sprung)pferd** [-e] vaulting-horse)

die Übersetzung [-en] translation

der Vortrag [ːe]; [university] **die Vorlesung** [-en] lecture (***halten** give)

das Wörterbuch [ːer] dictionary

das Zeugnis [-se] (school) report; certificate

der Zirkel [-] (pair of) compasses

Prüfungen Examinations

das Abitur [-e] *sing* = A-levels (**das Abitur machen** = take A-levels)

die Arbeit/Klassenarbeit [-en]; **der Test** [*pl* -s or -e] test (***schreiben** take; **schreiben *lassen** give)

das Attest [-e] doctor's certificate

das Diplom [-e] diploma; first science degree

der Doktorgrad [-e] doctorate; PhD (**die Doktorarbeit** [-en] PhD thesis)

der Erfolg [-e] success

das Ergebnis [-se] result

der Fehler [-]; **der Irrtum** [¨er] mistake

der Fortschritt [-e] *often pl* progress

der Grad [-e] degree

der Hochschulabschluß [¨sse] first degree [at university]

die Leistung [-en] performance; achievement

der Magister master's degree (**Magister Artium/rerum naturalium** MA/MSc; **den Magister machen** get one's master's degree)

die Mindestpunktzahl [-en] pass-mark

die mittlere Reife leaving certificate from *Realschule*

die Note [-n] mark (**ungenügend** unsatisfactory; **mangelhaft** poor; **befriedigend** fair; (**sehr**) **gut** (very) good)

der Preis [-e] prize (**die Preisverleihung** [-en] prize-giving; award ceremony)

das Problem [-e] problem

der/die Prüfer/in [-/-nen] examiner

die Prüfung [-en]; **das Examen** [*pl* - or **Examina**]; **die Klausur** [-en] examination (**machen**/**schreiben** take; **be'stehen** pass; **durch|fallen in** + D fail; **schriftlich** written; **mündlich** oral)

der Schulabschluß [¨sse] school-leaving qualification

das Staatsexamen finals [at university]

die Urkunde [-n] certificate

Das Schul- und Universitätsjahr
The academic year

der Feiertag [-e] (day's) holiday (**der freie Tag** day off; **heute haben wir schulfrei** there's no school today)

die Ferien *pl* holidays (**die Schulferien** school holidays; **die großen Ferien/die Sommerferien** summer holidays; **die Weihnachts-/Oster-/Herbstferien** Christmas/Easter/autumn holidays)

das Halbjahr [-e] [school] term
die Klassenfahrt [-en] school trip
der Schulanfang first day at school; school starting time
das Schuljahr [-e] school year (**das Universitätsjahr** university
  year)
der Schulschluß end of school (**nach Schulschluß** after school)
der Schultag [-e] school day
das Semester [-] [university] term (**das Trimester [-]** term [three
  per year]; **das Quartal** term [-e] [four per year])
der Stundenplan [-̈e] timetable

SEE ALSO: **Identity; Reading and Writing; Science**

17. Feelings Gefühle

die **Empfindlichkeit** [-en] sensitivity
das **Gefühl** [-e] feeling; emotion (die **Ergriffenheit** [deep] emotion)
der **Geisteszustand** [¨e] state of mind
die **Leidenschaft** [-en] passion
die **Sentimentalität** sentimentality
die **Stimmung** [-en]; die **Laune** [-n] mood (die **Verstimmung** [-en]; die **schlechte Laune** bad mood; **Launen *haben** be moody)
das **Temperament** disposition

Glück Happiness

die **Befriedigung**; die **Genugtuung** satisfaction
die **Begeisterung** enthusiasm
die **Ekstase** [-n] ecstasy
die **Freude** [-n] joy
die **Fröhlichkeit** cheerfulness
die **gehobene Stimmung** *sing* high spirits
das **Gelächter**; das **Lachen** laughter (**ein lautes Lachen** a loud laugh; die **Lachsalve** [-n] roar of laughter; **in Gelächter *aus|brechen** burst out laughing)
die **Gelassenheit** serenity
das **Glück** happiness; luck (**Glück *haben** be lucky/in luck; **Glück *bringen** bring good luck)
die **Heiterkeit** cheerfulness
die **Hoffnung** [-en] hope
der **Humor** humour
das **Lächeln** *no pl* smile
die **Leidenschaft** [-en] passion
die **Lust** [¨e] desire
der **Optimismus** optimism
die **Ruhe** calm
die **Seligkeit/Glückseligkeit** bliss

die Sorglosigkeit carefreeness
der Spaß [≈e] joke; (piece of) fun; prank (**Spaß machen** be fun; **Spaß *haben an** + D take pleasure in)
das Vergnügen [-]; **die Vergnügung** [-en] pleasure; delight (**ein Vergnügen** a treat)
die Verzückung rapture
der Witz [-e] joke
die Zufriedenheit contentment

sich amüsieren enjoy oneself
auf|heitern cheer (sb) up
sich be'geistern für + A be enthusiastic about
ent'zücken enchant
er'freuen delight; gladden
freuen please (**es freut mich, zu** . . . I'm pleased/glad to . . .)
*ge'nießen enjoy
guter Laune f ***sein** be in a good mood
hoch erfreut *sein be delighted
kichern giggle (**der Kicheranfall** [≈e] fit of the giggles)
lächeln smile
lachen (über + A) laugh (about)
scherzen joke

begeistert enthusiastic
erfreut (über + A) delighted (at)
freudig; freudvoll joyful
froh; fröhlich; heiter cheerful
gelassen serene
glücklich happy; lucky
lustig merry
munter lively
optimistisch optimistic
selig blissful (**selig *sein über** + A be over the moon about)
sorglos happy-go-lucky
strahlend radiant
überglücklich overjoyed
zufrieden; vergnügt pleased; content

Unglück Unhappiness

die **Angst** [⸚e] anxiety
das **Bedauern** regret
die **Bedrängnis** affliction
die **Depression** [-en] (fit of) depression
die **Desillusionierung** disillusionment
das **Elend** misery
die **Enttäuschung** [-en] disappointment
die **Erregung** agitation
das **Heimweh** homesickness
der **Kummer**; das **Leid** grief; sorrow (**es tut mir sehr leid** I'm very
  sorry)
das **Leiden** [-] suffering
die **Melancholie** melancholy
die **Niedergeschlagenheit** dejection
die **Not** need; hardship; poverty
das **Pech** bad luck
die **Qual** [-en] torment (**die Qualen** *pl* anguish; torture)
die **Rastlosigkeit** restlessness
die **Reue** remorse
der **Schluchzer** [-] sob
der **Seufzer** [-] sigh
die **Sorge** [-n] worry; sorrow; trouble; preoccupation
die **Träne** [-n] tear (**in Tränen *aus|brechen** burst into tears)
die **Trauer** sadness
das **Unglück** [-e] misfortune
die **Unruhe** disquiet
die **Unzufriedenheit** dissatisfaction
das **Versagen** *no pl* failure
die **Verzweiflung** despair

be'**kümmern** trouble
be'**stürzen** dismay
betroffen *sein von + D be affected by
be'**unruhigen** worry; disturb
deprimieren depress

ent'täuschen disappoint
*er'tragen suffer; put up with
fehlen be missing (**du fehlst mir** I miss you)
klagen (**über** + A) complain (of/about)
kränken hurt (sb's) feelings
den Mut *ver'lieren lose heart (**der Mut** courage)
*nahe|gehen + D; *mit|nehmen distress
schlechter Laune *f* *sein be in a bad mood
schluchzen sob
schmerzen pain
schockieren shock
seufzen sigh
sich sorgen; sich [D] Sorgen machen worry
stöhnen; auf|stöhnen groan
stören disturb
trösten comfort
ver'stören disconcert
ver'zweifeln despair (**die Hoffnung *auf'geben auf** + A despair of
  sth; give up hope of sth)
weinen weep

ängstlich anxious
bedrückt despondent
bekümmert worried; distressed
berührt touched
besorgt preoccupied
bestürzt upset
betrübt gloomy; dismayed
deprimiert depressed
elend miserable; wretched
entsetzt appalled
enttäuscht disappointed
ernüchtert disenchanted
frustriert frustrated
gequält pained
im Stich gelassen let down (**der Stich** the lurch)
leidvoll distressed

melancholisch melancholy; gloomy
mißmutig sullen; morose
mitgenommen worn out; grieved (**schwer mitgenommen** shattered)
niedergeschlagen dejected
rastlos restless
traurig sad
trübsinnig gloomy
überwältigt overwhelmed
unglücklich unhappy; miserable
unleidlich; grantig grumpy
untröstlich disconsolate
unzufrieden dissatisfied
verletzt hurt
verzweifelt despairing

Überraschung Surprise

das Erstaunen astonishment
die Überraschung [-en] surprise
die Verblüffung amazement; stupefaction
die Verwirrung bewilderment
die Verwunderung amazement

Aufsehen *n* **er'regen; Sensation** *f* **machen** make a sensation
be'eindrucken; Eindruck machen auf + A impress (**der Eindruck**
  [∺e] impression)
*durcheinander|bringen throw into confusion
er'schrecken startle (***er'schrecken** be startled)
er'staunen astonish
mit offenem Mund *m* **staunen** stand open-mouthed (in
  amazement)
die Sprache *ver'schlagen + D stupefy; stagger (sb)
über'raschen surprise
ver'blüffen amaze; take aback
ver'wirren bewilder; baffle
ver'wundern amaze; astonish
sich wundern wenn . . . /über + A be surprised if . . . /at

benommen dazed
erstaunt astonished (**erstaunlich** surprising)
mit großen Augen *n pl* wide-eyed
sprachlos dumbfounded
überrascht surprised
umgehauen *colloq* flabbergasted
verblüfft amazed; taken aback
verstört disconcerted
verwirrt bewildered
verwundert amazed
wie vom Donner gerührt thunderstruck
wie vor den Kopf geschlagen stupefied

Angst Fear

die Angst [≃e] fear; anxiety (**die panische Angst** terror)
die Besorgnis alarm; apprehension
die Bestürzung consternation
das Entsetzen; der Horror horror
die Furcht fear
die Hysterie hysteria
die Panik panic
der Schau(d)er [-] shiver; shudder
der Schreck [-e]; **der Schrecken** [-] fright
die Sorge [-n] worry
die Todesqualen *f pl* agony
das Unbehagen uneasiness
die Unruhe disquiet
das Zittern trembling

Angst haben vor + D be afraid of
ängstigen frighten
be'drohen threaten
be'unruhigen worry (sb); alarm
ein|schüchtern intimidate
er'schrecken frighten (**zu Tode erschrecken** scare to death)

fürchten fear (**ich fürchte, daß** ... I'm afraid that ... ; **sich fürchten vor** + D be afraid of)

schaudern shudder (**mich schaudert bei diesem Gedanken** I shudder at the thought)

schrecken fill with dread (**mich schreckt der Gedanke** I dread the thought)

vor Schreck *m* ***sterben** die of fright

zittern tremble; shiver

zum Fürchten ***sein be (quite) frightening

ängstlich anxious
bange afraid
bedroht threatened (**bedrohend** menacing)
bekümmert troubled
besorgt worried
beunruhigt alarmed
eingeschüchtert intimidated
entsetzt horrified
erschrocken frightened (**zu Tode erschrocken** terror-stricken)
furchtbar; **fürchterlich** dreadful
furchterregend frightening
furchtlos fearless
furchtsam timid
nervös nervous
starr (**vor** + D) petrified (with)
verängstigt scared
versteinert petrified
von Panik erfaßt panic-stricken

Zorn Anger

der Ärger annoyance
die Boshaftigkeit spite
die Entrüstung indignation
die Fassung self-control (**die Fassung ***ver'lieren** lose one's composure)

die Feindschaft enmity
die Feindseligkeit hostility; antagonism
der Groll *no pl* (**auf** + A) grudge (against)
die Reizbarkeit irritability
der Schrei [-e] cry
der Streß stress
die Verärgerung vexation
die Verzweiflung exasperation
die Wut fury; rage (**der Wutausbruch** [ːe] fit of rage)
der Zorn anger

ärgern irritate (**sich ärgern** get cross)
auf die Nerven *m pl* ***gehen** (+ D) get on (sb's) nerves
sich auf|regen get worked up
brüllen roar
sich ent'rüsten become indignant
er'zürnen; er'bosen incense
Luft *f* **machen** + D give vent to
meckern; mosern *colloq* grouse
***schreien** shout
***übel|nehmen** be resentful of
ver'ärgern vex
ver'zweifeln exasperate
vor Wut schäumen fume
wüten rage

böse angry; cross
boshaft malicious
entrüstet; indigniert indignant
erbost; erzürnt incensed
feindlich; feindselig hostile
fuchsteufelswild *colloq* hopping mad
haßerfüllt filled with hatred
jähzornig hot-tempered
mieser Laune *f* in a foul temper
mürrisch sullen
übelnehmerisch; nachtragend resentful
verärgert annoyed (**ärgerlich** cross; annoying)

wütend furious
zornig (very) angry

<small>SEE ALSO:</small> **Describing People; Liking, Dislike, Comparing**

18. Food Nahrungsmittel

die Beilage [-n] side-dish
der Fisch [-e] fish (**der Fischgang [=e]** fish course)
das Fleisch meat
das Gemüse [-] vegetable(s)
das Gericht [-e] dish (**das Haupt-/Tagesgericht** main course/dish of the day)
der Imbiß [-sse] snack
der Käse [-] cheese
die Konserven *f pl* preserved/canned food
der Nachtisch [-e]; die Nach-/Süßspeise [-n]; das Dessert [-s] dessert
die Nahrung food [= nourishment] (**die Lebensmittel** *pl* food [as commodity]; **das Essen** food [as eaten]; **das Futter** food [for animals])
der Salat [-e] salad (**grün** green; **gemischt** mixed)
die Suppe [-n] soup (**die Tagessuppe** soup of the day)
der/die Vegetarier/in [-/-nen] vegetarian (**vegetarisch** vegetarian *adj*)
die Vorspeise [-n] hors-d'œuvre; starter

Gerichte Dishes

der Aufschnitt [-e]; die kalte Platte assorted cold meats (and cheeses)
das Bauernfrühstück; das Hoppelpoppel fried potatoes and bacon in scrambled egg
der Bauernschmaus ['peasant's feast'] sauerkraut with pork, sausage, and dumplings
der Bismarckhering pickled herring with onions
die Bouillon; die Fleischbrühe broth
die Brühe-/Kraftbrühe mit Einlage *f* clear soup with meatballs/ dumplings
das Curry(gericht) curry

der Eintopf [÷e]; **das Ragout** [-s] stew

das Eisbein knuckle of pork

das/die Fondue fondue [melted cheese in white wine]

die Galantine galantine [cold meat in aspic]

das Geschnetzelte *adj n* small slices of veal in wine sauce

das/der Gulasch [*pl* -e or -s] goulash

der Hackbraten meat loaf

das Hacksteak [-s]; **die Frikadelle** [-n]; **die B(o)ulette** [-n] rissole; hamburger (**der Hamburger** [-] hamburger [in roll])

(der) Handkäse mit Musik marinaded curd-cheese

das Häppchen [-] canapé

(der) Himmel und Erde apple and potato purée with liver sausage and black pudding

das Holsteiner Schnitzel [-] veal ecalope with fried egg on top

das Jägerschnitzel escalope chasseur [veal escalope in mushroom and wine sauce] (**der Jäger** [-] huntsman)

der/das Kasseler Rippenspeer cured pork ribs

die Königsberger Klopse *m pl* meatballs in caper sauce

das Labskaus = lobscouse [beef and vegetable stew with gherkins, with fried egg]

der Leberkäse meat loaf [made with minced liver and eggs]

die Leberpastete [-n] liver pâté

das Matjesfilet fillet(s) of salted herring

die Pastete [-n] vol-au-vent; pâté; pie (**die Königinpastete** chicken vol-au-vent)

die Pizza [*pl* -s or **Pizzen**] pizza

das Pökelfleisch salt meat

das Roastbeef [-s] roast sirloin of beef

die Rouladen *f pl* beef/pork/veal olives

die russischen Eier *n pl* egg mayonnaise

der Sauerbraten braised beef marinaded in vinegar

der/das Schaschlik [-s]; **der Kebab** *no pl* kebab

der Schmorbraten pot-roast

der Spieß [-e] kebab; spit (**am Spieß** spit-roasted)

der stramme Max fried egg on spiced minced pork and onions, on bread

die Sülze brawn (**das Sülzkotelett** [-s] boned pork chop in aspic)

das Wiener Schnitzel [-] veal escalope fried in breadcrumbs
das Wiener Würstchen [-] frankfurter

Soßen Sauces

die Mayonnaise mayonnaise
nach Hausfrauenart in sour-cream sauce with wine and onions
[sometimes simply = home-made]
nach Jägerart in red-wine sauce with mushrooms and root
vegetables (for game)
die Minz-/Pfefferminzsoße mint sauce
die Remoulade tartare sauce [mustardy mayonnaise with
shallots or capers]
die Soße [-n]; **die Sauce** [-n] sauce (**die Braten-/Salatsoße** gravy/
vinaigrette dressing)
der/das Tomatenketchup tomato sauce

Fleisch Meat

der Braten [-] joint; roast (**der Schweine-/Rinderbraten** roast
pork/beef; **die Scheibe** [-n] slice)
das Bries [-e] sweetbread
die Brust breast [of chicken etc.]
das Eisbein [-e] pork knuckle
der Fleischkloß [ːe]; [smaller] **das Fleischklößchen** [-] meatball
die Hachse/Haxe [-n] shank; knuckle
das Hackfleisch mince
das Herz heart
die Innereien *pl* offal
die Kaldaune [-n] (piece of) tripe (**die Kutteln** *pl* tripe)
der Kamm; [as dish] **das (Schäl)rippchen** spare ribs
die Keule [-n] leg; haunch (**die Lamm-/Kalbskeule** leg of lamb/
veal)
das Kotelett [-s] chop; cutlet
die Leber [-n] liver (**die Geflügelleber** chicken liver)
das Lendenstück [-e] tenderloin (steak)
die Niere [-n] kidney (**das Nierenstück** [ːe] loin)

das Rippchen [-] pork rib
das Rippenstück [-e] rack [of lamb]
der Rostbraten grilled steak
das Rückenstück [-e] saddle (**der Lammrücken** saddle of lamb)
das Schnitzel [-] escalope [veal, pork]
die Schulter [-n] shoulder (**die Lamm-/Kalbsschulter** shoulder of
  lamb/veal)
das Steak [-s]; **das Beefsteak** [-s] steak (**das Filetsteak** fillet steak;
  das deutsche Beefsteak = beefburger; **das Tatarsteak** steak
  tartare [raw mince]; **englisch gebraten** rare; **halb durchgebraten**
  medium rare; **durchgebraten** well done; **verbraten** overdone)
die Zunge [-n] tongue

FLEISCHARTEN NAMES OF MEATS
die Ente [-n] duck (**die Mastente** specially fattened duck)
der Frühstücks-/Schinkenspeck bacon (**der Speck** bacon fat)
die Gans [ᴂe] goose
das Geflügel poultry
das Hammelfleisch mutton
das Huhn [ᴂer] chicken (**das (Brat)hähnchen** [-] roast chicken; **das
  junge Hähnchen** spring chicken; **das Masthuhn** fattened
  chicken)
das Kalbfleisch veal
der Kapaun [-e] capon
das Lammfleisch lamb
der Puter [-]; **der Truthahn** [ᴂe] turkey
das Rindfleisch beef
der Schinken [-] ham
das Schweinefleisch pork
die Wurst [ᴂe] sausage

WURSTSORTEN NAMES OF SAUSAGES
die Bierwurst smoked beef and pork sausage
die Blutwurst [cold] black pudding
die Bockwurst [hot] large frankfurter heated in water
die Bratwurst [hot] large fried or grilled sausage

die Currywurst sliced fried sausage served with curry and
  ketchup
der Fleischkäse bologna sausage
die Frankfurter [-] frankfurter
die Jagdwurst smoked sausage with garlic and mustard
die Knackwurst [hot] smoked minced-meat sausage in tight skin
  that snaps [**knacken**] when bitten
die Leberwurst liver sausage
die Nürnberger [hot] veal and pork sausage
die Regensburger spicy smoked sausage
die Salami [*pl* - or -s] salami
die Schinkenwurst ham sausage
die Weißwurst [hot] veal, bacon, and parsley sausage
das (Wiener) Würstchen [-] [hot] wiener; small frankfurter
die Zervelatwurst smoked pork, beef and bacon sausage
die Zungenwurst tongue sausage

Wild Game

der Fasan [G -(e)s *pl* -e(n)] pheasant
der Hase [-n] hare (**der Hasenpfeffer** jugged hare; **der falsche
  Hase** meat loaf)
das Kaninchen [-] rabbit
das Perlhuhn [≈er] guinea-fowl
das Rebhuhn [≈er] partridge
das Rehfleisch; der Hirsch venison
die Schnepfe [-n] snipe
die Taube [-n] pigeon
die Wachtel [-n] quail
das Waldhuhn [≈er] grouse
die Waldschnepfe [-n] woodcock
das Wild game
der Wildbraten roast venison
das Wildschwein [-e] wild boar

Fisch Fish

die **Fischfrikadelle** [-n] fishcake
der **Fischkloß** [⸚e] fish dumpling; fish ball
das **Fischstäbchen** [-] fish finger
die **Meeresfrüchte** *f pl* seafood; shellfish
die **Scheibe** [-n] (fish) steak

FISCHARTEN NAMES OF FISH

der **Aal** [-e] eel (der **Räucheraal** smoked eel)
die **Auster** [-n] oyster
der **Barsch** [-e] perch (der **Rotbarsch** rose-fish; red sea-bass)
der **Brachsen** [-] bream
die **Flunder** [-n] flounder
die **Forelle** [-n] trout
die **Garnele** [-n] shrimp; prawn
der **Hecht** [-e] pike
der **Heilbutt** [-e] halibut
der **Hering** [-e] herring (**mariniert** pickled)
der **Hummer** [-] lobster
die **Hummerkrabbe** [-n] king prawn
die **Jakobsmuschel** [-n] scallop
der **Kabeljau** [*pl* -e or -s]; der **Dorsch** [-e] cod
der **Kalmar** [-e] squid
der **Karpfen** [-] carp
die **Klaffmuschel** [-n] clam
die **Krabbe** [-n] crab; *colloq* prawn/shrimp
der **Krebs** [-e] crayfish; crab
der **Lachs** [-e]; der **Salm** [-e] salmon (der **Räucherlachs** smoked
 salmon)
die **Languste** [-n] langouste
die **Makrele** [-n] mackerel
die **Sprotte** [-n] sprat (**Kieler Sprotten** smoked sprats)
der **Steinbutt** [-e] turbot
der **Thunfisch** [-e] tuna
der **Wittling** [-e] whiting
der **Zander** [-] pike-perch

Eier Eggs

das Ei [-er] egg (**hart-/weichgekocht** hard-/soft-boiled; **verlorene Eier** poached eggs; **Eier mit Speck** *m*/**mit Schinken** *m* bacon/ ham and eggs)
das Eigelb [-] yoke
das Eiweiß [-] white of egg
das Omelett [*pl* -e or -s] omelette
das Rührei [-er] scrambled egg
das Spiegelei [-er] fried egg

Gemüse, Nüsse und Salate
Vegetables, nuts, and salads

das Gemüse [-] vegetable(s) (**eingemacht/tiefgekühlt** canned/ frozen)
die Nuß [≈sse] nut (**der Kern [-e]** kernel)
der Salat [-e] salad (**gemischter/russischer Salat** mixed/Russian salad; **an|machen** dress [salad])

GEMÜSESORTEN NAMES OF VEGETABLES

die Artischocke [-n] artichoke (**der/die Topinambur** [*pl* -s, -e or -en]** Jerusalem artichoke)
die Aubergine [-n] aubergine
die Avocado [-s] avocado
der Blumenkohl cauliflower
die Bohne [-n] bean (**die grüne Bohne** French bean; **die Stangen-/ Feuerbohne** runner bean; **die Saubohne**; **die dicke Bohne** broad bean; **die Garten-/Kidneybohne** kidney/red kidney bean)
die Brokkoli *pl* broccoli
der/die Chicorée chicory
die Endivie [-n] endive
die Erbse [-n] pea (**junge Erbsen** petits pois; **die Zuckererbse** sugar-pea; mange-tout; **die Schote [-n]**; **die Hülse [-n]** pod)

der Fenchel *no pl* fennel

der Grün-/Krauskohl kale

die Gurke [-n] cucumber (**die Essig-/Gewürzgurke** pickled gherkin)

die Kartoffel [-n] potato (**die Salz-/Brat-/Petersilienkartoffeln** boiled/fried/parsley potatoes; **die Pellkartoffeln** pototoes boiled in their jackets; **der Kartoffelbrei/das Kartoffelpüree** mashed potatoes; **der Kartoffelpuffer [-]** potato pancake; **der Kartoffelsalat** potato salad; **die Pommes frites** *pl* chips; **das (Kartoffel)stäbchen [-]** [single] chip; **der Chip [-s]** crisp)

der Kohl cabbage (**der Rotkohl/das Blaukraut** red cabbage; **der Weißkohl** white cabbage)

der Kohlrabi [*pl* **- or -s]** kohlrabi

die Kohl-/Steckrübe [-n] turnip

der Kopfsalat [-e] lettuce

die Kresse cress (**die Brunnenkresse** watercress)

das Leipziger Allerlei mixed vegetables [peas, carrots, celery, beans, kohlrabi, and asparagus]

die Linse [-n] lentil

der Mais/Zuckermais sweetcorn (**der Maiskolben [-]** corncob; corn-on-the-cob)

der Mangold *no pl* spinach beet/Swiss chard

der Meerrettich horse-radish

die Möhre [-n]; die Mohrrübe [-n]; die Karotte [-n] carrot

die Olive [-n] olive

die Paprikaschote [-n] (sweet) pepper

der Pfifferling [-e] chanterelle (mushroom)

der Pilz [-e]; [cultivated] **der Champignon [-s]** mushroom

der Porree [-s]; der Lauch [-e] leek(s) (**magst du Porree?** do you like leeks? [*German sing = English pl*])

das Radieschen [-]; [larger] **der Rettich [-e]** raddish (**das Bund [-e]** bunch)

der Reis rice

der Rosenkohl *no pl* Brussels sprouts

die rote Rübe [-n]/Be(e)te [-n] beetroot

das Sauerkraut pickled white cabbage (**das Kraut [⁼er]** herb; [in S. Germany] cabbage)

die **Schalotte** [-n] shallot
die **Schwarzwurzel** [-n] salsify
der/die **Sellerie** celeriac (der/die **Stangensellerie** celery; die
  Stange [-n] stick; der **Kopf** [ᵐe] head)
der **Spargel** [-] asparagus; stick of asparagus (die **Spitze** [-n] tip)
der **Speisekürbis** [-se] marrow (der **Kürbis** [-se] pumpkin)
der **Spinat** spinach
der **Steinpilz** [-e] cepe (mushroom)
die **Tomate** [-n] tomato
die/der **Trüffel** [-n] truffle
der **Zucchino** [pl **Zucchini**] courgette
die **Zwiebel** [-n] onion

NUSSARTEN NAMES OF NUTS
die **Cashewnuß** [ᵐsse] cashew nut
die **Erdnuß** [ᵐsse] peanut
die **Haselnuß** [ᵐsse] hazelnut
die **Kastanie** [-n] chestnut
die **Mandel** [-n] almond
die **Muskatnuß** [ᵐsse] nutmeg
die **Paranuß** [ᵐsse] Brazil nut
die **Pistazie** [-n] pistachio
die **Walnuß** [ᵐsse] walnut

Brot und Teigwaren Bread and pasta

das **Brot** [-e] bread; loaf (das **Butterbrot** slice of bread and
  butter; der/das **Sandwich** [-(e)s] sandwich; das **belegte Brot**
  open sandwich; das **Schinkenbrot** ham sandwich)
die **Corn-flakes** pl cornflakes
das **Getreide** [-] cereal (die **Getreideflocken** f pl breakfast cereal)
der **Kloß** [ᵐe]; der **Knödel** [-]; [smaller] das **Klößchen** [-] dumpling
die **Krume** [-n] crumb
die **Kruste** [-n] crust
der **Laib** [-e] loaf (ein **Laib Brot** a loaf of bread)
das **Mehl** flour

das Nockerl [G -s *pl* -n] semolina dumpling (**Salzburger Nockerl**
sweet vanilla soufflé)
die Nudeln *f pl*; **die Teigwaren** *f pl* pasta
der Pfann-/Eierkuchen [-] pancake
der Teig [-e] dough; pastry (**der Blätterteig** puff pastry)
die Waffel [-n] wafer

BROTARTEN NAMES OF BREADS

das Brötchen [-]; **die Semmel** [-n] roll
das Graubrot brown bread [made with rye and wheat flour]
das Hörnchen [-] croissant
das Knäckebrot [-e] crispbread
der Pfefferkuchen [-] gingerbread
der Pumpernickel pumpernickel [rich black rye bread]
das Roggenbrot rye bread
das Schwarzbrot black bread; rye bread
der Toast [*pl* -e or -s] toast
das Vollkornbrot wholemeal bread
das Weißbrot white bread
der Zwieback [*pl* -e or ⸚e] (breakfast) rusk

TEIGWARENARTEN NAMES OF PASTA

die Makkaroni *pl* macaroni
die Nudeln *f pl* pasta; [in soup] noodles
die Ravioli *pl* ravioli
die Spaghetti *pl* spaghetti
die Spätzle *pl* spaetzle; homemade gnocchi

Käse Cheeses

der Altenburger Altenburger cheese [mild; made from goat's
milk]
der Emmentaler Emmenthal cheese [boiled, with holes]
der Frischkäse fromage frais
der Kümmelkäse cheese with caraway seeds
der Münsterkäse Münster cheese [hard, yellow]

der Quark curd cheese
der Räucherkäse smoked cheese
der Tilsiter Tilsit cheese [mild]
der Ziegenkäse goat's cheese

Obst Fruit

die Beere [-**n**] berry
das Dörr-/Backobst dried fruit
die Frucht [**¨e**] fruit [of a plant]
der Kern [-**e**] pip; stone
das Obst *no pl* fruit (**ein Stück** *n* **Obst** a piece of fruit)
die Schale [-**n**] peel; skin

OBSTSORTEN NAMES OF FRUITS

die Ananas [*pl* - or -**se**] pineapple
der Apfel [¨] apple
die Aprikose [-**n**] apricot
die Back-/Dörrpflaume [-**n**] prune
die Banane [-**n**] banana
die Birne [-**n**] pear
die Brombeere [-**n**] blackberry
die Dattel [-**n**] date
die Erdbeere [-**n**] strawberry (**die Walderdbeere** wild strawberry)
die Feige [-**n**] fig
der Granatapfel [¨] pomegranate
die Grapefruit [-**s**]; **die Pampelmuse** [-**n**] grapefruit
die Heidel-/Blaubeere [-**n**] bilberry; blueberry
die Himbeere [-**n**] raspberry
die Kirsche [-**n**] cherry
die Kiwifrucht [**¨e**] kiwi
die Korinthe [-**n**] currant
die Limone [-**n**] lime
die Mandarine [-**n**] tangerine; mandarin
die Mango [-**s**] mango

die **Melone** [-n] melon
die **Mirabelle** [-n] mirabelle plum
die **Nektarine** [-n] nectarine
die **Orange** [-n]; die **Apfelsine** [-n] orange
der **Pfirsich** [-e] peach
die **Pflaume** [-n]; die **Zwetsch(g)e** [-n] plum
die **Preiselbeere** [-n] cranberry
die **Quitte** [-n] quince
die **Reineclaude** [-n] greengage
der **Rhabarber** rhubarb
die **Rosine** [-n] raisin
die **schwarze/rote/weiße Johannisbeere** [-n] black/red/white
  currant
die **Stachelbeere** [-n] gooseberry
die **Sultanine** [-n] sultana
die **Wassermelone** [-n] watermelon
die **Weintraube** [-n] grape (**eine Traube** a bunch of grapes)
die **Zitrone** [-n] lemon

Nachtische und Süßwaren
Puddings and sweets

der **Apfelkuchen** [-] apple flan/cake
der **Apfelstrudel** [-] apfelstrudel
die **Apfeltasche** [-n] apple turnover
das **Baiser** [-s] meringue
der **Berliner** [-] jam doughnut
der **Bienenstich** [-e] honey and almond cake
der/das **Bonbon** [-s] sweet (der **Pfefferminzbonbon** mint)
der **Cracker** [-s] cracker (biscuit)
die **Cremeschnitte** [-n] cream slice
das **Eclair** [-s] éclair
das **Eis** [-] ice-cream (der **Eisbecher** [-] ice-cream sundae; das **Eis
  am Stiel** ice-lolly; das **Eishörnchen** [-] cornet; das **Mokkaeis**
  coffee-ice; die **Eisbombe** [-n] bombe glacée)

der Honig honey (**der Honigkuchen** [-] honey cake)

das Gebäck [-e] cakes; pastries; biscuits

die Götterspeise [-n] jelly

der Gugelhupf [-e] large ring-shaped raisin cake

der/das Joghurt [*pl* - or -s] yogurt

die Kaltschale [-n] chilled fruit-and-wine soup

der Käsekuchen [-] cheesecake

der Kaugummi chewing-gum

der Keks [G - or -es; *pl* - or -e]; **das Plätzchen** [-] biscuit

das Kompott stewed fruit

der Kuchen [-] cake

die Makrone [-n] macaroon

die Marmelade [-n]; [better quality] **die Konfitüre** [-n] jam (**die Orangenmarmelade** marmalade)

das Marzipan marzipan

der Mohrenkopf [ᵉe] chocolate whipped-cream meringue

das Mus [-e] purée (**das Apfelmus** puréed apple)

der Obstsalat fruit salad

der Pfannkuchen [-] pancake

die Printe [-n] sweet spiced honey-cake

der Pudding [*pl* -e or -s] = blancmange

die Quarkspeise curd cheese and fruit dessert

die rote Grütze red-fruit blancmange

das Rumbaba [-s] rum baba

die Sahne; **der Rahm** cream (**die Schlagsahne** whipped cream)

die Schokolade chocolate (**die Tafel** [-n] bar; **eine Praline** [-n] a chocolate; **halbbitter** plain; **Milch-** milk)

der/das Sorbet [-s] sorbet; water-ice

das Soufflé [-s]; **der Auflauf** [ᵉe] soufflé

der Spekulatius [-] spiced figure-shaped Christmas biscuit

der Stollen [-] nut and fruit Christmas cake

der Streuselkuchen [-] cake topped with crumble

die Torte [-n] flan; gateau (**die Obsttorte** fruit flan; **die Schwarzwälder Kirschtorte** Black Forest gateau; **die Sachertorte** rich chocolate gateau)

das Trifle trifle

die **Vanillesoße** = custard
der **Windbeutel** [-] cream puff

SEE ALSO: **Cooking and Eating; Drinks; The Home; The Senses; Tobacco and Drugs**

19. Furniture Möbel

die Einrichtung [-en] furnishings; *pl* fittings
das Möbelstück [-e]; das Möbel [-] piece of furniture (**die Möbel**
  pl furniture)
die Tapete [-n] wallpaper
der Teppichboden [ː] fitted carpet
der Umzug [ːe] removal

aus|räumen clear out
*aus|ziehen move out
*ein|ziehen move in
möblieren furnish
um|räumen rearrange
*um|ziehen move house

bequem/unbequem comfortable/uncomfortable
eng cramped
geräumig roomy

Die Diele The hall

der Briefkasten [ː] letter-box
die Fußmatte [-n]; der Abtreter [-] doormat
die Kleiderablage [-n]; die Garderobe [-n] coat-rack (**der
  Kleiderhaken [-]** coat-hook)
der Läufer [-] [long, narrow] rug
der Schirmständer [-] umbrella-stand
das Telefon [-e] telephone
die Truhe [-n] chest
die Türklingel [-n] doorbell

Das Wohnzimmer The living-room

das Bild [-er] picture (**das Gemälde [-]** painting; **der Rahmen [-]**
  frame)

das Brett [-er]; **das Bord** [-e] shelf
das Büchergestell [-e] (set of) bookshelves
der Bücherschrank [ᵁe] bookcase
die Chaiselongue [*pl* -n or -s] *chaise longue*
der Couchtisch [-e] coffee-table
der Fernsehapparat [-e]; **der Fernseher** [-] television
das Foto [-s] photograph
der Heizkörper [-]; *colloq* **die Heizung** [-en] radiator (**der Speicherofen** [ᵁ] storage heater)
der Kaffeetisch [-e] = tea table (**den Kaffeetisch decken** lay the table for coffee and cakes)
der Kamin [-e] fireplace (**das Feuer** fire; **an|zünden** light; **der Kohleneimer** [-] coal-scuttle; **die Schürstange** [-n]; **das Schüreisen** [-] poker)
das Kissen [-] cushion
das Klavier [-e] piano (**der Flügel** [-] grand piano; **der Klavierschemel** [-] piano-stool)
die Lampe [-n] lamp (**die Stehlampe** standard lamp; **die Wandlampe** wall-light; **der (Lampen)schirm** [-e] lampshade; **die Birne** [-n] bulb)
der Lehnstuhl [ᵁe]; **der Sessel** [-] armchair
die Liege [-n] sofa-bed
der Plattenspieler [-] record-player (**die (Schall)platte** [-n] record; **die CD-Platte** CD; **der CD-Spieler** [-] CD player)
die Polstergarnitur [-en] three-piece suite
das Radio [-s] radio (**das Transistorrradio** transistor)
das Regal [-e] (set of) shelves; shelving
der Schaukelstuhl [ᵁe] rocking-chair
der Schmuckgegenstand [ᵁe] ornament
der Schreibschrank [ᵁe]; **der Sekretär** [-e] writing-bureau
das Sofa [-s]; **die Couch** [-es] sofa; settee
die Stereoanlage [-n] stereo (**der Verstärker** [-] amplifier; **der Lautsprecher** [-] loudspeaker)
der Teppich [-e] rug; carpet (**der Teppichboden** wall-to-wall carpeting)
das Tonbandgerät [-e] tape recorder (**die Kassette** [-n] cassette)

die Uhr [-en] clock (**die Kuckucks-/Standuhr** cuckoo/grandfather
clock)
die Vase [-n] vase
der Videorecorder [-] video (recorder) (**die Videokassette [-n]**
video cassette)
die Vitrine [-n] display cabinet
der Vorhang [≃e] curtain (**die Gardine [-n]** net curtain; ***auf|ziehen**
open; draw back; ***zu|ziehen** draw)
der Wandschirm [-e] (folding) screen
der Zeitschriftenständer [-] magazine rack; canterbury
die Zimmerpflanze [-n] house-plant

an|zünden light (**das Feuer** fire)
ein|schalten switch on (**aus|schalten** switch off)
sich ent'spannen relax
*fern|sehen watch television
hören/an|hören listen to
*lesen read
*schreiben write

Das Eßzimmer The dining-room

die Anrichte [-n]; das Sideboard [-s]; das Büfett [*pl* -s or -e]
sideboard; dresser
der Eßtisch [-e] dining-table
der Hochstuhl [≃e] [baby's] high chair
der Kerzenhalter [-] candlestick (**die Kerze [-n]** candle)
der Servierwagen [-] trolley
die Serviette [-n] (table) napkin
der Stuhl [≃e] chair
der Tisch [-e] table (**die Platte [-n]**; [for inserting] **das Einlegebrett**
[-er] leaf; **bei Tisch** at table)
das Tischtuch [≃er] table-cloth

ab|räumen clear [table]
decken lay [table]
*heran|ziehen draw up [chair]
sich zu Tisch setzen sit down at table

Die Terrasse The patio

die Bank [∺e] bench
der Blumentopf [∺e] flowerpot
der Grill [-s]; **das Barbecue** [-s] barbecue (**die Holzkohle**
charcoal)
der Klappstuhl [∺e] folding chair
der Liegestuhl [∺e] deck-chair
die Markise [-n] awning
der Sonnen-/Gartenschirm [-e] sunshade; garden umbrella
die Terrasse [-n] patio; terrace (**die Terrassengarnitur** patio
furniture)
die Veranda [*pl* **Veranden**] veranda; porch; patio

Die Küche The kitchen

das Abflußrohr [-e] drain
das Brett [-er]; **das Bord** [-e] shelf
das Element [-e] unit (**das Hängeelement** wall-unit)
das Gestell [-e] clothes-horse; wine-rack
die Heizungsanlage central heating
der Herd [-e] stove; cooker (**der Elektro-/Gasherd** gas/electric
cooker; **der (Back)ofen** [∺] oven; **der Grill** [-s] grill; **die
Kochplatte** [-n] hotplate; **die Abzugshaube** [-n] cooker hood)
der Hochstuhl [∺e] [baby's] high chair
der Hocker [-] stool
die Kaffeemühle [-n] coffee-grinder
der Kühlschrank [∺e] refrigerator
der Mikrowellenherd [-e] microwave
der Schrank [∺e] cupboard
das Spülbecken [-]; **die Spüle** [-n] sink
die Spül-/Geschirrspülmaschine [-n]; **der Geschirrspüler** [-] dishwasher
die Spül-/Abwaschschüssel [-n] washing-up bowl
das Tablett [*pl* -s or -e] tray (**das Teebrett** [-er] tea-tray)
die Tiefkühltruhe [-n]; [upright] **der Tiefkühlschrank** [∺e] deep-
freeze; freezer

der **Toaster** [-] toaster
der **Ventilator** [G -s *pl* -en] ventilator; fan
die **Waschmaschine** [-n] washing-machine
der **Wäschetrockner** [-] tumble-drier (die **Wäscheschleuder** [-n]
spin-drier)
der **Wasserhahn** [≃e] tap

Das Schlafzimmer The bedroom

das **Bett** [-en] bed
die **Bettwäsche** bed-linen
das **Bettzeug** bedclothes
die **Brücke** [-n] rug
das **Bücherregal** [-e] (set of) bookshelves
das **Daunenbett** [-en] eiderdown
die **Decke** [-n] blanket
das **Federbett** [-en] duvet
die **Frisierkommode** [-n]; die **Frisiertoilette** [-n] dressing-table
die **Heizdecke** [-n] electric blanket
der **Kassettenrecorder** [-] cassette recorder (die **Kassette** [-n]
cassette)
das **Kinderbett** [-en] cot; child's bed
das **Kissen/Kopfkissen** [-] pillow (der **Kissenbezug** [≃e] pillowcase)
der **Kleiderschrank** [≃e] wardrobe (der **Kleiderbügel** [-] coat-
hanger; die **Kleiderbürste** [-n] clothes-brush)
die **Kommode** [-n] chest of drawers (die **Schublade** [-n]; das
Schubfach [≃er] drawer)
das **Laken** [-]; das **Bettuch** [≃er] sheet
die **Matratze** [-n] mattress
das **Nachtlicht** [-er] night-light
der **Nachttisch** [-e] bedside table (die **Nachttischlampe** [-n]
bedside lamp)
die **Nackenrolle** [-n]; [wedge-shaped] das **Keilkissen** [-] bolster
die **Nähmaschine** [-n] sewing-machine (die **Strickmaschine**
knitting-machine)
der **Papierkorb** [≃e] waste-paper basket
das/der **Poster** [*pl* - or -s] poster

der Schrank [ˑe] cupboard
der Schreibtisch [-e] writing-desk
der Spiegel [-] mirror
die Steppdecke [-n] continental quilt
die Tagesdecke [-n] quilt; coverlet; bedspread
die Truhe [-n] chest
die Wärmflasche [-n] hot-water bottle
der Wecker [-] alarm clock (**der Radiowecker** radio alarm; **stellen auf** + A set for)
die Wiege [-n] cradle

auf|räumen tidy up
das Bett machen make the bed
im Bett *sein/*liegen be in bed
ins Bett/zu Bett *gehen go to bed
weg|räumen put away (**seine Sachen** *f pl* one's things)

Das Badezimmer The bathroom

die Badematte [-n] bath-mat
die Badewanne [-n] bath (**ein Bad** [ˑer] ***nehmen** take a bath)
der Badezimmerschrank [ˑe] bathroom cabinet
das Bidet [-s] bidet
die Dusche [-n] shower
die Haarbürste [-n] hairbrush
der Haartrockner [-]; **der Fön**® [-e] hair-drier
das Handtuch [ˑer] towel (**das Badetuch** bath towel; **der Handtuchhalter** [-] towel-rail)
der Heißwasserbereiter [-] immersion heater (**das Kontrollämpchen** [-] pilot-light)
die Jalousette [-n]; **die Jalousie** [-n] Venetian blind
der Kamm [ˑe] comb
der Rasierapparat [-e] razor; shaver (**die Klinge** [-n] blade; **der Rasierpinsel** [-] shaving-brush; **der Rasierspiegel** [-] shaving-mirror)
das Rouleau [-s] blind
das Schaumbad [ˑer] bubble bath

der Schwamm [≃e] sponge
die Seife [-n] soap
das Shampoo(n) shampoo
der Stöpsel [-] plug
die Toilette [-n] lavatory (**auf die Toilette *gehen** go to the
  lavatory; **das Klo** [-s] *colloq* loo; **das Klo-/Toilettenpapier** toilet-
  roll; **spülen** flush the lavatory)
die Waage [-n] scales
das Waschbecken [-] wash-basin
der Waschlappen [-] flannel
die Zahnbürste [-n] toothbrush
die Zahnpasta [*pl* **-pasten**] toothpaste

baden; ein Bad *nehmen have a bath
sich [D] **die Haare bürsten/kämmen** brush/comb one's hair
sich duschen have a shower (**sich kalt duschen** have a cold
  shower)
putzen clean (**sich** [D] **die Zähne putzen** clean one's teeth)
sich rasieren shave
trocknen dry [hair] (**sich ab|trocknen** dry oneself; **sich** [D] **die
  Hände ab|trocknen** dry one's hands)
sich *waschen wash (**sich** [D] **die Hände waschen** wash one's
  hands)

SEE ALSO: **The Home; Materials**

20. Greetings and Replies
Grüße und Antworten

Ankunft Arrival

bitte, nehmen Sie Platz! please take a seat
darf ich mal vorbei, bitte? may I get past?
Entschuldigung! excuse me!
grüß (dich) Gott! hello! [in S. Germany]
guten Abend good evening
guten Morgen good morning
guten Tag good day/morning/afternoon; hello
hallo! hi!; hello!
herein! come in!
verzeihen Sie bitte, können Sie mir sagen . . . ? excuse me, can
  you tell me . . . ?
Vorsicht!; Achtung!; paß auf! watch out!
was darf es sein? can I help you? [in shop]
wie geht es Ihnen?; wie geht's how are you? ((es geht mir) gut,
  danke, und Ihnen/dir? very well, thank you, and you?; **so lala**
  so-so)
willkommen (bei + D) welcome (to)

Abfahrt Departure

alles Gute! all the best!
bis gleich/bis bald see you soon
bis heute abend/morgen [etc.] see you tonight, tomorrow [etc.]
bis später see you later
grüße(n Sie) X von mir all the best to X
gute Nacht good night
gute Reise!; gute Fahrt! safe journey!
hau ab! clear off!
ich muß mich verabschieden I have to go now
raus! get out!

schlaf gut! sleep well! (**gut geschlafen?** did you sleep well?
ausgeschlafen? did you have a long enough sleep?)

tschüs! bye!

viel Spaß! have a good time!

(auf) Wiedersehen goodbye (**auf Wiederhören** goodbye [on
phone])

(auf) Wiedersehen in Köln/nächsten Montag goodbye, see you in
Cologne/next Monday

Vorstellung Introduction

darf ich vorstellen: X? can I introduce X? (**darf ich mich
vorstellen? Ich heiße . . .** may I introduce myself? My name
is . . .)

kennen Sie X? do you know X? (**kennen Sie sich?** do you know
each other?; **nur vom Sehen** only by sight)

möchten Sie . . . ? would you like to . . . ?

(sehr) angenehm; (es) freut mich pleased to meet you

Entschuldigungen Apologies

bedaure! sorry!

entschuldigen Sie, bitte! please excuse me (**die Störung** for
disturbing you; **die späte Störung** for disturbing you at this
hour)

Entschuldigung!; Verzeihung! excuse me (**oh, Verzeihung!** sorry!;
Verzeihung? (I beg your) pardon?)

es tut mir (sehr) leid I'm (very) sorry

es war nicht böse gemeint I didn't mean it nastily

ich bedaure sehr, daß . . . I'm very sorry that . . .

lassen Sie sich nicht stören don't let me disturb you

Pardon! I beg your pardon

seien Sie mir bitte nicht böse, aber . . . please don't be angry
with me, but . . .

störe ich? am I intruding/disturbing you?

stört es, wenn ich rauche? do you mind if I smoke?

verzeihen Sie, daß ich es sage, aber ... forgive me for saying so, but ...

wie bitte? what?; pardon?

Einladungen Invitations

bedienen Sie sich! serve yourself

darf ich dich/Sie hereinbitten/herüberbitten/zu mir einladen? may I invite you in/over/round? (**zu** + D for)

darf ich dich/Sie nach Hause begleiten? may I see you home?

erlauben Sie? may I?; would you mind?

gehen wir! let's go

ich möchte Ihnen keine Umstände machen I don't want to put you to any trouble

machen Sie sich nicht allzuviel Umstände don't go to a lot of trouble (**das macht keine Umstände** it's no trouble)

nur zu! go ahead!

was möchten Sie trinken? what will you have?

werden wir uns wiedersehen? shall we see each other again?

Festliche Anlässe Special occasions

alles Gute (zum Geburtstag etc.**)** all the best (for your birthday, etc.)

bravo! well done

frohe Ostern! happy Easter

fröhliche/frohe Weihnachten! merry Christmas

Gesundheit! bless you! [after sneeze]

gute Besserung! get well soon

gute Reise! safe journey (**gute Heimfahrt!** safe journey home)

guten Appetit!; Mahlzeit! enjoy your meal!

herzlichen Glückwunsch (zum Jahrestag etc.**)!** happy anniversary etc.

herzliches/aufrichtiges Beileid! heartfelt/sincere condolences (**darf ich Ihnen mein Beileid aussprechen?** may I offer you my sympathy?; **zu** + D on)

ich gratuliere! congratulations!

mit den besten Wünschen (zu + D) with best wishes (for; on)
pros(i)t! cheers!
pros(i)t Neujahr!; ein glückliches neues Jahr!; frohes neues Jahr!; guten Rutsch (ins neue Jahr)! happy New Year (**der Rutsch** [-e] slide)
viel Glück! best of luck!
viel Spaß!; viel Vergnügen! have a good time!
zum Wohl! good health!

Antworten Replies

aber doch [contradicting negative statement] you're wrong, it is
aber nein [contradicting positive statement] no, you're wrong, it isn't
(ach) du lieber Himmel! good heavens!
ach je!; ach du liebe (Zeit)! oh dear!
also so was! well, really!
beruhige dich! calm down!
besser nicht better not
bitte (sehr/schön) please; here you are [offering sth]; don't mention it (**bitte nicht!** please don't!)
danke (schön/sehr/vielmals) thank you (very much) (**danke; danke, ja** yes thank you; **danke; danke, nein** no thank you)
danke, gleichfalls thank you, and the same to you [not rude]
das/es ist mir egal/einerlei/gleich it's all the same to me
das ist sehr nett von Ihnen that's very kind of you
das kann ich mir vorstellen I can quite believe it
das macht mir nichts aus I don't mind
das soll wohl ein Witz sein you must be joking
(das) stimmt nicht that's not so
das tut mir sehr leid I'm sorry to hear it
das versteht sich (von selbst) that goes without saying
desto besser so much the better
einverstanden! agreed!
es geht it's all right
es ist nicht der Mühe wert it's not worth it
es kommt darauf an it depends

(es) macht nichts it doesn't matter
ganz im Gegenteil quite the reverse
ganz recht quite right
gar nicht; durchaus nicht not at all
gern geschehen my pleasure
genau! exactly!
Gott sei Dank! thank God!
großartig terrific
hocherfreut delighted
ich habe es satt I'm fed up with it
ich habe nichts dagegen I don't mind
ich komme gleich I'm just coming
ich weiß nicht so recht I'm not really sure
im Gegenteil quite the reverse
in Ordnung OK
ja bitte; bitte ja yes please
(ja) doch oh yes (it is)
ja sicher of course
ja, stimmt! that's right!
jawohl certainly
keine Ahnung no idea
keineswegs by no means; not at all
keine Ursache not at all (**die Ursache [-n]** cause)
kein Problem! no problem!
kommt nicht in Frage out of the question
laß mich in Ruhe! leave me alone
leider nicht unfortunately not
lieber nicht better not
mach dir keine Sorgen don't worry
macht keine (großen) Umstände please don't go to any trouble
  (**das macht gar keine Umstände** it's no trouble at all)
mein Gott! good Lord!
mit Vergnügen with pleasure
na gut; also gut OK then
na bitte! there you are!
(na/nein/also) so was! well I never!
nanu well, there's a surprise

natürlich of course
na, und? well, so what?
na und ob! and how!
nein danke no thank you
nichts zu danken don't mention it
nichts zu machen! nothing doing!
nicht wahr? absolutely!; how true!
nie im Leben! not on your life!
noch besser so much the better
noch schlimmer even worse
okay OK
Pech gehabt! hard luck!
prima!; Klasse! great!
recht/gut so right, that's fine
schön fine
sei doch nicht so! don't be like that!
so? really?
so eine Frechheit! what cheek!
so ein Pech! too bad!
so ist es that's right (**so ist es nun einmal** that's the way it is)
so, so! oh, I see
so, und nun? right, and now what?
tatsächlich? really?
um Gottes/Himmels willen! for God's/heaven's sake!
um so besser so much the better
verflucht (noch mal)! blast it! (**verdammt!** bloody hell!; **verflixt!** [weaker] damn it all!)
vielen Dank (für + A) thank you very much (for)
was du nicht sagst! you don't say!
was ist zu tun? what shall we do?
was kümmert mich das? I should worry!
weiß Gott!; weiß der Himmel! heaven knows!
wie ärgerlich! what a nuisance!
(wie) bitte? what?
(wie) schade! what a pity!

wie schrecklich! how dreadful!
wirklich? really?

SEE ALSO: **Directions; Identity; Post and Telephone; Reading and Writing; Shops and Shopping**

21. Hair Haar

der Backenbart side-whiskers
der Bart [ː̈e] beard (**bärtig** bearded; **glatt rasiert** clean-shaven)
die Glatze [-n] bald head (**eine Glatze *haben** be bald; **der Skinhead** [-s] skinhead)
das Haar [-e] *often pl* hair
die Koteletten *pl* sideboards
der Schnurrbart [ː̈e] moustache

Wie man es beschreibt How to describe it

blond blond; fair
braun brown
dunkel dark
dunkelblond light brown
dunkelbraun dark brown
grau grey
graumeliert [**grau meliert** after verb] greying
kastanienbraun chestnut
rot red
rotblond sandy
rötlichbraun auburn
silbern silver
schwarz black
weiß white

bis in den Nacken down the back of one's neck
blondiert bleached
dicht thick
dünn thin
fein fine
fettig greasy
gefärbt dyed
geflochten plaited

gestutzt cropped
gewellt; wellig wavy
glänzend glossy
glatt straight
-haarig -haired
kahl bald
kraus frizzy
kurz short
lang long
lockig curly
matt dull
mittellang medium-length
trocken dry

Wie man es trägt How it's worn

die Bürste [-n] crew cut
die Frisur [-en] hairstyle; hair-do
das Haarteil [-e] hair-piece
der Knoten [-] bun
die Locke [-n] curl
die Perücke [-n] wig
der Pferdeschwanz [ᵉe] pony-tail
der Pony [-s] fringe
der Scheitel [-] parting
der Schnitt/Haarschnitt [-e] cut/haircut
das Strähnchen [-] highlight (**die Strähne** [-n] streak; strand)
der Zopf [ᵉe] plait; pigtail

blondieren bleach
bürsten brush (**sich** [D] **die Haare bürsten** brush one's hair)
sich [D] **die Haare auf|drehen** put one's hair in rollers
färben dye
sich frisieren; sich [D] **das Haar machen** do one's hair
kämmen comb (**sich** [D] **die Haare kämmen** comb one's hair)
sich rasieren shave

Was man darauf verwendet What's used on it

das After-shave; das Rasierwasser aftershave
das Frisiermittel [-] conditioner
das Gel [-e] gel
das Haarband [¨er] hairband
die Haarbürste [-n] hairbrush
der Haarfestiger [-] setting-lotion
die Haarnadel [-n] hairpin
die Haarspange [-n] hair-slide
das/der Haarspray [-s] hair-spray
der Haartrockner [-]; der Fön® [-e] hair-drier (**mit dem Fön trocknen; fönen** blow-dry)
der Kamm [¨e] comb
der Lockenstab [¨e] (electric) curling-tongs
der Lockenwickler [-] hair-curler/roller
der Rasierapparat [-e] shaver
die Rasierklinge [-n] razor-blade
das Rasiermesser [-] razor
der Rasierpinsel [-] shaving-brush
der Rasierschaum shaving-foam
das Shampoo(n) [-s] shampoo (**shampoonieren** shampoo; **die Schuppen** *f pl* dandruff)
die Schere [-n] (pair of) scissors

Beim Friseur At the hairdresser's

die Dauerwelle [-n] perm (**sich [D] eine Dauerwelle machen *lassen** have one's hair permed)
das Einlegen set
das Farbmittel [-] dye (**die Aufhellung** bleach; **die Farbspülung** colour-rinse; **die Farbtabelle [-n]** colour chart)
der Friseur/Frisör [-e]/die Friseuse/Frisöse [-n] hairdresser (**zum Friseur *gehen** go to the hairdresser's)
der Friseursalon [-s] hairdressing salon
die Frisur [-en] hair-do
der Haarschnitt [-e] haircut

das Strähnchen [-] highlight
der Termin [-e] appointment (**sich** [D] **einen Termin geben
  *lassen** make an appointment)
die Tönung [-en] rinse (**der Töner** [-] rinse [the substance])
die Trockenhaube [-n] [hairdresser's] drier

sich an|melden make an appointment
sich [D] **das Haar färben *lassen** have one's hair dyed
sich [D] **das Haar in Locken** *f pl* **legen *lassen** have one's hair
  curled
ein|legen set
frisieren do sb's hair (**mit dem Fön frisieren *lassen** have a blow-
  dry)
legen shape
*nach|schneiden; stutzen trim
*schneiden cut (**sich** [D] **die Haare schneiden *lassen** have one's
  hair cut)
tönen tint

an der Seite [-n] at the side
hinten at the back
im Nacken at the neck
oben on top

SEE ALSO: **Adornment; Colours; Describing People; The Human
  Body**

22. Health and Sickness
Gesundheit und Krankheit

Symptome Symptoms

was hast du?; was fehlt dir? what's wrong?

der Abszeß [-sse] abscess
die Allergie [-n] allergy
der Anfall [¨e] attack; fit
die Ansteckung contagion
der Ausschlag [¨e] rash (**Ausschlag *be'kommen** break out in spots)
die Beule [-n]; [cancerous] **der Knoten [-]** lump
das Bewußtsein consciousness (**das Bewußtsein *ver'lieren** lose consciousness; **wieder zum Bewußtsein *kommen** regain consciousness)
die Bißwunde [-n] bite
die Blase [-n] blister
das blaue Auge [-n] black eye
der blaue Fleck [-e]; **die Quetschung [-en]** bruise
die Blindheit blindness
der Blutdruck blood pressure (**hoch** high; **niedrig** low)
die Blutung haemorrhage; bleeding
die Brandwunde [-n] burn
der Bruch [¨e] fracture
das Eitern suppuration
die Entzündung [-en] inflammation
das Erbrechen vomiting
die Erfrierung frost-bite
die Erschöpfung exhaustion
das Fieber fever; high temperature (**Fieber *haben** have a temperature)
die Frostbeule [-n] chilblain
der/das Furunkel [-] boil

die **Gebrechlichkeit** infirmity
die **Gehirnerschütterung** [-en] (case of) concussion
das **Geschwür** [-e] ulcer
die **Halsschmerzen** *m pl*; das **Halsweh** sore throat
das **Herzklopfen** *no pl* palpitations
das **Hühnerauge** [-n] corn
der **Husten** [-] cough (**Husten *haben** have a cough)
die **Infektion** [-en] infection
das **Jucken** itch(ing) (**es juckt mich** I itch)
der **Katarrh** catarrh
das **Koma** coma (**im Koma *liegen** be in a coma)
die **Kopfschmerzen** *m pl*; das **Kopfweh** headache
der **Krampf** [ː̈e] cramp; spasm
die **Krampfader** [-n] varicose vein
der **Kratzer** [-]; die **Schramme** [-n] scratch
die **Lahmheit** lameness (die **Lähmung** paralysis)
die **Lebensmittelvergiftung** food poisoning
die **Magenschmerzen** *m pl*; die **Bauchschmerzen** *m pl* stomach-
  ache (die **Magenverstimmung** [-en] stomach upset)
die **Mikrobe** [-n] microbe
die **Muskelzerrung** [-en] muscle strain; pulled muscle
die **Narbe** [-n] scar
das **Nasenbluten** nosebleed
die **Ohnmacht** [-en] faint (**in Ohnmacht *fallen** faint; **ohnmächtig
  *werden** pass out)
der **Pickel** [-] spot
die **Rückenschmerzen** *m pl* backache
der **Rückfall** [ː̈e] relapse (**einen Rückfall *be'kommen** have a
  relapse)
der **Rülpser** [-] belch
der **Schmerz** [-en] pain; ache (**Schmerzen *haben** be in pain;
  dumpf dull; **scharf** sharp; **anhaltend** constant; **unregelmäßig**
  irregular)
die **Schnittwunde** [-n] cut
der **Schock** [-s] shock (**unter Schock *stehen** be in shock)
die **Schürfwunde** [-n]; die **Abschürfung** [-en] graze
die **Schwäche** [-n] weakness

der Schweiß sweat
die Schwellung [-en] swelling
der Schwindel giddiness; dizziness (**das Schwindelgefühl** feeling of dizziness)
das Seitenstechen *no pl* stitch (**Seitenstechen *haben** have a stitch)
der Splitter [-] splinter
der Stich [-e] sting; insect bite
das Symptom [-e] symptom
die Todesqualen *f pl* agony; death throes
der Tumor [G -s *pl* -en] tumour
die Übelkeit nausea
die Unpäßlichkeit indisposition; upset
die Unterernährung malnutrition
die Verbrennung [-en] burn
die Verdauungsstörung [-en] (attack of) indigestion
die Vergiftung [-en] (case of) poisoning (**das Gift** poison)
die Verletzung [-en] injury
die Verstauchung [-en] sprain
das Virus [*pl* Viren] virus (**die Virusinfektion** [-en] virus infection)
die Warze [-n] wart; verruca
die Wehwehchen *n pl* aches and pains
die Wunde [-n] wound
die Zahnschmerzen *m pl*; **das Zahnweh** toothache
das Zittern trembling; shivering

Krankheiten Diseases

(**das**) **AIDS**; (**das**) **Aids** Aids (**die HIV-Infektion** [-en] HIV infection; **HIV-negativ** HIV-negative; **HIV-positiv** HIV-positive)
die Akne acne
die Angina pectoris angina
die Arthritis arthritis
das Asthma asthma
die Bindehautentzündung conjunctivitis
die Blähungen *f pl* flatulence

die **Blasenentzündung** cystitis
die **Blinddarmentzündung** appendicitis
die **Blutarmut; die Anämie** anaemia
die **Bronchitis** bronchitis
der **Bruch** [ᵕe] hernia
die **Brustfellentzündung** pleurisy
die **Cholera** cholera
die **Diphtherie** diphtheria
der **Durchfall** diarrhoea
die **Epidemie** [-n] epidemic
die **Epilepsie** epilepsy
die **Erkältung** [-en] cold; chill (**erkältet *sein** have a cold)
der **Gallen-/Nierenstein** [-e] gall/kidney stone
die **Gastritis** gastritis
die **Geisteskrankheit** insanity
die **Gelbsucht** jaundice
die **Geschlechtskrankheit** venereal disease
die **Gicht** gout
die **Grippe** flu
die **Hämorrhoiden** *pl* haemorrhoids
der **Herzanfall** [ᵕe]; der **Herzinfarkt** [-e]; [fatal] der **Herzschlag**
  [ᵕe] heart attack
der **Heuschnupfen; das Heufieber** hay fever
der **Hexenschuß** lumbago
der **Hitzschlag** [ᵕe] heat-stroke
der **Keuchhusten** whooping cough
die **Kinderlähmung** polio
die **Kolik** colic
die **Krankheit** [-en] illness
der **Krebs** cancer
die **Lebensmittelvergiftung** [-en] (case of) food poisoning
das **Leiden** [-] illness; complaint (**ein Herzleiden** a heart
  complaint)
der **Leistenbruch** [ᵕe] hernia
die **Lepra** leprosy (**der/die Leprakranke** *adj n* leper)
die **Leukämie** leukaemia
die **Lungenentzündung** pneumonia

die **Mandelentzündung** tonsillitis
die **Masern** *pl* measles
die **Migräne** [-n] migraine
der **Mumps** mumps
der **Nervenschmerz** neuralgia
der **Nervenzusammenbruch** [ˆe] nervous breakdown
die **Pocken** *f pl* smallpox
die **Reisekrankheit** travel sickness (**die See-/Luftkrankheit** sea/air
  sickness)
der **Rheumatismus; das Rheuma** rheumatism
die **Röteln** *pl* German measles
die **Ruhr** dysentery
die **Salmonellenvergiftung** (case of) salmonella poisoning
der **Scharlach** scarlet fever
die **Schlaflosigkeit** insomnia
der **Schlaganfall** [ˆe] stroke
der **Schluckauf** hiccups (**den/einen Schluckauf *be|kommen** get
  hiccups)
der **Schnupfen** (head) cold ((**den) Schnupfen *haben; sich** [D]
  einen Schnupfen holen have/catch a cold)
die **Sepsis** septicaemia
die **Seuche** [-n] plague (**die Pest** bubonic plague)
das **Sodbrennen** heartburn
der **Sonnenbrand** sunburn (**der Sonnenstich** sunstroke; **einen
  Sonnenstich *be'kommen** get sunstroke)
der **Starrkrampf/Wundstarrkrampf** tetanus
die **Tollwut** rabies
die **Tuberkulose** tuberculosis
der **Typhus** typhoid
die **Verdauungsstörungen** *f pl* (chronic) indigestion
die **Verstopfung** constipation
der **Wahnsinn** madness
die **Windpocken** *f pl* chicken-pox
die **Zuckerkrankheit** diabetes

Wie man ist How you are

allergisch gegen + A allergic to
anämisch anaemic
ansteckend contagious; infectious
asthmatisch asthmatic
atemlos breathless
behindert disabled; handicapped (**körperbehindert** physically
  handicapped; **geistig behindert** mentally handicapped; **der/die
  Behinderte** *adj n* handicapped person)
bewußtlos unconscious
blind blind (**der/die Blinde** *adj n* blind person; **der Blindenstock**
  [ᵂe] white stick; **der Blindenhund** [-e] guide-dog)
bucklig humpbacked
deprimiert depressed
diabetisch diabetic
einäugig one-eyed
epileptisch epileptic
ernst serious
erschöpft exhausted
farbenblind colour-blind
fiebrig feverish
fit fit
gebrechlich frail
gebrochen broken
geheilt cured
geisteskrank mentally ill
gelähmt lamed; crippled; paralysed
gerissen torn
geschwollen swollen
gestochen stung
gesund/ungesund healthy/unhealthy
heiser hoarse
infiziert infected
krank ill (**kränklich** sickly)
lahm lame
müde tired

reisekrank travel-sick (**see-/luftkrank** sea-/airsick)
schläfrig sleepy
schlecht; schlimm bad (**mir ist schlecht** I feel sick; **ich fühle mich schlecht** I feel unwell)
schmerzhaft painful
schwach weak
schwanger pregnant
schwerhörig hard of hearing (**das Hörgerät [-e]** hearing-aid)
schwindlig dizzy (**mir ist schwindlig** I feel dizzy)
stark strong
taub deaf (**taubstumm** deaf and dumb)
träge lethargic
übel sick (**mir ist/wird übel** I feel sick)
unversehrt unscathed
verkrüppelt crippled
verletzt hurt
verrenkt dislocated
verstaucht sprained
verstopft constipated
wach alert
wahnsinnig insane; mad
wohl/unwohl well/unwell (**mir ist nicht wohl** I'm not feeling well)
zuckerkrank diabetic

Was man tut What you do

sich an|melden bei + D make an appointment to see
sich an|stecken (bei + D) catch sth (from)
***an|schwellen** swell
aus|renken; aus|kugeln dislocate
sich aus|ruhen take a rest
***be'kommen** catch
***besser|gehen** + D improve (**mir geht es besser** I'm better; **auf dem Wege der Besserung *sein** be getting better)
bluten bleed
***brechen** break (**sich [D] das Bein** etc. **brechen** break one's leg etc.)

*ein|reiben rub in
sich ent'zünden become infected
*er'brechen bring up (sich erbrechen; sich *über'geben vomit; be
  sick)
sich er'holen von + D; *ge'nesen von + D recover from
sich er'kälten catch a cold (erkältet *sein have a cold)
*er'tragen; *aus|halten bear; put up with
fiebern be feverish
sich fühlen feel (krank ill; besser better)
*ge'nesen recover
holen *lassen send for
husten cough
eine Kur machen take a cure/take the waters
leichtes/hohes Fieber *haben run a slight/high temperature
*leiden an + D suffer from
mir ist kalt/warm/schwind(e)lig I feel cold/hot/dizzy
*nehmen; *ein|nehmen take [medicines]
niesen sneeze
ohnmächtig *werden faint
operiert *werden (an + D) have an operation (on)
schwitzen sweat
stöhnen; ächzen groan
ver'heilen heal up
sich ver'letzen injure oneself (sich am Bein verletzen hurt one's
  leg)
ver'renken twist (sich [D] den Knöchel etc. verrenken twist one's
  ankle etc.)
sich ver'schlimmern; sich ver'schlechtern get worse (mir geht es
  schlechter I'm getting worse)
ver'stauchen sprain (sich [D] den Knöchel etc. verstauchen sprain
  one's ankle etc.)
sich ver'wöhnen coddle oneself
warm *bleiben; sich warm *halten keep warm
sich [D] weh *tun hurt oneself (es tut weh it hurts)
zittern shiver
*zu|nehmen put on weight (*ab|nehmen lose weight)

Ärzte Doctors

der Arzt [∺e]/die Ärztin [-nen] doctor (**der/die praktische Arzt/
Ärztin** general practioner; **der Hausarzt/die Hausärztin** family
doctor; **den Arzt *rufen; den Arzt kommen *lassen** call the
doctor)

der Augenarzt [∺e]/die Augenärztin [-nen] oculist; eye-specialist

der Chefarzt [∺e]/die Chefärztin [-nen] consultant

der/die Chirurg/in [-en/-nen] surgeon

der Frauenarzt [∺e]/die Frauenärztin [-nen] gynaecologist

der/die Fußpfleger/in [-/-nen] chiropodist

der Hals-Nasen-Ohren-Arzt [∺e]/-Ärztin [-nen] ear, nose, and
throat specialist

der Hautarzt [∺e]/die Hautärztin [-nen] dermatologist

der Kinderarzt [∺e]/die Kinderärztin [-nen] paediatrician

der Nervenarzt [∺e]/die Nervenärztin [-nen] neurologist

der Orthopäde [-n]/die Orthopädin [-nen] orthopaedist

der/die Psychiater/in [-/-nen] psychiatrist

der Psychologe [-n]/die Psychologin [-nen] psychologist

der Quacksalber [-] quack

der/die Spezialist/in [-en/-nen] specialist

der Zahnarzt [∺e]/die Zahnärztin [-nen] dentist

Was sie tun What they do

ab|horchen sound the chest

ärztlich ver'sorgen give medical care to

be'handeln treat

diagnostizieren diagnose

eine Diät *ver'schreiben + D put on a diet

heilen cure [disease or person]

impfen vaccinate

ins Krankenhaus schicken send to hospital

*messen measure (**den Blutdruck/den Puls/die Temperatur
messen** take sb's blood pressure/pulse/temperature)

operieren + A operate on

*raten + D advise

sorgen für + A; **pflegen** look after
jm einen Termin *geben give sb an appointment
unter'suchen examine
*ver'binden bandage
ver'ordnen; *ver'schreiben prescribe

Beim Arzt At the doctor's

die Behandlung [-en] (course of) treatment
die Beratung [-en] consultation
der Blutdruck blood pressure
die Blutgruppe [-n] blood group
die Blutprobe [-n] blood test/sample (**die Harnprobe** urine test/
  sample; **das Blut** blood; **der Harn** urine)
die Diagnose [-n] diagnosis
die Empfängnisverhütung contraception
die Erste Hilfe first aid (**Erste Hilfe leisten** give first aid)
die Gesundheit health
die Impfung [-en] vaccination (**der Impfstoff [-e]** vaccine)
der/die Kranke *adj n* sick person
die Krankenkasse [-n] health insurance scheme/company (**der
  Krankenschein [-e]** health insurance certificate)
das Medikament [-e] medicine (**die Medizin** medecine [the
  science])
die Menstruation menstruation (**menstruieren** menstruate)
das Mittel/Heilmittel [-] [thing that cures]; **die Heilung**
  [restoration to health] cure
der/die Patient/in [-en/-nen] patient
die Pille [-n] the [contraceptive] pill
die Praxis/Arztpraxis [*pl* -**praxen**] practice; surgery
der Puls pulse (**fühlen** feel; ***messen** take)
das Rezept [-e]; die Verschreibung [-en] prescription
das Sprechzimmer [-] consulting room (**die Sprechstunden** *pl*
  surgery; surgery hours)
die Spritze [-n]; die Injektion [-en] injection
das Stethoskop [-e] stethoscope

die **Temperatur** temperature (***messen** take; (**erhöhte**) **Temperatur *haben** be running a temperature)
der **Termin** [-e] appointment
das **Thermometer** [-] thermometer
die **Untersuchung** [-en] examination
das **Wartezimmer** [-] waiting-room
der **Zustand** [ˁe] condition

Im Krankenhaus At the hospital

die **Abmagerungskur** [-en] slimming diet (**eine Abmagerungskur machen** go on a diet; **die Diät** [-en] special diet; **auf Diät setzen** put on a diet)
die **Abtreibung** [-en] abortion (**die Fehlgeburt** [-en] miscarriage)
die **Armbinde** [-n] sling
der **Arzt** [ˁe]/die **Ärztin** [-nen] doctor (**der diensthabende Arzt/die diensthabende Ärztin** duty doctor)
die **Bahre/Tragbahre** [-n]; die **Trage** [-n] stretcher
die **Besserung** improvement; recovery (**gute Besserung!** get well soon!)
die **Besuchszeit** [-en] visiting hours/period
die **Bettpfanne** [-n] bedpan
die **Bluttransfusion** [-en] blood transfusion (**das Blutbild** blood count)
die **Entlassung** discharge [from hospital]
die **Erholung** recovery
die **Genesung** convalescence
der **Gipsverband** [ˁe] plaster cast
die **Hygiene** hygiene
die **Intensivpflege** intensive care (**die Intensivstation** [-en] intensive-care unit; **auf der Intensivstation *sein** be in intensive care)
die **Klinik** [-en] hospital; clinic
das **Krankenhaus** [ˁer] hospital
der **Krankenwagen** [-] ambulance
die **Krücke** [-n] crutch
die **Kur** [-en] health cure (**der Kurort** [-e] health spa)

der Masseur [-e] masseur (**die Masseurin** [-nen] masseuse)
die Narkose general anaesthetic **die örtliche Betäubung** local
  anaesthetic)
der Notfall [ᵉe] emergency
die Oberin [-nen]; **die Oberschwester** [-n] matron
die Operation [-en] operation
der Operationssaal [*pl* -säle] operating-theatre
der/die Patient/in [-en/-nen] patient
die Poliklinik out-patients' department
der Rollstuhl [ᵉe] wheelchair
die Röntgenaufnahme [-n] X-ray
der Rückfall [ᵉe] relapse
die Ruhe rest
das Sanatorium [*pl* Sanatorien] sanatorium
die Schiene [-n] splint
das Schlammbad [ᵉer] mud-bath (**das Dampfbad** steam bath)
die Schlinge [-n] sling
die Schwangerenfürsorge antenatal care
die Schwester/Krankenschwester [-n] nurse (**der (Kranken)pfleger**
  [-] male-nurse; **die diensthabende Schwester** duty nurse)
die Station [-en]; **der Krankensaal** [*pl* -säle] ward (**die
  Unfallstation** casualty (ward))
die Therapie [-n] therapy
der Ultraschall ultrasound; ultrasonics (**mit Ultraschall
  unter'suchen** give an ultrasound scan)

be'handeln treat
massieren massage
operieren operate (on sb) (**jn am Bein** etc. **operieren** operate on
  sb's leg etc.; **opereriert *werden; sich operieren *lassen** have an
  operation)
röntgen X-ray
sorgen für + A look after
*ver'binden; ver'sorgen dress [wound]

In der Apotheke At the chemist's

das Abführmittel [-] laxative
das Antibiotikum [*pl* **Antibiotika**] antibiotic
das Antidepressivum [*pl* **Antidepressiva**] antidepressant
das Antiseptikum [*pl* **Antiseptika**] antiseptic (**antiseptisch** antiseptic)
die Apotheke [-n] (dispensing) chemist's; pharmacy
der/die Apotheker/in [-/-nen] (dispensing) chemist; pharmacist
die Augentropfen *m pl* eye-drops (**die Ohrentropfen** ear-drops)
das Beruhigungsmittel [-] tranquilizer
die Damenbinde [-n] sanitary towel
die Droge [-n] drug
die Drogerie [-n] (non-dispensing) chemist's
das Einreib(e)mittel [-] liniment
das Gurgelmittel [-] gargle (**gurgeln** gargle)
das homöopathische Mittel [-] homoeopathic remedy
das Hühneraugenpflaster [-] corn-plaster
die Husten-/Halspastillen *f pl* cough-drops
der Hustensaft cough mixture
das/der Kondom [-e] condom
die Kopfschmerztablette [-n] headache tablet; aspirin
das Kortison cortisone
das Medikament [-e] medicine
das Mittel [-] remedy
der Mull lint; gauze
das Mundwasser mouthwash
die Pastille [-n] lozenge
das Pflaster/Heftpflaster [-] sticking plaster
die Salbe [-n] ointment
die Schlaftablette [-n] sleeping-pill
das Schmerzmittel [-] pain-killer
die Tablette [-n] pill; tablet
der Tampon [-s] tampon
das Tonikum [*pl* **Tonika**] tonic
die Vaseline vaseline®

der **Verband** [ːe] bandage; dressing
der **Verbandskasten** [ː] first-aid kit
die **Vitamintablette** [-n] vitamin pill
die **Watte** cotton wool
die **Wundsalbe** [-n] antiseptic cream
das **Zäpfchen** [-] suppository

auf|**lösen** dissolve
kauen chew
schlucken swallow

**dreimal täglich/nach dem Essen/auf nüchternen Magen einzu-
nehmen** to be taken three times a day/after meals/on an empty
stomach
ich möchte etwas gegen + A I'd like something for . . .
nicht zur innerlichen Anwendung not be taken internally

Beim Zahnarzt At the dentist's

der **Abszeß** [-sse] abscess
der **Backenzahn** [ːe] molar
der **Eck-/Augenzahn** [ːe] canine/eye-tooth
die **Füllung** [-en] filling
das **(künstliche) Gebiß** [-e]; die **Zahnprothese** [-n] (set of)
dentures/false teeth
die **Infektion** [-en] infection
die **Karies** caries
die **Krone** [-n] crown
der **Milchzahn** [ːe] milk-tooth
die **Spritze** [-n] injection
der **Weisheitszahn** [ːe] wisdom tooth
die **Wurzel** [-n] root
der **Zahn** [ːe] tooth (**Vorder-** front; **Hinter-** back; **locker** loose)
der **Zahnarzt** [ːe]/die **Zahnärztin** [-nen] dentist
die **Zahnarztpraxis** [*pl* -praxen] dental surgery
der **Zahnbelag**; die **Plaque** plaque
das **Zahnfleisch** gum(s) (**wund** sore)
die **Zahnspange** [-n]; die **Zahnklammer** [-n] brace

der Zahnstein tartar
das Zahnweh; die Zahnschmerzen *m pl* toothache

an|passen fit [dentures]
***an|schlagen** chip
füllen fill
spülen; aus|spülen rinse (**bitte mal (aus)spülen!** please rinse)
***ziehen** draw; take out (**ziehen *lassen** have out)

Beim Optiker At the optician's

das Auge [-n] eye (**sich** [D] **die Augen *ver'derben** ruin one's
eyesight)
die Brille [-n] (pair of) spectacles (***tragen** wear)
das Brillenetui [-s] spectacle case
das Fernglas [≈er] (pair of) binoculars
das Gestell/Brillengestell [-e] frame
das Glas [≈er] lens [in spectacles] (**getönt** tinted)
das Glaukom; der grüne Star glaucoma (**der graue Star** cataract)
der Kneifer [-] pince-nez
die Kontaktlinse [-n] contact lens (**hart** hard; **weich** soft)
die Lupe [-n] magnifying glass
das Monokel [-] monocle
der/die Optiker/in [-/-nen] optician (**der/die Augenoptiker/in**
ophthalmic optician)
der Sehtest [*pl* -s or -e] eye-test (**unter'suchen; testen** test)
das Sehvermögen sight (**gut** good; **schwach** weak; **der Verlust des
Sehvermögens** loss of sight)
die Sonnenbrille [-n] (pair of) sun-glasses

bebrillt wearing glasses
farbenblind colour-blind
kurzsichtig short-sighted (**weitsichtig** long-sighted)

SEE ALSO: **Accidents; Disasters; The Human Body; Science; The
Senses; Tobacco and Drugs**

23. History Geschichte

die Antike; das Altertum antiquity (**im Altertum; in der Antike** in antiquity)
die Ära [*pl* **Ären**] era
der Archäologe [**-n**]/**die Archäologin** [**-nen**] archaeologist
die Archäologie; die Altertumskunde archaeology (**die Unterwasser-/Industriearchäologie** marine/industrial archaeology)
die Ausgrabung excavation [action] (**die Ausgrabungsstätte** [**-n**] excavation [place])
die Chronologie chronology
das Denkmal [**¨er**] monument
das Dokument [**-e**]; **die Urkunde** [**-n**] document
die Eiszeit Ice Age (**die Stein-/Bronze-/Eisenzeit** Stone/Bronze/Iron Age)
die Entwicklung [**-en**] development
die Epoche [**-n**] epoch
das Ereignis [**-se**] event
der Feudalismus feudalism (**feudalistisch; Feudal-** feudal)
die Gegenwart present (**gegenwärtig** present)
die Geschichte [**-n**] history; story (**geschichtlich; historisch** historical)
der/die Historiker/in [**-/-nen**]; [writer] **der/die Geschichtsschreiber/in** [**-/-nen**] historian
der Höhepunkt [**-e**] high point
der Imperialismus imperialism
das Jahrhundert [**-e**] century (**im neunzehnten Jahrhundert** in the nineteenth century)
das Jahrzehnt [**-e**] decade
der Kreuzzug [**¨e**] crusade
das Mittelalter Middle Ages (**im Mittelalter** in the Middle Ages; **mittelalterlich** medieval)
das Museum [*pl* **Museen**] museum
die Periode [**-n**] period
die Quelle [**-n**] source

die **Reformation** Reformation
die **Renaissance** Renaissance
die **Revolution** [-en] revolution
die **Ruine** [-n] ruin
die **Tatsache** [-n] fact
der **Untergang** [⸚e] fall
der **Ursprung** [⸚e] origin
der **Verfall** *no pl* decline
die **Vergangenheit** past (**in der Vergangenheit** in the past;
 vergangen past)
die **Verschwörung** [-en] conspiracy (**die Pulververschwörung**
 Gunpowder Plot)
die **Vorgeschichte** prehistory (**vorgeschichtlich** prehistoric)
die **Zeit** [-en] time (**zu der Zeit** at that time; **in früheren Zeiten** in
 former times; **das waren noch Zeiten** those were the days; **das
 Zeitalter** [-] age; **das goldene Zeitalter** golden age)
die **Zivilisation** [-en] civilization (**zivilisiert** civilized)
die **Zukunft** future ((**zu)künftig** future)

dauern last
*****ent'stehen aus** + D originate from
*****ge'schehen; passieren** happen
stammen aus + D date from
*****ver'gehen** pass [of time]
*****vor|kommen** occur

aktuell current
chronologisch chronological
damals at that time
ehemalig former
einmal once (**es war einmal . . .** once upon a time there was . . .)
früher former(ly); in the past
heutzutage nowadays
in diesem/dem Moment at the/that moment
legendär; sagenhaft legendary
modern modern
seit + D since (**seit X Jahren** for X years)
traditionell; [handed down] **überkommen** traditional

vor/nach Christus; v./n. Chr. BC/AD
vor X Jahren X years ago

SEE ALSO: **Art and Architecture; Politics; Time; War, Peace, and the Armed Services**

24. Holidays Ferien

Vorbereitungen Preparations

die Anzahlung [-en]; **die Kaution** [-en] deposit
der Aufenthalt [-e] stay
die Bestätigung confirmation
die Broschüre [-n]; **der/das Prospekt** [-e] brochure
die Fahrkarte [-n] ticket (**die Flugkarte** plane ticket)
das Gepäck luggage
das Hotelverzeichnis [-se] hotel guide
die Karte [-n] map; ticket
der Koffer/Reisekoffer [-] suitcase
der Kulturbeutel [-] sponge-bag
die Liste [-n] list
der Paß/Reisepaß [ˉsse] passport (**ver'längern** renew; **das Visum**
  [*pl* **Visen**] visa)
der Rabatt [-e] discount
die Reise [-n] journey; trip
das Reisebüro [-s] travel agent's
der Reisescheck [-s] traveller's cheque
die Reiseroute [-n] itinerary
die Reiseversicherung travel insurance (**eine Versicherung**
  *ab|schließen take out insurance; **die grüne Karte** green card)
die Reservierung [-en] reservation
der Rucksack [ˉe] rucksack
die Saison [-s] (holiday) season (**während/außerhalb der Saison**
  during the season/off-season)
die Unterkunft [ˉe] accommodation
der Urlaub; **die Ferien** *pl* holiday(s) (**in Urlaub *fahren** go on
  holiday; **auf/in/im Urlaub *sein**; **Urlaub machen** be on holiday;
  urlaubsreif *sein need a holiday; **der freie Tag** [-e]; [public
  holiday] **der Feiertag** day's holiday)

ab'sagen cancel
be'stätigen confirm (**schriftlich** in writing)

buchen; [rooms] **vor|be'stellen** book (**voll belegt; ausgebucht** fully booked)

sich er'kundigen (nach + D) enquire (about)

*fahren; reisen travel

sich impfen *lassen be vaccinated

mieten rent

*mit|nehmen take (with you)

packen pack (**die Koffer** *m pl* **packen** pack one's bags)

Reiseziele Destinations

der Austausch/Schüleraustausch [-e] exchange/school exchange

der Campingplatz [ᵂe] campsite

die Ferien *pl* **auf dem Lande** country holiday

die Ferienreise [-n] holiday trip/journey

die Ferienwohnung [-en] holiday flat

die Frühstückspension [-en] bed-and-breakfast place (**ein Zimmer** *n* **mit Frühstück** bed and breakfast; ***unter|bringen** put up)

der Gasthof [ᵂe] inn

das Hotel [-s] hotel (**das Hotel garni** [G - -; *pl* -s -s] bed-and-breakfast hotel)

die Jugendherberge [-n] youth hostel

die Kreuzfahrt [-en] cruise (**eine Kreuzfahrt machen** go on a cruise)

der Kurort [-e] health resort; spa

das Motel [-s] motel

die Pauschalreise [-n] package tour (**die Gruppe** [-n] group)

die Pension [-en]; **das Fremdenheim** [-e] guest-house

die Selbstversorgung self-catering

der Urlaubs-/Aufenthalts-/Ferienort [-e] resort (**der Skiurlaubsort** ski resort; **das Seebad** [ᵂer] seaside resort)

Was man dort findet What you find there

der Aufenthalt [-e] stay (**ein fünftägiger Aufenthalt** a five-day stay)

der Ausflug [ᴂe] outing; excursion (**das Ausflugsziel** [-e] destination; **das Ausflugsziel am Ort** local beauty-spot)

der Besuch [-e] visit (**der/die Besucher/in** [-/-nen] visitor)

die Busreise [-n] coach trip

der/die Fremde *adj n* foreigner; stranger; visitor

das Fremdenverkehrsbüro [-s] tourist office (**die Broschüre** [-n]; **der/das Reiseprospekt** [-e] brochure)

die Führung [-en] guided tour

die Gastfreundlichkeit hospitality

die Gastronomie gastronomy

die Grenze [-n] frontier; border

der Karneval [*pl* -e or -s]; [pre-Lent] **der Fasching** [*pl* -e or -s] carnival

das Konsulat [-e] consulate

die Küche cuisine; cooking

das Kunsthandwerk crafts

das Picknick [*pl* -e or -s] picnic (**Picknick machen/*halten** have a picnic)

der Reiseführer [-] guide(book)

der/die Reiseleiter/in [-/-nen] guide [the person]

die Rundfahrt [-en] tour

die Sehenswürdigkeit [-en] sight (**die Sehenswürdigkeiten be'sichtigen** see the sights)

das Souvenir [-s]; **das Reiseandenken** [-] souvenir

der Spaziergang [ᴂe] walk

die Spezialität [-en] (**des Hauses**) speciality (of the house)

der Sprachführer [-] phrase-book

der Tourismus tourism

der/die Tourist/in [-en/-nen] tourist (**ermäßigte Preise für Touristen** tourist rates)

der Zoll customs (**der Zollbeamte** *adj n*/**die Zollbeamtin** [-nen] customs officer; **die Zollkontrolle** customs check; **zollfrei** duty-free; **ver'zollen** pay duty on)

sich amüsieren; sich ver'gnügen enjoy oneself (**sich vergnügen damit, et zu tun** enjoy oneself doing sth)

be'suchen visit

neppen rip off

beeindruckend impressive
berühmt famous
häßlich ugly
malerisch picturesque
romantisch romantic
Touristen- tourist
vergnügt having a good time

Im Hotel At the hotel

das Anmeldeformular [-e] registration form (**aus|füllen** fill in)
das Badezimmer [-] bathroom
der Balkon [*pl* -s or -e] balcony (**die Aussicht** [-en] view)
die Bar [-s] bar
die Bedienung service (**der Zimmerservice; die Zimmerbedienung**
   room service; **mit/ohne Bedienung** including/excluding service)
die Beschwerde [-n]; **die Reklamation** [-en] complaint
das Bett [-en] bed (**das Kinderbett** cot)
das Büro [-s] office
der Direktor [G -s *pl* -en]**/die Direktorin** [-nen] manager (**die
   Direktion** the management)
das Einzelzimmer [-] single room (**das Doppel-/Zweibettzimmer**
   double/twin-bedded room)
der Empfang reception
der Empfangschef [-s]**/die Empfangsdame** [-n] receptionist
die Empfangshalle [-n]; **das Foyer** [-s] foyer
das Essen [-]; **die Mahlzeit** [-en] meal
der Fahrstuhl [ːe]; **der Aufzug** [ːe]; **der Lift** [*pl* -e or -s] lift
das Fremden-/Gästebuch [ːer] hotel register (**sich ins Fremden-
   buch *ein|tragen** register)
das Fremdenzimmer [-] room (to let) (**Übernachtung** *f* **mit
   Frühstück** *n* bed and breakfast)
der Gast [ːe] guest; patron; resident
das Gasthaus [ːer]**/Gasthof** [ːe] inn
die Gaststätte [-n] public house; restaurant

die Heizung [-en] *colloq* heating; radiator
das Hotel [-s] hotel
die Hotelgarage [-n] hotel garage
der Hotelier [-s] hotelier
die Hotelpreise *m pl* tariff
der/die Inhaber/in [-/-nen] proprietor
die Klimaanlage air-conditioning
die Kneipe [-n]; die Schenke [-n] pub (**die Theke [-n]** bar
[counter])
der Küchenchef [-s] chef
die Kurtaxe [-n] (spa) visitor's tax
die Lounge [-s]; die Hotelhalle [-n] lounge
der Notausgang [-̈e] emergency exit
der Parkplatz [-̈e] car-park
die Pension [-en] full board (**halbe/volle Pension** half/full board)
der Portier [-s]; der Hausdiener [-] porter (**der Nachtportier**
night-porter)
die Quittung [-en] receipt
die Rechnung [-en] bill (**das Trinkgeld [-er]** tip; **die Mehrwertsteuer VAT**)
das Restaurant [-s] restaurant (**der Speisesaal** [*pl* -säle] dining-
room)
die Rezeption reception (desk/counter)
der/das Safe [-s] safe
das Schwimmbecken [-] swimming-pool (**das Freibad [-̈er]** open-
air swimming-pool)
der Stock [-] floor (**im ersten/obersten Stock** on the first/top floor;
im Erd-/Kellergeschoß *n* on the ground/basement floor)
der/die Telefonist/in [-en/-nen] switchboard operator
die Terrasse [-n] terrace
die Toilette [-n] toilet (**eine eigene Toilette** a private toilet)
die Treppe [-n] (flight of) stairs
das Waschbecken wash-basin (**der Stöpsel [-]** plug)
der Wäscheservice laundry service
der Wirt/Gastwirt [-e] host; landlord (**die Wirtin/Gastwirtin**
[-nen] hostess; landlady)

das Zimmer [-] **(mit Dusche** *f*/**mit Bad** *n*/**mit Frühstück** *n*) room
  (with shower/bath/breakfast) (**vorne/zur Straße** at the front;
  hinten/zum Hof at the back; **der Hof** [≃e] yard; **mit Blick
  auf** + A facing . . . ; **Zimmer frei** vacancies)
das Zimmermädchen [-] chambermaid (**das Zimmer machen** do
  the room)
die Zimmernummer [-n] room number
der Zimmerpreis [-e] price of room (**pro Tag** per day)
der Zimmerschlüssel [-] (room) key (**das Schloß** [≃sser] lock)
der Zuschlag [≃e] supplement

auf das Zimmer *bringen take up to one's room
sich be'schweren/sich be'klagen über + A complain
*bleiben bis + A stay until
*emp'fehlen recommend
fertig|machen make up; prepare [bill]
hinauf|-/hinunter|*tragen take up/down (**hinauf|-/hinunter-
  schicken** send up/down)
klingeln ring
*liegen zu + D **hin** look out on
nach|prüfen check [bill] (**richtig|stellen** put right)
reservieren *lassen; **vor|be'stellen** book
stören disturb
über'nachten put up; spend the night
wecken wake
zahlen pay (**im voraus zahlen** pay in advance)

auf open (**zu** closed)
ausgebucht full up
belegt hotel full; no vacancies
bequem comfortable
inbegriffen in + D included in
laut noisy
zur Verfügung available

Auf dem Campingplatz On the campsite

der Abfall [ѕe] *often pl* rubbish (**die Abfalltonne** [-n] rubbish bin)
das Abwaschbecken washing-up sink
der Anhänger [-] trailer
die Bodenplane [-n]; **der Zeltboden** [ѕ] groundsheet (**die Plane**
flysheet)
der/die Camper/in [-/-nen] camper
das Camping; **das Zelten** camping (**zum Camping *fahren** go
camping; **Zelten verboten** no camping)
der Campingbus [-se] motor-caravan; camper
der Campingführer [-] camping-guide (book)
das Campinggas camping-gas (**das Butangas** butane; **die**
Nachfüllflasche [-n] refill)
der Campinghocker [-] camp-stool
die Campingliege [-n] camp-bed
der Campingplatz [ѕe] campsite (**der Campingplatz für Wohn-**
wagen caravan site; **die Gebühren** *f pl* charges)
das Feldbett [-en] camp-bed
die Feldflasche [-n] water-bottle
das Freie *adj n* the open air (**im Freien über'nachten** spend the
night in the open)
der Herd [-e] stove
der Klapptisch [-e] folding table (**der Klappstuhl** [ѕe] folding
chair)
die Kühltasche [-n] cool box/bag
das Lagerfeuer [-] camp-fire
die Luftmatratze [-n] air-bed
das Mückennetz [-e] mosquito-net
der Preis [-e] charge (**der Tages-/Wochenpreis** daily/weekly
charge)
die sanitären Anlagen showers and toilets
das Seil [-e] rope
der Spielplatz [ѕe] playground
der Stromanschluß electricity connection
die Taschenlampe [-n] torch
das Taschenmesser [-] pocket-knife

das Trinkwasser drinking-water
der Waschsalon [-s] launderette
der Wasserkanister [-] water container
das Wohnmobil [-e] mobile home
der Wohnwagen [-] caravan (**Urlaub im Wohnwagen machen** go
  caravanning)
das Zelt tent
der Zeltpflock [≃e]; **der Hering** [-e] tent-peg
der Zeltplatz [≃e] (tent) site
die Zeltstange [-n] tent-pole

auf|bauen; ***auf|schlagen** put up; pitch (**ab|bauen**; ***ab|schlagen**
  take down; strike)
trampen hitch-hike
zelten; **campen** camp (**wild zelten** camp off-site)

In der Jugendherberge At the youth hostel

die Bettwäsche bed-linen (**die Decke** [-n] blanket; **das Laken** [-]
  sheet)
der Herbergsvater [≃]/**die Herbergsmutter** [≃] warden
die Jugendherberge [-n] youth hostel
die Kochgelegenheit *sing* cooking facilities (**die Waschgelegen-
  heit** *sing* washing facilities)
der Mitgliedsausweis [-e] membership card
der Schlafraum [≃e] dormitory
der Schlafsack [≃e] sleeping-bag
der Spielraum [≃e] games room
der Tagesraum [≃e] day-room
die Vorschriften *f pl* rules
der Waschraum [≃e] wash-room

SEE ALSO: **Cinema and Photography; Furniture; The Home;
  Leisure and Hobbies; Nature; Places, People, and Languages;
  Sports and Games; Transport; The Weather**

25. The Home Das Heim

der/die Eigentümer/in [-/-nen] owner
der/die Hausbesitzer/in [-/-nen] (home-)owner
der/die Hausverwalter/in [-/-nen] caretaker
die Hypothek [-en] mortgage (***auf|nehmen** take out)
die Miete [-n] rent (**der/die Mieter/in** [-/-nen] tenant; **der
  Mietvertrag** [=e] lease; **der/die Untermieter/in** [-/-nen] subtenant)
der/die Nachbar/in [-n/-nen] neighbour (**die unmittelbaren
  Nachbarn; die Nachbarn von nebenan** next-door neighbours)
der Umzug [=e] move; removal (**der Möbelpacker** [-] removal
  man)

ab|stellen cut off [electricity, gas]
***an|schließen (an die Strom-/Gasversorgung)** connect (the
  electricity/gas)
auf|drehen turn on [water, gas] (**zu|drehen** turn off)
bauen *lassen have built
sich ein|leben settle in
ein|ziehen** move in (aus|ziehen** move out)
heizen heat
kündigen give notice; foreclose [mortgage] (**jm die Wohnung
  kündigen** give sb notice to quit the flat)
***liegen** be situated
mieten rent
möblieren furnish
nach Hause *gehen go home (**zu Hause *sein** be at home)
räumen vacate
***um|ziehen** move house
ver'mieten let; rent out
wohnen (in + D) live (in)
***zu|schließen** lock (up)

außen outside
gemütlich cosy
innen inside

möbliert furnished (**möbliert wohnen** live in a furnished flat)
nebenan next door
oben upstairs (**die Treppe *hinauf|gehen** go upstairs)
schön gelegen nicely situated
unten downstairs (**die Treppe *hinunter|gehen** go downstairs)

Wohnungen Dwellings

der Altbau [*pl* -bauten] old house/building (**der Neubau** new
  house/building)
das Altersheim [-e]/**das Altenheim** [-e] old people's home
der Bauernhof [∸e] farm
der Bungalow [-s] bungalow
das Chalet [-s] chalet
das Cottage [-s] cottage (**strohgedeckt** thatched)
die Doppelhaushälfte [-n] semi-detached house (**das Doppelhaus**
  [∸er] pair of semis)
das Einfamilienhaus [∸er] private house [as opposed to **das
  Mehrfamilienhaus**, house split into flats]
das Einzelhaus [∸er] detached house
die Einzimmerwohnung [-en]; **das Apartment** [-s] studio flat
das Gebäude [-] building
das Haus [∸er] house; building
die Kellerwohnung [-en] basement flat
das Landhaus [∸er] country house
das Reihenhaus [∸er] terraced house
das Stadthaus [∸er] town house
die Villa [*pl* Villen] villa
der Wohnblock [-s] block of flats
die Wohnung [-en] flat (**die Sozialwohnung** = council flat)
der Wolkenkratzer [-] skyscraper

Teile eines Hauses Parts of a house

der Abstellraum [∸e] box-room
das Arbeitszimmer [-] study
das Bad [∸er]; **das Badezimmer** [-] bathroom

der Balken [-] beam (**freigelegt** exposed)

der Balkon [*pl* -s or -e] balcony

der Boden/Fußboden [=] floor (**das Parkett** [-e]; **der Parkettboden**
parquet floor)

die Bibliothek [-en] library

das Dach [=er] roof (**der Dachziegel** [-] roof tile; **die Schieferplatte**
[-n] slate; **der Dachboden** [=] attic; loft; **die Dachkammer** [-n]; **die
Mansarde** [-n] attic room; **der Dachausbau** [-bauten] loft
conversion; **das Dachfenster** [-] rooflight; skylight)

die Decke [-n] ceiling

die Diele [-n] hall(way); floor-board

das Erdgeschoß [-sse] ground floor (**im Erdgeschoß** on the
ground floor)

das Eßzimmer [-] dining-room (**die Eßecke** [-n] dining-area)

der Fahrstuhl [=e]; **der Aufzug** [=e] lift (**außer Betrieb** *m* out of order)

die Fassade [-n]; **die Front** [-en] façade; house front

das Fenster [-] window (**das Erker-/Mansarden-/Schiebe-/
Flügelfenster** bay/dormer/sash/casement window; **das franzö-
sische Fenster** French window)

die Fensterbank [=e] [internal]; **der/das Fenstersims** [-e] [external]
window-ledge

die Fensterscheibe [-n] window pane

die Fliese [-n] tile

der Flur [-e] entrance hall; corridor

der Gang [=e]; **der Korridor** [-e] corridor

die Garage [-n] garage

das Gast-/Gästezimmer [-] guest-room

der Giebel [-] gable (**die Giebelseite** [-n] gable-end)

das Haus [=er] house

der Kamin [-e] fireplace (**der/das Kaminsims** [-e] mantlepiece; **das
Feuer** [-] fire; **der Rauch** smoke; **die Kohle** [-n] coal; **das
Holzscheit** [*pl* -e or -er] log; **der Schornstein** [-e] chimney; **der
Schornsteinkopf** [=e] chimney-pot; **der Schornsteinfeger** [-]
chimney-sweep)

der Keller [-] cellar (**das Kellergeschoß** [-sse]; **das Souterrain** [-s]
basement)

das Kinderzimmer [-] children's room; nursery

die **Küche** [-n] kitchen
die **Mauer** [-n] [outside]; die **Wand** [ˌe] [inside] wall
das **Obergeschoß** [-sse] upper storey
das **Oberlicht** [-er] fanlight
die **Rumpelkammer** [-n] junk room
das **Schlafzimmer** [-] bedroom
die **Schwelle** [-n] threshold
der **Sparren** [-] rafter
die **Speisekammer** [-n] larder (der **Speiseschrank** [ˌe] larder
  cupboard)
der **Stock** [-]; das **Stockwerk** [-e]; die **Etage** [-n] floor; storey (**im
  ersten Stock** on the first floor)
die **Toilette** [-n]; das **WC** [pl - or -s] lavatory (das **Klo** [-s] colloq loo)
die **Trennwand** [ˌe] partition (wall)
die **Treppe** [-n] staircase; flight of stairs (die **Stufe** [-n] step; das
  Treppenhaus [ˌer] stairwell; das **Geländer** [-] (set of) bannisters;
  die **Treppe** *hinauf|-/hinunter|gehen go up-/downstairs; der
  Treppenabsatz [ˌe] half-landing; der **Treppenflur** [-e] landing;
  die **Wendeltreppe** spiral staircase)
die **Tür** [-en] door (die **Türstufe** [-n] doorstep; die **Eingangs-/
  Haus-/Hintertür** entrance/front/back door; die **Dreh-/Schiebe-/
  Pendel-/Doppeltür** revolving/sliding/swing/double door)
die **Veranda** [pl **Veranden**] veranda; patio
die **Vorderfront** [-en]; die **Frontseite** [-n] front; façade
der **Waschraum** [ˌe] laundry room (die **Wäscherei** [-en] laundry)
das **Wohnzimmer** [-] living-room; sitting-room
das **Zimmer** [-] room (der **Raum** [ˌe] room [especially
  unfurnished]; der **Saal** [pl **Säle**] (public) room)

Der Garten The garden

das **Beet** [-e] bed; plot (das **Blumenbeet** flower-bed)
der **Boden** soil
die **Erde** earth
der **Faulraum** [ˌe] septic tank
die **Gartenbank** [ˌe] garden seat
die **Gartenmöbel** n pl garden furniture

der **Gemüsegarten** [:] kitchen garden
der **Geräteschuppen** [-] garden shed
das **Gewächshaus** [:er] greenhouse
die **Gießkanne** [-n] watering-can
das **Gitter** [-] trellis
die **Hecke** [-n] hedge
der **Hof** [:e] courtyard (**der Hinterhof** backyard)
die **Laube/Gartenlaube** [-n]; das **Gartenhaus** [:er] summer-house;
  garden house
der **Obstgarten** [:] orchard
der **Pfad** [-e]; der **Weg** [-e] path
die **Pflanze** [-n] plant
die **Pforte** [-n] gate (**die Gartenpforte** [-n] garden gate)
die **Rabatte** [-n] border
der **Rasen** [-] lawn (**das Gras** [:er] grass; **der Rasenmäher** [-] lawn-
  mower)
der **Schlauch** [:e] hose
die **Schubkarre** [-n]/der **Schubkarren** [-] wheelbarrow
die **Sonnenuhr** [-en] sundial
der **Steingarten** [:] rockery
der **Teich** [-e] pond
die **Terrasse** [-n] terrace; patio
das **Unkraut** weeds
der **Vorgarten** [:] front garden (**der Hintergarten** back garden)
die **Walze** [-n] (garden) roller
der **Wintergarten** [:] conservatory
der **Zaun** [:e] fence (**der Gitterzaun** railings; lattice fence)

blühen blossom
jäten weed
mähen mow
pflanzen plant
pflücken pick
*****um|graben** dig over
*****wachsen** grow

SEE ALSO: **Plants; Tools**

Ausstattung und Installationen
Fixtures and fittings

der Abfluß [ː̈sse] waste-pipe
die Abwasserleitung [-en] drain-pipe; soil-pipe
die Antenne [-n] aerial
der Aschenbecher [-] ashtray
die Batterie [-n] battery
der Boiler [-] boiler; water-heater
der Briefkasten [ː̈] letter-box
die Dachrinne [-n] gutter
der Fensterladen [*pl* ː̈ or -] shutter (**der Rolladen** roller shutter)
die Fensterscheibe [-n] window pane
der Fensterverschluß [ː̈sse] window catch
die Fliese [-n] tile [floor/wall]
die Garderobe [-n] coat-rack
das Geländer [-] handrail; banisters
der Griff [-e] [bucket, jug, cup]; **der Henkel** [-] [broom, pan, axe]; **der Stiel** [-e] handle
der Hahn/Wasserhahn [ː̈e] tap (**der Abstellhahn** mains stopcock; **auf**|-/**zu**|**drehen** turn on/off)
der Haken [-] hook
der Hausrat household goods
der Heißwasserbereiter [-] water-heater (**der Heißwasserspeicher** [-] hot-water tank with immersion heater)
die Jalousette [-n]; **die Jalousie** [-n] Venetian blind
der Kachelofen [ː̈] tiled stove (**die Kachel** [-n] tile)
der Kamin [-e] fireplace
die Kanalisation sewage system
das Kissen [-] cushion
der Kleiderbügel [-] coat-hanger
die Lampe [-n] light; lamp (**die Birne** [-n] bulb; **die Fassung** [-en] (lamp) socket)
die Leitungen *f pl* wiring (**die Gas-/Wasserleitung** gas-/water-pipe; gas-/water-main)
die Lüftung ventilation

der Ofen [÷] stove; heater

der Putz/Verputz plaster; [external] rendering

der Riegel [-] bolt (**die Tür ver'riegeln** bolt the door)

das Rohr [-e] pipe (**das Regen(abfall)rohr** rain-water pipe)

das Rouleau [-s]; **das Rollo** [-s] (roller) blind

der Schalter [-] switch (**an|-/aus|schalten** switch on/off)

das Scharnier [-e] hinge

das Schloß [÷sser] lock (**der Schlüssel** [-] key; **das Schlüsselbund** [-e] bunch of keys; **das Schlüsselloch** [÷er] keyhole)

der Schnapper [-] door latch

die Schnur [÷e] lead (**die Verlängerungsschnur** extension lead)

der Schrank [÷e] cupboard

der Sicherungskasten [÷] fuse-box (**die Sicherung** [-en] fuse)

das Spülbecken [-]; **die Spüle** [-n] sink

die Steckdose [-n] socket (**die Zweifachsteckdose** double socket; adaptor; **der Stecker** [-] plug; ***an|schließen** plug in; **den Stecker *heraus|ziehen** unplug)

das Stromnetz [electric] mains (**der Hauptschalter** [-] mains switch; **die (Hoch-/Nieder)spannung** (high/low) voltage)

der Stromzähler [-] electricity meter (**der Gaszähler** gas meter; **die Wasseruhr** [-en] water meter)

die Tapete [-n] wallpaper

der Türgriff [-e]; **die Klinke/Türklinke** [-n] door-handle

die Türklingel [-n] doorbell

der Türklopfer [-] door-knocker

das Vorhängeschloß [÷sser] padlock

der Wetterhahn [÷e] weathercock

die Zentralheizung central heating (**die Gas-/Öl-/Elektroheizung** gas/oil/electric heating; **der Heizkörper** [-]; **der Radiator** [G -s *pl* -en]; *colloq* **die Heizung** [-en] radiator)

Hausarbeit Housework

WER SIE MACHT THOSE WHO DO IT

das Au-pair-Mädchen [-] au pair
der/die Babysitter/in [-/-nen] baby-sitter (**die Tagesmutter** [=]
  baby-minder)
das Dienstmädchen [-] maid
der/die Gärtner/in [-/-nen] gardener
die Hausfrau [-en] housewife
die Haushaltshilfe [-n] home help
der Hausmann [=er] house-husband
der/die Hausmeister/in [-/-nen] caretaker
die Putzfrau [-en]; **die Reinemachefrau** [-en] cleaning woman;
  daily

WAS SIE TUN WHAT THEY DO

ab|decken clear the table
ab|stauben dust [a piece of furniture] (**im Wohnzimmer Staub** *m*
  wischen dust the living room)
*ab|waschen; spülen wash up (**das Geschirr** the dishes)
auf|räumen tidy up
babysitten *only inf* baby-sit
die Betten machen make the beds
bügeln; plätten iron; do the ironing
fegen; kehren sweep (**zusammen|fegen; zusammen|kehren** sweep
  up)
flicken patch
die Hausarbeit machen do the housework
*helfen + D; **Hilfe** *f* **leisten** + D help
kochen cook
polieren; [floor] **bohnern** polish
reinigen [carpets, clothes]; **sauber|machen/putzen** [house, shoes]
  clean (**der Frühjahrsputz** spring-clean)
reparieren mend
scheuern scour
spülen rinse

staub|saugen vacuum
stopfen darn
den Tisch decken lay the table
trocknen dry (**im Automaten trocknen** tumble-dry; **ab|trocknen**
dry [dishes])
*waschen wash; do the washing
*weg|werfen throw away

WAS SIE GEBRAUCHEN WHAT THEY USE

der Abfalleimer [-] bin
das Abtropfbrett [-er] draining-board
die Abwaschschüssel [-n] washing-up bowl
der Besen/Kehrbesen [-] long-handled brush; broom
das Bleichmittel [-] bleach
der Bodenwischer [-] [for floors]; **der Fensterwischer** [for
windows] squeegee
das Bügel-/Plätteisen [-] iron (**das Bügel-/Plättbrett** [-er] ironing-
board)
die Bürste [-n] brush
das Desinfektionsmittel [-] disinfectant
der Eimer [-] bucket
der Geschirrspüler [-] dishwasher
das Geschirrtuch [̈er] tea-towel
der Handfeger [-]; **der Handbesen** [-] (short-handled) brush
die Kehrschaufel [-] dustpan
der Lappen [-] cloth (**der Putzlappen** floor-cloth)
der Mop [-s] mop
der Mülleimer [-] waste-bin (**der Müll**; **der Abfall** refuse; **die
Müllabfuhr** refuse collection)
die Mülltonne [-n] dustbin
die Nähmaschine [-n] sewing-machine
die Scheuerbürste [-n] scrubbing-brush
das Seifenpulver soap powder
die Spülbürste [-n] washing-up brush
das Spülmittel [-] washing-up liquid
der Staubsauger [-] vacuum cleaner

das **Staubtuch** [¨er] duster
der **Teppichkehrer** [-] carpet-sweeper
der **Topfreiniger** [-]; der **Topfkratzer** [-] scourer
die **Wäscheleine** [-n] washing-line (die **Wäscheklammer** [-n] peg)
der **Wäscheständer** [-] clothes-horse
die **Waschmaschine** [-n] washing-machine
das **Waschpulver** [-] washing-powder

SEE ALSO: **Accidents; Cooking and Eating; Furniture; Plants; Relationships**

26. The Human Body
Der menschliche Körper

Der Kopf The head

der Augapfel [∺] eyeball
das Auge [-n] eye
die Augenbraue [-n] eyebrow
das Augenlid [-er] eyelid
die Falte [-n] wrinkle
der Gaumen [-] palate (**hart** hard; **weich** soft)
das Gehirn *no pl* brain
das Gesicht [-er] face (**der Gesichtszug [∺e]** feature)
die Gesichtsfarbe [-n]; der Teint [-s] complexion
die Grimasse [-n] grimace (**eine Grimasse *schneiden** make a
  face)
das Grübchen [-] dimple
das Haar [-e] hair
der Hals [∺e] neck; throat
die Kehle [-n] throat
der Kiefer [-] jaw (**der Ober-/Unterkiefer** upper/lower jaw)
das Kinn [-e] chin (**das Doppelkinn** double chin)
der Kopf [∺e] head (**von Kopf bis Fuß** from head to foot)
die Lippe [-n] lip
die Miene [-n] look; facial expression
der Mund [∺er] mouth
der Nacken [-]; das Genick [-e] nape (of neck)
die Nase [-n] nose (**sich [D] die Nase putzen** blow one's nose; **das
  Nasenloch [∺er]** nostril)
das Ohr [-en] ear (**das Ohrläppchen [-]** ear-lobe)
die Pupille [-n] pupil
der Schädel [-] skull
die Schläfe [-n] temple
der Speichel [-] saliva
die Stimme [-n] voice

die Stirn [-en] forehead (**die Stirn runzeln** frown)
die Wange [-n]; die Backe [-n] cheek (**der Backenknochen** [-]
  cheekbone)
die Wimper/Augenwimper [-n] eyelash
der Zahn [⸚e] tooth (**der Milch-/Weißheitszahn** milk-/wisdom
  tooth)
das Zahnfleisch *sing* gum(s)
die Zunge [-n] tongue

Der Körper The body

die Achselhöhle [-n] armpit
die Ader [-n]; die Vene [-n] vein (**die Arterie** [-n]; **die Schlagader**
  artery)
der Arm [-e] arm (**der Unterarm** forearm)
der Atem breath (**ein Atemzug** [*m; pl* ⸚e] a breath)
das Atmen breathing
das Band [⸚er] ligament
die Bandscheibe [-n] (inter-vertebral) disc
die Bauchspeicheldrüse [-n] pancreas
das Becken [-] pelvis
das Bein [-e] leg
die Blase [-n] bladder
der Blinddarm [⸚e] appendix
das Blut blood (**der Kreislauf** circulation)
die Brust [⸚e] breast; chest (**die Büste** [-n]; **der Busen** [-] bust)
der Darm bowels
der Daumen [-] thumb
die Drüse [-n] gland
der Ell(en)bogen [-] elbow
die Faust [⸚e] fist (**der Faustschlag** [⸚e] punch)
die Ferse [-n] heel
die Figur [-en] figure
der Finger [-] finger (**der Zeige-/Mittel-/Ringfinger** index/middle/
  ring-finger; **der kleine Finger** little finger)
das Fleisch flesh
der Fuß [⸚e] foot (**zu Fuß** on foot; **barfuß** barefoot)

die Galle [-n] gall-bladder; bile
das Gelenk [-e] joint
das Gerippe [-]; **das Skelett** [-e] skeleton
die Geschlechtsorgane *n pl* genitals
das Glied [-er] limb
die Hand [⸚e] hand (**sich** [D] **die Hand *geben** shake hands)
die Handfläche [-n]; **der Handteller** [-] palm
das Handgelenk [-e] wrist
der Harn; der Urin urine
die Haut [⸚e] skin
das Herz [-en] heart (**klopfen** beat)
die Hinterbacke [-n] buttock
der Hintern [-]; **das Gesäß** [-e] backside; bottom
der Hoden [-] testicle
die Hüfte [-n] hip
der Kehlkopf [⸚e] larynx
das Knie [-] knee (**die Kniescheibe** [-n] kneecap)
der Knöchel [-] ankle; knuckle (**der Fußknöchel; die Fessel** [-n]
  ankle; **sich** [D] **den Knöchel ver'stauchen** sprain one's ankle)
der Knochen [-] bone
der Knorpel [-] cartilage
der Körper [-] body
die Leber [-n] liver
die Luftröhre [-n] windpipe
die Lunge [-n] lung
der Magen [*pl* ⸚ or -]; **der Bauch** [⸚e] stomach
die Mandel [-n] tonsil
die Menstruation menstruation (**die Periode** [-n]; **die Regel** [-n]
  period)
der Muskel [G -s *pl* -n] muscle
der Nagel [⸚] nail
der Nerv [-en] nerve (**das Nervensystem** nervous system)
die Niere [-n] kidney
das Organ [-e] organ
der Penis [-se] penis
die Rippe [-n] rib
der Rücken [-] back

das Rückgrat [-e] spine (**die Wirbelsäule** [-n] spinal column)
der Rumpf [ᵜe] trunk
die Scheide [-n] vagina
der Schenkel [-] thigh
das Schienbein [-e] shin
das Schlüsselbein [-e] collar-bone
die Schulter [-n]; **die Achsel** [-n] shoulder (**die/mit den Achseln zucken** shrug)
der Schweiß sweat
die Sehne [-n] sinew; tendon (**die Achillessehne** Achilles tendon)
die Seite [-n] side
die Sohle/Fußsohle [-n] sole
der Spann [-e]; **der Fußrücken** [-] instep
der Stoffwechsel; **der Metabolismus** metabolism
die Taille [-n] waist
das Trommelfell [-e] ear-drum
die Verdauung digestion
die Wade [-n] calf
der Zeh [-e]; **die Zehe** [-n] toe (**auf Zehenspitzen** on tiptoe)

Körperbewegungen Actions of the body

*an|sehen look at
atmen breathe
*auf|schrecken; ***auf|fahren** start
*auf|stehen stand/get up
aus|strecken stretch out (**sich ausstrecken** stretch (oneself))
ballen clench [fist]
sich be'eilen hurry (up)
*beißen bite
be'rühren touch
beugen bend
be'wegen move (**die Bewegung** [-en] movement)
blicken; **schauen** glance (**der Blick** [-e] glance)
blinzeln blink
boxen punch

*brechen break (**sich [D] das Bein** etc. **brechen** break one's leg etc.)

sich bücken bend down; stoop

eilen rush

er'sticken choke

*fallen fall

*fallen|lassen drop

*fangen catch

gähnen yawn (**das Gähnen** *no pl* yawn; yawning)

*gehen walk

gestikulieren gesture (**die Geste [-n]** gesture)

grinsen grin (**das Grinsen** *no pl* grin)

*halten hold

*heben raise

*herab|lassen; [gaze] **senken** lower

hinken limp

sich hin|legen lie down

sich hocken squat down

hören hear

hüpfen hop

kauen chew

keuchen pant

kosten; **schmecken** taste

kratzen scratch

lächeln smile (**das Lächeln** *no pl* smile)

lachen laugh (**das Lachen** *no pl* laugh; laughter)

laufen run; walk

sich lehnen lean (**gegen + A** against; **sich vor|-/zurück|lehnen** lean forwards/backwards)

*nehmen take

nicken nod (**das Nicken** *no pl* nod)

nieder|knien; **sich knien**; **sich hin|knien** kneel down

*riechen smell

ruhen; **sich aus|ruhen** rest

runzeln wrinkle (**die Stirn runzeln** frown)

*schlagen hit; slap; [heart] beat (**der Schlag [ᵋe]** blow)

schlucken swallow

schütteln shake (**den Kopf schütteln** shake one's head; **das Kopfschütteln** shake of the head)
schwanken stagger
*sehen see
sich setzen; sich hin|setzen sit down
*sprechen speak
*springen jump; leap
starren stare (**finster starren** glare; **finster** darkly)
stolpern (**über** + A) trip (over)
sich strecken stretch (**das Bein strecken** stretch one's leg)
*treten kick (**der Tritt** [-e] kick)
sich um|drehen turn round
ver'dauen digest
ver'stauchen sprain
weinen (**vor** + D) weep (with) (**die Träne** [-n] tear)
*werfen throw
winken wave
zeigen (**auf** + A) point (at) (**das Zeichen** [-] sign)
zu|hören listen
*zurück|treten step back
zwinkern wink; blink (**das Zwinkern** *no pl* wink)

Stellungen Positions

Arm *m* **in Arm** arm in arm
ausgestreckt stretched out
hängend hanging
gebückt bent
gekrümmt bent double
gelehnt gegen + A; **angelehnt an** + A or D leaning against/on
Hand *f* **in Hand** hand in hand
hängend hanging
hockend squatting
kauernd crouching
kniend; auf den Knien kneeling (**auf allen vieren** on all fours)
krumm bent [finger]
liegend lying (**auf dem Bauch** face down)

nebeneinander side by side
Schulter *f* **an Schulter** shoulder to shoulder
sitzend sitting
stehend standing
verschränkt [arms]; **gefaltet** [hands] folded

SEE ALSO: **Accidents; Adornment; Clothing; Describing People; Hair; Health and Sickness; Identity; The Senses; Tobacco and Drugs**

27. Identity Identität

Name Name

ich heiße . . . my name is . . .

wie heißen Sie?; wie nennen Sie sich?; wie ist Ihr Name? what is your name?

wie heißen Sie mit Vor-/Nachnamen? what is your first name/surname?

wie schreiben Sie sich? how do you spell your name?

die Identität [-en] identity
die Initiale [-n] initial
der Name [G -ns _pl_ -n] name (**der Vor-/Mädchen-/Ehename** first/maiden/married name; **der Familien-/Nach-/Zuname** surname; **der Schriftsteller-/Künstlername** pen-/stage-name; **der Spitz-name** nickname)
die Unterschrift [-en] signature

Frau X Mrs/Ms X
Fräulein/Frl. X Miss X
Herr [A, G, D -n] X Mr X
Herr/Frau Doktor X Dr X [**Frau Doktor** also found meaning 'wife of Dr X']

(die) Damen _f pl_ ladies (**meine Damen und Herren** ladies and gentlemen)
(die) Herren _m pl_ gentlemen

buchstabieren spell
*heißen be called
*nennen name (**sich nennen** be called)
paraphieren initial
taufen christen
*unter'schreiben sign

Adresse Address

wo wohnen Sie? where do you live?
**ich wohne in der Bismarckstraße Nummer 17; ich wohne
  Bismarckstraße 17** I live at 17 Bismarckstraße

die Adresse [-n]; die Anschrift [-en] address
die Allee [-n]; die Avenue [-n]; der Boulevard [-s] avenue
das Branchenverzeichnis [-se] trade directory
die Etage [-n]; der Stock [-]; das Stockwerk [-e] storey
der Geburtsort [-e] place of birth
die Hausnummer [-n] number
der/die Mieter/in [-/-nen] tenant (**der/die Untermieter/in** subtenant)
der Ort [-e] place [town]
der Platz [ᵂe] square
die Postleitzahl [-en] postcode
die Staatsangehörigkeit [-en] nationality
die Straße [-n] street
das Telefonbuch [ᵂer] telephone directory (**die Telefonnummer [-n]**
  phone number)
der Vermieter [-]; der Hauswirt [-e] landlord (**die Vermieterin
  [-nen]; die Hauswirtin [-nen]** landlady)
der Wohnort [-e] place of residence

*be'sitzen own
leben live
mieten rent
teilen mit + D share with
ver'mieten let
wohnen live [in a specific place]

am Meer *n*; **an der See** by the sea (**die Seestadt [ᵂe]** seaside town;
  der Badeort [-e] seaside resort; spa)
am Stadtrand on the edge of town; in the suburbs
auf dem Lande in the country
bei X [D] at X's
in der Stadt in town

Alter Age

wie alt sind Sie? how old are you?
ich bin 17 Jahre alt I'm 17
ich bin Mitte (der) Dreißig I'm in my mid-thirties

die Adoleszenz adolescence (**der/die Heranwachsende** *adj n*
adolescent)
der/die Alte *adj n* old man/woman (**die Alten** *pl* the old; **alte
Leute** *pl* old people)
das Alter [-] age; old age (**im Alter von** + D at the age of; **ein
älterer Herr/eine ältere Dame** an elderly man/woman; **in
fortgeschrittenem Alter** at an advanced age)
die Altersgrenze [-n] age limit
das Baby [-s] baby
der/die Erwachsene *adj n* adult
die Geburt [-en] birth (**das Geburtsdatum** [*pl* -daten] date of birth;
der Geburtstag [-e] birthday; **gebürtige(r) Deutsche(r)** *adj n*
German by birth)
der/die hundertjährige Greis/in [-e/-nen] centenarian; hundred-
year-old
das Jahr [-e] year
die Jugend youth [the state] (**der/die Jugendliche** *adj n* youth;
young person; **junge Leute** *pl* young people)
die junge Dame [-n] young woman/lady
der junge Mann [¨er] young man
das Kid [-s] kid
das Kind [-er] child
die Langlebigkeit longevity
das Mädchen [-] girl
der Monat [-e] month
der Teenager [-]; der Teen [-s] teenager
der Zeitgenosse [-n]/die Zeitgenossin [-nen] contemporary

altern age; grow old
*auf|wachsen; [reach maturity] **erwachsen *werden** grow up
geboren *sein be born
mündig/volljährig *werden come of age

*sterben die

alt old (**älter** elderly; **älter als** older than)
altersschwach; senil senile
erwachsen adult
jugendlich; [derogatory] **infantil** juvenile
jung young (**jünger als** younger than)
kindlich; [derogatory] **kindisch** childish
-jährig -year-old (**siebenjährig** seven-year-old)
mit X Jahren at the age of X
mittleren Alters middle-aged
reif mature (**im reiferen Alter** of mature years)
unmündig; minderjährig under-age
zeitgenössisch; gleichaltrig contemporary

Geschlecht Sex

die Dame [-n] lady; woman
der Feminismus feminism
die Frau [-en] woman
der Herr [A, G, D *sing* **-n**; *pl* **-en**] (gentle)man
der Junge [-n] boy
das Mädchen [-] girl
der Mann [ᵉer] man
die Männlichkeit masculinity
die Weiblichkeit femininity

damenhaft ladylike
gentlemanlike gentlemanly
heterosexuell heterosexual
homosexuell homosexual (**der/die Homosexuelle** *adj n* homosexual; **schwul** *colloq* gay)
lesbisch Lesbian (**die Lesbierin [-nen]** Lesbian)
männlich male; masculine
weiblich female; feminine

SEE ALSO: **Birth, Marriage, and Death; Describing People; The Human Body; Jobs; Places and Languages; Relationships**

28. Jobs Arbeit

Wie man sich ernährt What you do for a living

Feminine forms are given where these are in everyday use.

der/die **Abgeordnete** *adj n* MP
der/die **Ansager/in** [-/-nen] announcer
der/die **Anstreicher/in** [-/-nen] painter; decorator
der/die **Apotheker/in** [-/-nen] chemist; pharmacist
der/die **Architekt/in** [-en/-nen] architect
der **Arzt** [ːe]/die **Ärztin** [-nen] doctor
der/die **Astronaut/in** [-en/-nen] astronaut
der/die **Astronom/in** [-en/-nen] astronomer
der/die **Ausbilder/in** [-/-nen] instructor
der **Autor** [G -s *pl* -en]/die **Autorin** [-nen] author
der/die **Bäcker/in** [-/-nen] baker
der/die **Bankangestellte** *adj n* bank clerk
der/die **Bauarbeiter/in** [-/-nen] builder
der **Bauer** [-n]/die **Bäuerin** [-nen] countryman/-woman; farmer
der **Bauunternehmer** [-] building contractor
der **Beamte** *adj n*/die **Beamtin** [-nen] official; civil servant; police
  officer
der/die **Berater/in** [-/-nen] counsellor (der/die **Eheberater/in**
  marriage guidance counsellor; der/die **Berufsberater/in** careers
  advisor)
der **Bergarbeiter** [-]; der **Bergmann** [*pl* **Bergleute**] miner
der/die **Bergführer/in** [-/-nen] mountain guide
der/die **Bettler/in** [-/-nen] beggar
der/die **Bibliothekar/in** [-e/-nen] librarian
der/die **Bildhauer/in** [-/-nen] sculptor
der/die **Blumenhändler/in** [-/-nen] florist
der **Brauer** [-] brewer
der/die **Briefträger/in** [-/-nen] postman/-woman
der/die **Buchhalter/in** [-/-nen] bookkeeper
der/die **Buchhändler/in** [-/-nen] bookseller

der/die Büchsenmacher/in [-/-nen] gunsmith
der/die Büroangestellte *adj n* office worker
der/die Busfahrer/in [-/-nen] bus driver
der/die Cartoonist/in [-en/-nen]; **der/die Karikaturist/in** [-en/-nen] cartoonist
der/die Caterer/in [-/-nen] caterer
der/die Chirurg/in [-en/-nen] surgeon
der/die Dichter/in [-/-nen] poet; writer
der/die Diener/in [-/-nen] servant
das Dienstmädchen [-] maid
der/die Dolmetscher/in [-/-nen] interpreter
der/die Dozent/in [-en/-nen] lecturer
der/die Drogist/in [-en/-nen] chemist
der/die Drucker/in [-/-nen] printer
der/die Effektenmakler/in [-/-nen] stockbroker
der Eisenbahner [-] railwayman
der/die Eisenwarenhändler/in [-/-nen] ironmonger
der/die Elektriker/in [-/-nen] electrician
der Empfangschef [-s]/**die Empfangsdame** [-n] receptionist
der/die Fahrer/in [-/-nen] driver
der/die Fahrschullehrer/in [-/-nen] driving-instructor
der/die Fensterputzer/in [-/-nen] window cleaner
der Feuerwehrmann [*pl* ⁼er or **-leute**] fireman
der Fischer [-] fisherman
der/die Fischhändler/in [-/-nen] fishmonger
der/die Fleischer/in [-/-nen]; **der/die Metzger/in** [-/-nen] butcher
der Förster [-] forester
der/die Fotograf/in [-en/-nen] photographer
das Fotomodell [-e] photographic model
der/die Fremdenführer/in [-/-nen] tourist guide
der Friseur [-e]/**die Friseuse** [-n] hairdresser
der/die Gärtner/in [-/-nen] gardener
der Gasmann [⁼er] gasman (**der/die Gasintallateur/in** [-e/-nen] gas-fitter)
der/die Geistliche *adj n* clergyman; minister
der/die Gelehrte *adj n*; **der/die Wissenschaftler/in** [-/-nen] scholar
der/die Gemüseanbauer/in [-/-nen] market gardener

der Geschäftsinhaber/in [-/-nen] shopkeeper
der Geselle [-n]/**die Gesellin** [-nen] journeyman/-woman (**der Maurergeselle** journeyman bricklayer)
der/die Goldschmied/in [-e/-nen] goldsmith
der/die Großhändler/in [-/-nen] wholesaler
der/die Grundschullehrer/in [-/-nen] primary-school teacher
der/die Handelsvertreter/in [-/-nen] sales rep(resentative)
der/die Hausierer/in [-/-nen] hawker
der/die Hausmeister/in [-/-nen] caretaker
die Hebamme [-n] midwife
der Hirte [-n] (*obsolete f* **die Hirtin** [-nen]); **der/die Schäfer/in** [-/-nen] shepherd
der/die Hochschullehrer/in [-/-nen] university teacher
der/die Ingenieur/in [-e/-nen] engineer
der/die Innenausstatter/in [-/-nen] interior decorator
der/die Installateur/in [-e/-nen]; **der/die Klempner/in** [-/-nen] plumber
der/die Journalist/in [-en/-nen] journalist
der Juwelier [-e] jeweller
der Kameramann [¨er] cameraman
der Kaufmann [*pl* -leute]/**die Kauffrau** [-en] businessman/-woman; grocer
der Kellner [-] waiter (**die Kellnerin** [-nen] waitress)
der/die Kindergärtner/in [-/-nen] nursery-school teacher
das Kindermädchen [-] nanny
der Koch [¨e]/**die Köchin** [-nen] cook (**der/die Küchenchef/in** [-s/-nen] chef)
der/die Kohlenhändler/in [-/-nen] coal-merchant
der/die Komiker/in [-/-nen] comedian
der Konditor [G -s *pl* -en]/**die Konditorin** [-nen] pastry-cook
die Krankenschwester [-n] nurse (**der Krankenpfleger** [-] male nurse)
der/die Künstler/in [-/-nen] artist
der/die Kurzwarenhändler/in [-/-nen] haberdasher
der/die Ladenbesitzer/in [-/-nen] shopkeeper
der/die Landarbeiter/in [-/-nen] farm worker
der/die Landstreicher/in [-/-nen] tramp

der/die **Lebensmittelhändler/in** [-/-nen] grocer

der/die **Lehrer/in** [-/-nen] teacher

der/die **Lieferant/in** [-en/-nen] delivery man/woman

der/die **LKW-/Lkw-Fahrer/in** [-/-nen] lorry driver

der **Lokführer** [-] engine driver

der **Lumpensammler** [-] rag-and-bone man

der/die **Maler/in** [-/-nen] painter

das **Mannequin** [-s]; das **Model** [-s] fashion model (der **Dressman** [*pl* -men] male model)

der **Matrose** [-n] sailor

der **Maurer** [-] bricklayer

der/die **Mechaniker/in** [-/-nen] mechanic

der **Messerschmied** [-e] cutler

der/die **Metallarbeiter/in** [-/-nen] metalworker

der/die **Militärangehörige** *adj n* serviceman/-woman

der/die **Minister/in** [-/-nen] (cabinet) minister (der/die **Premierminister/in** prime minister)

der **Möbelpacker** [-] removal man

der **Moderator** [G -s *pl* -en]/die **Moderatorin** [-nen] (radio, TV) presenter

der/die **Modeschöpfer/in** [-/-nen] fashion designer

der/die **Modist/in** [-en/-nen]; der **Putzmacher/in** [-/-nen] milliner

der **Mönch** [-e] monk

der/die **Müller/in** [-/-nen] miller

der **Müllmann** [ᵂer] dustman

der/die **Musiker/in** [-/-nen] musician

die **Nonne** [-n] nun

der/die **Notar/in** [-e/-nen] notary

der **Ober** [-] waiter

der/die **Obst- und Gemüsehändler/in** [-/-nen] greengrocer

der **Offizier** [-e] officer (**bei der Armee/der Luftwaffe/der Marine** in the army/air force/navy; der/die **Offiziersanwärter/in** [-/-nen] officer cadet)

der/die **Optiker/in** [-/-nen] optician (der/die **Augenoptiker/in** ophthalmic optician)

der/die **Pfarrer/in** [-/-nen] [protestant] minister; [catholic] parish priest

der/die Physiker/in [-/-nen] physicist
der/die Pilot/in [-en/-nen] pilot
der Platzanweiser [-] usher (**die Platzanweiserin** [-nen] usherette)
der/die Politiker/in [-/-nen] politician
der/die Polizist/in [-en/-nen] policeman/-woman
der Postbeamte *adj n*/**die Postbeamtin** [-nen] post-office clerk
der Priester [-] priest (**die Priesterin** [-nen] priestess)
der/die Produzent/in [-en/-nen] producer
der/die Programmierer/in [-/-nen] computer programmer
der/die Psychiater/in [-/-nen] psychiatrist
der Psychologe [-n]/**die Psychologin** [-nen] psychologist
die Putzfrau [-en]; **der/die Raumpfleger/in** [-/-nen] cleaner
das Ratsmitglied [-er] councillor (**der Stadtrat** [⁼e]/**die Stadträtin**
  [-nen] town councillor)
der/die Raumgestalter/in [-/-nen] interior decorator
der Rechtsanwalt [⁼e]/**die Rechstsanwältin** [-nen] lawyer
der/die Rennfahrer/in [-/-nen] racing river
der/die Reporter/in [-/-nen] reporter
der/die Richter/in [-/-nen] judge
der/die Sänger/in [-/-nen] singer
der/die Sanitäter/in [-/-nen] ambulance man/woman
der/die Schaffner/in [-/-nen] ticket inspector; guard
der Schauspieler [-] actor (**die Schauspielerin** [-nen] actress)
der Schiff(s)bauer [-] shipbuilder
der/die Schlosser/in [-/-nen] locksmith
der Schmied [-e] blacksmith
der/die Schneider/in [-/-nen] tailor/dressmaker
der/die Schornsteinfeger/in [-/-nen] chimney-sweep
die Schreibkraft [⁼e] typist [male or female] (**der/die Phonotypist/in**
  [-en/-nen] audio typist; **der/die Stenotypist/in** shorthand typist)
der/die Schreibwarenhändler/in [-/-nen] stationer
der/die Schriftsteller/in [-/-nen] writer
der Schuster [-]; **der Schuhmacher** [-] cobbler
der Seemann [*pl* Seeleute] seaman
der/die Sekretär/in [-e/-nen] secretary
der/die Silberschmied/in [-e/-nen] silversmith
der/die Soldat/in [-en/-nen] soldier

der/die Sozialarbeiter/in [-/-nen] social worker
der/die Spion/in [-e/-nen] spy
die Sprechstundenhilfe [-n] (medical/dental) receptionist
der Staatsbeamte *adj n*/**die Staatsbeamtin** [-nen] civil servant
der Star [-s] star [male or female]
der Steinmetz [-en] stonemason
der Steward [-s] steward (**die Stewardeß** [-ssen] stewardess; air hostess)
der/die Straßenfeger/in [-/-nen] street-sweeper
der/die Straßenhändler/in [-/-nen] costermonger; street-trader
der/die Stricker/in [-/-nen] knitter
der/die Student/in [-en/-nen] student
der Studienrat [⸚e]/**die Studienrätin** [-nen] secondary-school teacher
der/die Taxifahrer/in [-/-nen] taxi-driver
der/die Telefonist/in [-en/-nen] switchboard operator
der Tierarzt [⸚e]/**die Tierärztin** [-nen] vet
der Tischler [-] joiner (**der Kunst-/Möbeltischler** cabinet-maker)
der/die Töpfer/in [-/-nen] potter
der/die Übersetzer/in [-/-nen] translator
der/die Uhrmacher/in [-/-nen] watch/clockmaker
der/die Verkäufer/in [-/-nen] sales assistant
der/die Verleger/in [-/-nen] publisher
der/die Vertreter/in [-/-nen] representative; agent (**der/die Versicherungsvertreter/in** insurance agent)
der Wäschemann [⸚er]/**die Wäschefrau** [-en] laundryman/-woman
der/die Weber/in [-/-nen] weaver
der/die Weinhändler/in [-/-nen] wine-merchant
der/die Winzer/in [-/-nen] winegrower
der/die Wirtschaftsprüfer/in [-/-nen] chartered accountant
der/die Wissenschaftler/in [-/-nen]/**Naturwissenschaftler/in** scientist
der Zahnarzt [⸚e]/**die Zahnärztin** [-nen] dentist
der/die Zeichner/in [-/-nen] draughtsman/-woman; graphic artist
der/die Zeitungshändler/in [-/-nen] newsagent
das Zimmermädchen [-] chambermaid
der Zimmermann [*pl* -leute]; **der Zimmerer** [-] carpenter
der Zollbeamte *adj n*/**die Zollbeamtin** [-nen] customs officer

Was man ist What you are

der/die Angestellte *adj n* employee; white-collar worker (**der/die leitende Angestellte** *adj n* executive; **leiten** manage)

der/die Arbeiter/in [-/-nen] worker

der/die Arbeitgeber/in [-/-nen] employer

der/die Arbeitnehmer/in [-/-nen] employee

der/die Arbeitslose *adj n* unemployed person

der/die Arbeitssuchende *adj n* job-seeker

der/die Aufseher/in [-/-nen] overseer; supervisor

der/die Azubi [-s] [= **Auszubildende**]; **der Lehrling** [-e]/**das Lehrmädchen** [-] apprentice; trainee (**die Lehrstelle** [-n] apprenticeship [= place]; **die Lehre** apprenticeship [= training]; **die Lehrzeit** [-en] apprenticeship [= training period])

der/die Betriebsleiter/in [-/-nen]; **der/die Geschäftsführer/in** [-/-nen]; **der/die Geschäftsleiter/in** manager; managing director

der/die Büroangestellte *adj n* office worker

der/die Chef/in [-s/-nen] boss

der Direktor [G -s *pl* -en]/**die Direktorin** [-nen] director; manager; headmaster/-mistress

der Fachmann [*pl* -leute]/**die Fachfrau** [-en] expert

der Geschäftsmann [*pl* -leute]/**die Geschäftsfrau** [-en] businessman/-woman

der/die Gewerkschaft(l)er/in [-/-nen] trade-unionist

das Gewerkschaftsmitglied [-er] union member

der Handwerker [-] tradesman; craftsman

der/die Herrsteller/in [-/-nen] manufacturer

der/die Hilfsarbeiter/in [-/-nen] unskilled worker; labourer

der/die Industrielle *adj n* industrialist

der Kollege [-n]/**die Kollegin** [-nen] colleague

der/die Lohnempfänger/in [-/-nen] wage-earner

der/die Manager/in [-/-nen] manager

der Profi [-s] professional

der/die Rentner/in [-/-nen]; **der/die Ruheständler/in** [-/-nen] retired person; pensioner

der/die Spezialist/in [-en/-nen] specialist

der/die Streikbrecher/in [-/-nen] blackleg

der/die **Streikende** *adj n* striker
der/die **Techniker/in** [-/-nen] technician
der **Verwaltungsbeamte** *adj n*/die **Verwaltungsbeamtin** [-nen]
administrator
der/die **Vorarbeiter/in** [-/-nen]; der/die **Werkmeister/in** [-/-nen]
foreman/-woman; charge-hand
die **Zeitarbeits-/Aushilfskraft** [ᵘe]; die **Aushilfe** [-n] temporary
worker; temp (**Zeitarbeit** *f* **machen** to temp)

Wo man arbeitet Where you work

die **Baustelle** [-n] building site
das **Büro** [-s] office
die **Fabrik** [-en]; das **Werk** [-e] factory; works
die **Firma** [*pl* **Firmen**]; der **Betrieb** [-e] firm
das **Geschäft** [-e] business; shop (die **Geschäftsreise** [-n] business
trip; die **Geschäftswelt** business world)
die **Gesellschaft** [-en] company (**Co.** [**Compagnie**] co.; **GmbH**
[**Gesellschaft mit beschränkter Haftung**] = plc; **beschränkt**
limited; die **Haftung** liability)
der **Handel** trade; commerce (die **Hotelbranche** [-n] the hotel
trade; der **Groß-/Einzelhandel** wholesale/retail trade)
die **Hauptverwaltung**; [banking] die **Hauptgeschäftsstelle**;
[commerce] das **Hauptbüro** head office
die **Industrie** [-n] industry (die **Schwer-/Leichtindustrie** heavy/
light industry)
das **Labor** [*pl* -s or -e] laboratory (die **Forschung** research)
der **Laden** [ᵘ] shop
das **Lagerhaus** [ᵘer] warehouse
die **Landwirtschaft** agriculture (**auf dem Feld** *n* **arbeiten** work in
the fields)
die **Leitung** management
das **Unternehmen** [-] company
die **Werkstatt** [ᵘen]; die **Werkstätte** [-n] workshop
die **Zweigstelle** [-n]; die **Filiale** [-n] branch

Was man tut What you do

sich ab|arbeiten toil; slog
arbeiten work
arbeitslos *sein be unemployed
Arbeit *f* **suchen/*finden** look for/find work
*aus|scheiden (aus + D); in Rente/in den Ruhestand *gehen retire
  (from)
sich *be'werben für + A (bei + D) apply for (with)
ein|stellen take on
*ent'lassen sack; make redundant; dismiss
führen run
kündigen (bei + D) give in one's notice (to) **(kündigen + D give
  sb notice)**
leiten manage
eine Stelle [-n] *an|nehmen/ab|lehnen accept/refuse a job
streiken strike
ver'dienen earn **(sich er'nähren von + D; seinen Lebensunterhalt
  verdienen mit + D** earn a/one's living by)
ver'walten administer
*zurück|treten resign

Die Arbeitswelt Industrial life

der Abschluß [⸚sse] qualification
die Akkordarbeit piece-work
der Antrag [⸚e] application
die Arbeit [-en] work; job
die Arbeiterschaft; die Arbeitskräfte *f pl* labour **(ungelernt**
  unskilled; **angelernt** semi-skilled; **ausgebildet** skilled)
das Arbeitslosengeld unemployment benefit
der Arbeitsplatz [⸚e] place of work; job **(den Arbeitsplatz
  *ver'lieren/wechseln** be made redundant/change jobs)
der Arbeitsvertrag [⸚e] contract of employment
die Ausbildung training
die Aussperrung [-en] lock-out

der Beruf [-e] profession; job (**von Beruf** by profession; **die Berufsberatung** careers advice)

die Beschäftigung employment (**die Ganztagsbeschäftigung** full-time work; **die Halbtagsbeschäftigung**: **die Teilzeit-/Halbtags-arbeit** part-time work; **die Kurzarbeit** short time)

die Betriebsferien *pl* company holidays

der Betriebsrat [≃e] works committee

die Bewerbung [-en] (um + A) application (for)

die Bezahlung payment; pay

die Branche [-n] industry; branch of industry

die Demonstration [-en] demonstration

die Einstellung appointing; taking on

die Entlassung [-en] dismissal

die Erfahrung [-en] experience

der Feierabend end of work [for the day] (**nach Feierabend** after work; **Feierabend machen** knock off)

die Fort-/Weiterbildung further training

das Gehalt [≃er] salary (**die Gehaltserhöhung [-en]** pay rise)

die Geschäftsleitung management

die Gewerkschaft [-en] trade union

die Gleitzeit flexitime (**gleitende Arbeitszeit *haben** be on flexitime)

das Handwerk [-e] craft

das Interview [-s]; **das Vorstellungsgespräch [-e]** job interview

die Laufbahn [-en] career

der Lebenslauf [≃e] curiculum vitae; CV

der Lehrgang [≃e] training course (**einen Lehrgang machen** go on a course)

der Lohn [≃e] wage (**die Lohnsteuer** income tax; **die Lohnerhö-hung [-en]** pay increase; **der Lohnstopp [-s]** pay freeze)

die Mittagspause [-n] lunch-break

die Pensionskasse [-n] pension fund

das Personal staff

die Rente [-n] pension (**die Invalidenrente** disability pension)

der Ruhestand retirement

die 36-Stunden-Woche 36-hour week

die soziale Sicherheit social security (**die Sozialhilfe** social security benefit)

die Stelle [-n]; die Stellung [-en]; *colloq* **der Job [-s]** job; post (**fest** permanent; **vorübergehend** temporary; **die freie Stelle** vacancy; **die Stellenangebote** *n pl* situations vacant; **eine ruhige Kugel *schieben** have a soft job)

der Streik [-s] strike (**in den Streik/einen Bummelstreik *treten** come out on strike/go on a go-slow; **zum Streik *auf|rufen** call out on strike; **mit Streik drohen** threaten to strike; **der wilde Streik** wildcat strike; **der Dienst nach Vorschrift** work-to-rule)

der Streit [-e] dispute

die Überstunden *pl* overtime

die Verwaltung [-en] administration

der Vorstand [⸚e] board

*an|treten start [a job] (**zur Arbeit antreten** report for work)

sich *be'werben um + A apply for

krank gemeldet *sein be off sick (**sich krank melden** report sick)

Überstunden machen work overtime

<small>SEE ALSO:</small> **Describing People; Education; Identity; Tools**

29. Justice and Law
Gerechtigkeit und Gesetz

Verfolgung des Verbrechers
Pursuit of the criminal

die Anzeige [-n] report (**gegen jn Anzeige er'statten** report sb to
the police)

der Ausbruch [⸚e] escape

die Auskunft [⸚e] (piece of) information

die Aussage [-n] statement (**eine Aussage machen** make a
statement)

der Ausweis [-e] identity card

die Belohnung [-en] reward

der Bericht [-e] report; account

die Beschreibung [-en] description (**der Beschreibung** [D]
*ent'sprechen fit the description)

die Beschwerde [-n] complaint

die Beute loot

der Bulle [-n]; **der Polyp** [-en] *both colloq* cop

der/die Detektiv/in [-e/-nen] (private) detective

der/die Entflohene *adj n* escaped prisoner

der/die Ermittler/in [-/-nen] investigator

die Festnahme [-n] capture; arrest

der Fingerabdruck [⸚e] fingerprint

die Flucht [-en] escape (**die Flucht *er'greifen** take flight)

der/die Flüchtige *adj n* fugitive

die Gefahr [-en] danger

der/die Gefangene *adj n* prisoner

der/die Geheimagent/in [-en/-nen] secret agent

das Geständnis [-se] confession

die grüne Minna [-s] Black Maria

der Haftbefehl [-e] warrant [for arrest] (**der Durchsuchungsbefehl**
search-warrant)

die Handgreiflichkeiten *f pl* scuffle
die Handschellen *f pl* handcuffs (**jm Handschellen an|legen**
 handcuff sb)
der Helm [-e] helmet
der/die Informant/in [-en/-nen] informer (**der Spitzel** [-] *colloq*
 grass)
die Klage [-n] complaint (**eine Klage führen** make a complaint)
der Kriminalbeamte *adj n*/**die Kriminalbeamtin** [-nen] detective
die Kripo [= **die Kriminalpolizei**] CID
das Lösegeld [-er] ransom
die Nachforschung [-en] investigation
der Nachtwächter [-] night-watchman
das Opfer [-] victim
die Pistole [-n] pistol
die Polizei police (**die Bereitschaftspolizei** riot police)
der Polizeibeamte *adj n*/**die Polizeibeamtin** [-nen] police-officer
der Polizeihund [-e] police dog
der Polizeiinspektor [G -s *pl* -en] police inspector
der Polizeikommisar [-e] police superintendent
das Polizeipräsidium police headquarters
die Polizeiwache [-n] police station
der Polizeiwagen [-]; **das Polizeiauto** [-s] police car
der/die Polizist/in [-en/-nen] policeman/woman (**der/die Polizist/in**
 in Zivil plain-clothes policeman/woman)
die Razzia [*pl* **Razzien**] (**in** + D) raid (on)
der/die Retter/in [-/-nen] rescuer
die Rettung [-en]; **die Befreiung** [-en] rescue
der Schild [-e] shield
die Schlägerei [-en]; **die Rauferei** [-en] fight; brawl
der Schlagstock [ͤe]; **der Knüppel** [-] truncheon
die Spur [-en] track (**jm auf der Spur *sein** be on sb's track)
der Strafzettel [-] parking-ticket
der Streifenwagen [-] patrol car
der Streit [-e] dispute
das Tränengas tear-gas
die Überwachung surveillance
die Untersuchung [-en] enquiry; examination

das Verbrechen [-] crime
der Verdacht [-] suspicion (**verdächtig** suspicious; **der/die
  Verdächtige** *adj n* suspect)
die Verhaftung [-en] arrest
die Verkehrspolizei traffic police
der Versuch [-e] attempt
die Wache [-n] guard [group] (**der Wachtposten** [-] guard
  [person]; **der/die Wächter/in** [-/-nen] security guard;
  warder)
der Wacht(haupt)meister [-] constable

*ab|fangen; [conversation] **ab|hören** intercept
an|klagen wegen + G charge with
*an|rufen challenge
be'freien free (***frei|lassen** set free)
*be'gehen commit
be'lohnen reward
be'schlagnahmen; **konfiszieren** confiscate
*be'stechen bribe
durch'suchen search
*ein|ge'stehen; ***zu|geben** admit
ein|sperren imprison
*ent'kommen escape
ent'waffnen disarm
er'tappen catch (**auf frischer Tat** red-handed)
*fest|nehmen arrest (**festgenommen** under arrest)
*gefangen|nehmen take prisoner
holen *lassen send for
melden report
retten rescue
stören disturb
über'wachen watch
über'wältigen overpower
unter'suchen investigate
ver'hören interrogate
*ver'nehmen question
*zurück|weisen deny

*zusammen|schlagen beat up
zusammen|stellen compile

Prozeß und Strafe Trial and punishment

das Alibi [-s] alibi
der/die Angeklagte *adj n* accused
die Anklage [-n] charge; prosecution
die Anklagebank dock
der Anwalt [-e]/die Anwältin [-nen]; der Rechtsanwalt [-e]/die
  Rechtsanwältin [-nen] lawyer
die Begnadigung pardon
der Beweis [-e] proof; piece of evidence (**das Beweismaterial**
  evidence)
das Delikt [-e]; die Straftat [-en] offence
der Eid [-e] oath (**unter Eid** on oath; **vereidigt *werden** take the
  oath)
der Einspruch [-̈e] (**gegen** + A) appeal; objection (to) (**die**
  Berufung [-en] appeal [to a higher court]; **das Berufungsgericht**
  Court of Appeal)
die Einzelhaft solitary confinement
der Fall [-̈e] case
das Fallbeil [-e] guillotine
der Freispruch [-̈e] acquittal
der/die Gefangene *adj n* prisoner
die Gefangenschaft imprisonment
das Gefängnis [-se] prison; imprisonment
der/die Gefängniswärter/in [-/-nen] prison officer
die Geldstrafe [-n] fine (**jn mit einer Geldstrafe be'legen** fine sb)
die Gerechtigkeit justice (**um der Gerechtigkeit willen** in order
  that justice be done)
das Gericht [-e] court (**jn vor Gericht stellen wegen** + G try sb
  for; **das Zivilgericht** civil court)
der Gerichtsdiener [-] usher
der Gerichtshof [-̈e] law court
die Gerichtskosten *pl* costs

der Gerichtssaal [*pl* -säle] courtroom

der/die Geschworene *adj n* juror (**die Geschworenen** *pl* jury)

das Gesetz [-e] law (**ein Gesetz** a law; **das Gesetz** *no pl*; **das Recht** *no pl* the law)

die Haft; die Gefangenschaft imprisonment

der Henker [-] hangman; executioner

die Hinrichtung [-en] execution

die Jugendkriminalität juvenile delinquency

der Justizirrtum [¨er] miscarriage of justice

die Kaution bail

der Kerker [-] dungeon

die Klage [-n] accusation; complaint

die Körperstrafe corporal punishment

der/die Notar/in [-e/-nen] notary

der Prozeß [-sse]; **der Fall** [¨e] trial; case (**jm den Prozeß machen** take sb to court)

der Randalierer [-] delinquent

das Recht [-e] right; law (**das Zivilrecht** civil law; **das Strafgesetz** penal law)

der/die Richter/in [-/-nen] judge

der Schaden(s)ersatz damages

das Schafott [-e] gallows; scaffold

der Scharfrichter [-] executioner

der/die Schiedsrichter/in [-/-nen] arbitrator; magistrate (**das Schiedsgericht** [-e] = magistrates' court)

der Schöffe [-n]/**die Schöffin** [-nen] [in Germany] lay judge [= jury member]

die Schuld guilt (**schuldig** guilty)

der Staatsanwalt [¨e]/**die Staatsanwältin** [-nen] prosecutor

der Strafaufschub [¨e] reprieve

die Strafe [-n] punishment; sentence (**die Freiheitsstrafe** prison sentence; **die Strafe mit Bewährung** *f* suspended sentence; **lebenslänglich** life *adj*; **lebenslänglich *be'kommen** get life)

der/die Strafgefangene *adj n* convict

die Todesstrafe death penalty (**die Hinrichtung durch den Strang** hanging; **der elektrische Stuhl** electric chair)

die **Unschuld** innocence (**unschuldig** innocent)
die **Untat** [-en] misdeed
die **Untersuchungshaft** remand (**in Untersuchungshaft *be'halten** remand in custody)
das **Urteil** [-e] verdict; sentence; judgement (**mild** lenient; die **Verurteilung** sentencing; das **Todesurteil** death sentence)
das **Verfahren/Gerichtsverfahren** [-]; die **Verhandlung** [-en] trial
die **Verteidigung** defence
die **Vorladung** [-en] summons
der **Vorsatz** premeditation (**vorsätzlich** premeditated)
die **Zelle** [-n] cell
der **Zeuge** [-n]/die **Zeugin** [-nen] witness (der **Augenzeuge/die Augenzeugin** eye-witness)
die **Zeugenaussage** testimony
der **Zeugenstand** witness-box
das **Zuchthaus** [ːer] (long-stay) prison
die **Zwangsarbeit** hard labour

*ab|geben pass [judgement]
*ab|sitzen; ver'büßen serve [sentence]
an|klagen wegen + G accuse of
be'gnadigen pardon
*be'stechen bribe; suborn
*be'weisen prove
Bürge *m* ***sein (für** + A) stand bail (for)
*ent'lassen (von + D) release (from) (**auf Bewährung** *f* **entlassen** release on parole)
*frei|lassen set free
*frei|sprechen acquit
ge'horchen [+ D] obey
hin|richten execute
Jura studieren study law (das **Jus** [*pl* **Jura**] law [as subject])
plädieren plead (**sich schuldig *be'kennen** plead guilty)
schuldig/unschuldig *sein be guilty/innocent
strafen punish
strafrechtlich ver'folgen (wegen + G) prosecute (for)
ver'haften imprison

ver'handeln try [case]
*ver'stoßen gegen + A contravene
ver'teidigen defend
ver'urteilen (zu + D) sentence (to)

SEE ALSO: **Arguments For and Against; Crimes and Criminals**

30. Leisure and Hobbies
Freizeit und Hobbys

die **Begeisterung** enthusiasm (**für/über** + A for)
die **Einladung** [-en] invitation
die **Freizeit** leisure; free time (**in der Freizeit** in one's free time;
 die **Freizeitbeschäftigung** [-en] leisure pursuit)
der **Gast** [ᵉ] guest [male or female] (**der ungebetene Gast**
 gatecrasher; **der/die Gastgeber/in** [-/-nen] host/hostess)
das **Hobby** [-s] hobby
das **Interesse** [-n] interest
das **Mitglied** [-er] member (**der Mitgliedsbeitrag** [ᵉ] subscription)
das **Taschengeld** pocket-money
das **Treffen** [-] meeting
der **Treffpunkt** [-e] meeting-place
das **Verein** [-e]; der **Klub** [-s] club
die **Versammlung** [-en] meeting
der **Zeitvertreib** [-e] pastime

sich **amüsieren** enjoy oneself
an|ge'hören + D belong to [club]
***aus|gehen** go out
be'gleiten accompany; go with
be'suchen visit
***ein|laden** invite
faulenzen laze about
et gern ***tun** enjoy doing sth
sich **interessieren für** + A be interested in (**interessiert an** + D
 interested in)
sich **langweilen** be bored (die **Langeweile** boredom)
***mit|bringen** bring (along)
Spaß *m* **machen** be fun
***teil|nehmen an** + D take part in
vorbei|schauen (**auf** + A) come round/over (for + *time*)

wild *sein auf + A be keen on
Zeit *f* ***ver'bringen mit** + D spend time on
*zusammen|kommen meet [club, group]

faszinierend fascinating
interessant interesting
langweilig boring
spannend exciting

Freizeitbeschäftigungen Leisure-time activities

der Ausflug [˝e]; [longer] **die Reise** [-n] trip
die Ausstellung [-en] exhibition (**der Eintritt** admission; **die
Ermäßigung** [-en] reduced rate)
die Autofahrt [-en] drive
das Ballett [-e] ballet (**der/die Tänzer/in** [-/-nen] dancer)
die Bar [-s] bar; night-club
die Blaskapelle [-n] brass band
der botanische Garten [˝] botanical garden(s)
die Bowlingbahn [-en] (ten-pin) bowling-alley
das Café [-s] café
die Diskothek [-en] disco (**der Diskjockey** [-s] DJ; **der Diskotanz**
disco dancing; **die Juke-/Musikbox** [-en] juke-box)
die Eisbahn [-en] ice-rink (**Schlittschuh *laufen** skate)
die Ferienkolonie [-n]; **das Ferienlager** [-] vacation camp
das Fernsehen television (***fern|sehen** watch TV; **im Fernsehen** on
television; **der Kanal** [˝e] channel; **um|schalten** change channels;
der Videorecorder [-] video recorder)
das Feuerwerk [-e] firework display (**der Feuerwerkskörper** [-]
firework)
der Freund [-e] boyfriend (**die Freundin** [-nen] girlfriend; **der/die
Brieffreund/in** pen-friend)
die Gemäldegalerie [-n] art gallery (**die Sammlung** [-en]
collection)
der Jahrmarkt [˝e] fun-fair (**die Messe** [-n] trade fair)
der Jazzklub [-s] jazz club (**der Jazz** jazz; **die Jazzband** [-s] jazz
band)

der Jugendklub [-s] youth club
das Kasino/Spielkasino [-s] casino
die Kegelbahn [-en] bowling-alley [for skittles]
das Kino [-s] cinema (**ins Kino *gehen** go to the cinema; **der Film**
  [-e] film)
das Konzert [-e] concert
das Kreuzworträtsel [-] crossword
das Minigolf minigolf(-course)
das Museum [*pl* **Museen**] museum
der Nachtklub [-s]; **das Nachtlokal** [-e] night-club (**der**
  Rausschmeißer [-] bouncer)
die Oper [-n] opera
der Park [-s] park (**der Vergnügungspark** amusement park)
die Party [-s]; **die Fete** [-n] party (**die Geburtstagsfeier** [-n]; **die**
  Geburtstagsparty birthday party; **die Einladung** [-en] invitation;
  das Geschenk [-e] present; **das Betriebsfest** [-e] office party;
  *geben/feiern throw)
der Pfadfinder [-] scout (**die Pfadfinderin** [-nen] guide)
das Picknick [*pl* -e or -s] picnic (**Picknick machen/*halten** have a
  picnic)
der Plattenspieler [-] record-player (**die Box** [-en] speaker; **die**
  CD-Platte [-n] CD; **eine Platte auf|legen** put a record on; **hören**
  listen to)
das Popkonzert [-e] pop concert (**der/die Popsänger/in** [-/-nen]
  pop singer; **der Schlager** [-] pop song; hit; **der Fan** [-s] fan; **die**
  Hitparade [-n] hit parade)
das Radfahren cycling (**das Fahrrad** [¨er] bicycle; ***rad|fahren**
  cycle; **eine Radtour** [-en] **machen** go for a cycle ride/a cycling
  tour)
das Radio [-s] radio [set] (**das Radio/der Rundfunk/der Hörfunk**
  radio [sound broadcasting]; **im Radio/Rundfunk** on the radio;
  der Transistor [G -s *pl* -en] transistor; **Radio hören** listen to the
  radio)
die Rennbahn [-en] racecourse (**das Pferd** [-e] horse; **der/die**
  Rennbesucher/in [-/-nen] racegoer; **das (Pferde)rennen** [-] horse-
  race)
das Restaurant [-s] restaurant

die Rollschuhbahn [-en] roller-skating rink (**Rollschuh *laufen** roller-skate)

das Schwimmbad [̈er] swimming-pool (**das Frei-/Hallenbad** open-air/indoor pool)

die Show [-s]; die Schau [-en] show (**der Showmaster [-]** compère)

der Spaziergang [̈e] walk (***spazieren|gehen/einen Spaziergang machen** go for a walk)

das Spiel [-e]; [football, tennis, also] **das/der Match [***pl* **-s** or **-e]**; [boxing] **der Kampf [̈e]** match

der Spielautomat [-en] gaming-machine

der Sport [*pl* **Sportarten]** sport (**Sport *treiben** do sport; play games; **der Wintersport** winter sports)

das Sportstadion [*pl* **-stadien]** sports stadium

der Tanzabend [-e] dance (**tanzen** dance; **tanzen *gehen** go dancing; **der Tanzsaal [***pl* **-säle]** ballroom; dance-hall; **die Tanzfläche [-n]** dance-floor; **ein Tanz** *m* a dance; **zum Tanz auf|fordern** ask for a dance)

das Theater [-] theatre (**das Stück [-e]; das Schauspiel [-e]** play; **im/ins Theater** at/to the theatre)

das Varieté [-s] variety theatre

das Wandern hiking (**eine Wanderung [-en]** a hike)

der Zirkus [-se] circus (**der Clown [-s]** clown)

der Zoo [-s] zoo (**im/in den Zoo** at/to the zoo)

ab|setzen drop off

be'suchen visit

*ein|laden invite

*gehen in + A go to (**gehen mit** + D go out with; **nach Hause gehen** go home)

*mit|gehen go with

(sich) *treffen meet (one another)

verabredet *sein mit + D be meeting; have a date with

sich/einander *wieder|sehen meet again

Hobbys Hobbies

das Amateurtheater amateur theatre (**die Theatergruppe** [-n],
   drama group; **der/die Amateur-/Laienschauspieler/in** [-/-nen]
   amateur actor/actress)

das Angeln fishing

der Ausflug [⸚e] outing; trip

die Band/Rockband [-s] band (**die Gruppe** [-n] group; **der/die**
   Sänger/in [-/-nen] singer; **das (Demo)band** [⸚er] (demo) tape)

das Basteln model-making; handicraft (**das Modell** [-e] model;
   der/die Bastler/in [-/-nen] handicraft enthusiast)

der Bildteppich [-e] tapestry (***weben** weave)

das Bingo bingo

das Briefmarkensammeln stamp-collecting

der Chor [⸚e] choir

die Computertechnik computing (**der (Mikro)computer** [-]
   (micro)computer; **das Computerspiel** [-e] computer game;
   programmieren program)

der Drachen [-] kite (**steigen *lassen** fly)

die Fahrt/Autofahrt [-en] drive

die Fotografie photography (**der Fotoapparat** [-e]; **die Kamera**
   [-s] camera; **die Filmkamera** ciné-camera; **der Film** [-e] film; **das**
   Foto [-s] photo; **der Abzug** [⸚e] print; **das Dia** [-s] slide)

die Gartenarbeit gardening (**der Kleingarten** [⸚] allotment; **das**
   Gartencenter [-] garden centre)

das Heimwerken; **das Do-it-yourself** DIY; do-it-yourself

das Kartenspielen card-playing (**das Kartenspiel** [-e] card-game;
   ein Spiel Karten *f pl* a pack of cards)

das Kochen cooking

die Kunst art

das Lesen reading (**der Roman** [-e] novel; **die Zeitschrift** [-en];
   die Illustrierte [-n] magazine; **der Krimi** [-s] thriller; **das**
   Taschenbuch [⸚er] paperback)

die Malerei painting (**das Gemälde** [-] picture; **die Farbe** [-n]
   paint; **der Pinsel** [-] brush)

der Modellbau model-making

die Musik music

die Pfadfinderei scouting (**der/die Pfadfinder/in** [-/-nen] scout/ guide)

das Puzzle [-s]; **das Puzzlespiel** [-e] jigsaw

das Reiten/Pferdereiten horse-riding

das Sammeln collecting (**die Sammlung** [-en] collection; **das Album** [*pl* **Alben**] album)

das Schneidern dressmaking (**die Nadel** [-n] needle; **der Faden** [̈] thread; **die Nähmaschine** [-n] sewing-machine)

das Segeln sailing; yachting

das Singen singing (**das Lied** [-er] song; **der Chor** [̈e] choir)

das Spazierengehen walking

das Spiel [-e] game (**das Gesellschaftsspiel** party game)

die Stickerei embroidery

das Stricken knitting (**die Stricknadel** [-n] knitting-needle)

die Töpferei pottery (**der/die Töpfer/in** [-/-nen] potter)

das/der Toto/Fußballtoto pools (**im Toto spielen** do the pools)

das Video video (**die Videokamera** [-s] camcorder; **das Videoband** [̈er] videotape)

die Vogelkunde; **die Vogelbeobachtung** bird-watching

das Wandern rambling

der Wettbewerb [-e]; [in magazine] **das Preisausschreiben** [-] competition

das Zeichnen [the activity]; **die Zeichnung** [-en] [the product] drawing

angeln fish

basteln make things

bauen build

fotografieren take photos; photograph (sb)

gärtnern garden

kochen cook

*lesen read

malen paint

nähen sew

*rad|fahren cycle

*reiten ride [horse]

sammeln collect (**tauschen** swap)

*schreiben write
segeln sail
*singen sing
*spazieren|gehen walk
spielen play; act
sticken embroider
stricken knit
zeichnen draw

SEE ALSO: **Art and Architecture; Cinema and Photography; Cooking and Eating; Holidays; The Media; Music; Nature; Reading and Writing; Sports and Games; Theatre; Tools; Transport**

31. Liking, Dislike, Comparing
Vorliebe, Abneigung, Vergleichen

Vorliebe Liking

die Anhänglichkeit (an + A) attachment (to)
das Bedürfnis [-se] (nach + D) need (for)
die Freundschaft [-en] friendship
der Geschmack [≈e] taste (**nach meinem Geschmack** to my taste)
das Interesse [-n] interest
die Kameradschaft comradeship
die Leidenschaft [-en] passion
die Liebe [-n] love (**auf den ersten Blick** at first sight)
die Liebenswürdigkeit kindness
das Mitgefühl sympathy
die Neigung [-en] inclination
die Sehnsucht [≈e] longing; desire
das Vergnügen [-]; die Vergnügung [-en] pleasure (**mit Vergnügen** with pleasure)
die Vertraulichkeit familiarity
die Vorliebe (für + A) (special) liking (for); partiality
der Wunsch [≈e] wish
die Zärtlichkeit tenderness; fondness
die Zuneigung affection

be'nötigen require
be'wundern admire (**bewundernswert** admirable)
brauchen need
freuen please (**es freut mich** I'm pleased; **erfreulich** agreeable)
***ge'fallen** + D please (**es gefällt mir** I like it)
gern *haben like (**gern *essen/*trinken** like [eating/drinking])
hegen cherish
hoffen hope
lieben love (**innig/abgöttisch lieben** adore/dote on; **sich ver'lieben in** + A fall in love with; **bis über beide Ohren** head over heels)

Lust *f* ***haben (auf + A/et zu tun)** feel like (sth/doing sth)
*mögen like; be fond of (**ich möchte (gern)** I should like)
schätzen value (**richtig ein|schätzen** appreciate)
schwärmen für + A be mad about
ver'göttern idolize
*vor|haben intend
*vor|ziehen; lieber *haben/*mögen prefer
*wollen want (**wohlwollend** benevolent)
sich [D] wünschen wish for (**wünschenswert** [thing]/**begehrenswert**
  [person] desirable)

angenehm pleasant
freundlich friendly
großartig great
herrlich magnificent
köstlich delicious; delightful
nett; liebenswürdig kind
prima *inv*; **toll** *both colloq* fantastic; terrific
reizend charming
sagenhaft; fabelhaft fabulous
schön lovely
unwahrscheinlich incredible
verliebt (in + A) in love (with)
wohlgesinnt (+ D) well-disposed (towards)
wunderbar marvellous
wundervoll wonderful

Abneigung Dislike

die Abneigung [-en] (gegen + A) aversion (to); dislike (of)
der Abscheu revulsion
die Antipathie antipathy
die Beanstandung [-en]; die Beschwerde [-n]; die Klage [-n]
  complaint
die Boshaftigkeit spite
die Böswilligkeit ill will
der Ekel disgust

die Feindschaft hostility; enmity
die Feindseligkeit animosity
die Gleichgültigkeit indifference
der Groll resentment (**jm grollen** bear a grudge against sb)
der Haß hate
der Horror horror (**einen Horror *haben vor** + D have a horror of)
die Unzufriedenheit dissatisfaction
die Verachtung scorn
die Verärgerung annoyance

ab|lehnen reject
sich be'klagen/sich be'schweren über + A complain about
hassen hate (**wie die Pest** like the plague)
miß'billigen (+ A) disapprove of (sth)
nicht *er'tragen; nicht *aus|halten not stand (**das kann ich nicht ertragen/aushalten** I can't stand it)
nicht *mögen; nicht leiden *können dislike
sich schämen wegen + G be ashamed of
ver'abscheuen detest (**verabscheuenswert** detestable)
ver'achten despise
widerstrebend/ungern *tun do reluctantly

abscheulich hateful; abominable
ärgerlich annoying
boshaft; bösartig spiteful; malicious
entrüstet (über + A) indignant (at)
gleichgültig indifferent
langweilig boring
nachtragend vindictive
scheußlich dreadful
übelgesinnt (+ D) ill-disposed (towards)
übelnehmerisch resentful
unerwünscht undesirable
unzufrieden (mit + D) dissatisfied (with)
widerwärtig repulsive

Vergleichen Comparing

die Ähnlichkeit [-en] similarity
das Gegenteil contrary; opposite (**im Gegenteil** on the contrary)
der Kontrast [-e] contrast
der Unterschied [-e] difference
das Urteil [-e] judgement
der Vergleich [-e] comparison (**im Vergleich zu/mit** + D in comparison with/to)
die Vorliebe [-n] (für + A) preference (for)
die Wahl [-en] choice; election

*ab|wägen weigh [ideas]
*be'schließen decide
sich *ent'scheiden (zwischen + D) decide (between)
sich *ent'schließen make up one's mind
neigen zu + D incline towards
über'legen consider
*ver'gleichen compare (**vergleichbar mit** + D comparable with/to)
*vor'ziehen; lieber *haben prefer (**vorzuziehen;** [before noun] **vorzuziehend-** preferable)
wählen choose
zögern hesitate

ähnlich (+ preceding D) similar (to)
anders als different from
besser als better than
gleich equal(ly); same (**der/die/das gleiche; der-/die-/dasselbe** the same; **wie** as)
identisch (mit + D) identical (to)
in bezug auf + A concerning
lieber rather (**ich gehe lieber** I'd rather go)
Lieblings- favourite (**meine Lieblingsfarbe [-n]** my favourite colour)
mehr als more than
schlimmer als worse than

soviel . . . wie as much . . . as (**genau-/ebensoviel . . . wie** just as much . . . as; **(nicht) so viel wie** (not) as much as; **ebensoviel** just as much)

so . . . wie as . . . as (**genau-/ebenso . . . wie** just as . . . as)

verschieden; [before noun] **ander-;** [after verb] **anders** different (**als** from)

viel much; a lot (of); *pl* many

weniger als less than

SEE ALSO: **Arguments For and Against; Describing People; Feelings**

32. Materials Materialien

die Flüssigkeit [-en] liquid
das Gas [-e] gas (das Erdgas natural gas)
der Körper/feste Körper [-] solid
der Kristall [-e] crystal
das Material [*pl* Materialien] material (das Rohmaterial; der
  Rohstoff [-e] raw material)
das Metall [-e] metal
das Mineral [*pl* -e or Mineralien] mineral
das Produkt [-e] product
der Stoff [-e] fabric; material; substance
die Zusammensetzung composition

dicht dense
echt real
farbecht colour-fast
fest firm
flüssig liquid; runny
gasförmig gaseous
geschnitzt [from wood]; gemeißelt [from stone] carved
glatt smooth
handgearbeitet handmade
hart hard
kompakt compact
künstlich artificial
leicht light
natürlich natural
plastisch plastic; malleable
porös porous
rauh rough
schwer heavy
solide solid
stabil sturdy
steinartig stony

synthetisch synthetic
versteinert petrified
weich soft
zerbrechlich fragile

Names of materials Namen von Materialien

das Aluminium; das Alu *colloq* aluminium
der Asphalt asphalt
der Backstein [-e]; der Ziegelstein [-e] brick
der Bambus [-se] bamboo
der Beton concrete
der Bindfaden string (**die Schnur** [ˮe] piece of string)
das Bitumen bitumen
das Blech sheet metal
das Blei lead (**bleiern** leaden; lead *adj*)
die Bronze bronze (**bronzen** bronze *adj*)
der Draht [ˮe] wire
das Eisen iron (**das Schmiedeeisen** wrought iron;
  (schmiede)eisern (wrought) iron *adj*)
die Erde earth (**irden** earthen; earthenware *adj*)
das Erz [-e] ore
der Faden [ˮ] (piece of) thread
der Fels [-en] rock
der Feuerstein [-e] flint
der Filz felt
der Gips plaster
das Glas [ˮer] glass (**gläsern** glass *adj*)
der Glimmer mica
das Gold gold (**golden** golden; gold *adj*)
der Granit granite
das/der Gummi rubber (**das/der Kreppgummi** crêpe)
das Holz [ˮer] wood (**hölzern** wooden; **das Sperrholz** plywood;
  dreilagig three-ply)
der Kalk lime (**der Kalkstein** limestone)
das Kaolin kaolin
die Keramik [-en]; die Töpferware [-n] (piece of) pottery

der **Kies** gravel
der **Kitt** putty
der **Klebstoff**; der **Leim** glue
die **Kohle** coal (die **Steinkohle** (hard) coal; die **Braunkohle** brown
  coal; lignite)
der **Koks** coke
das **Korbgeflecht** wickerwork
das **Kristall** crystal [glass] (**kristallen** crystalline)
das **Kupfer** copper (**kupfern** copper *adj*)
die **Lava** lava
der **Lehm** clay; loam (**lehmig** clayey)
die **Luft** air
der **Marmor** marble (**marmoriert** marbled)
das **Messing** brass
der **Mörtel** mortar
das **Öl** [-e] oil
das **Papier** [-e] paper
die **Pappe**; der **Karton/Pappkarton** cardboard
das **Petroleum** paraffin
der **Pewter**; das **Zinn/Hartzinn** pewter (das **Zinn** [also] tin)
das **Plastik**; der **Kunststoff** plastic
das **Porzellan** [-e] (piece of) porcelain/china (die **Porzellanerde**
  china clay)
das **Rohr** cane
der **Sand** sand; grit (**sandig** sandy; der **Sandstein** sand-/gritstone)
das **Seil** [-e]; das **Tau** [-e] rope
das **Silber** silver (**silbern** silver *adj*; das **Silberpapier** silver paper)
der **Stahl** steel (**stählern** steel *adj*)
der **Stein** [-e] stone (**steinern** stone *adj*; der **Edelstein** precious
  stone)
das **Steingut** earthenware
das **Stroh** straw
der **Teer** tar (der **Makadam** tar macadam)
der **Ton** [-e] clay (**tönern** clay *adj*; die **Tonwaren** *f pl* earthenware)
der **Torf** peat
das **Wachs** wax (**wächsern** waxen)
das **Wasser** [=] water (**wäßrig** watery)

das Weißblech tin-plate
der Zement cement

SEE ALSO: **Adornment** (for jewels); **Clothing** (for textiles); **Plants** (for woods); **Science** (for gases and chemicals)

33. The Media Die Medien

Fernsehen, Funk und Video
Television, radio, and video

die Antenne [-n] aerial
die Aufnahme [-n] recording
der Bericht [-e] report
das Bild [-er] vision; picture (**der (Bild)schirm [-e]** screen)
der Decoder [-] decoder (**das Abonnement [-s]** subscription; **der/die Abonnent/in [-en/-nen]** subscriber)
der Empfang reception (**der Empfänger [-]** receiver)
die Fernbedienung remote control
das Fernsehen television (**der Fernseher [-]**; **das Fernsehgerät [-e]** television [set]; **im/beim Fernsehen** on/in television; **das Werbe-/Farb-/Schwarzweiß-/Kabel-/Satellitenfernsehen** commercial/colour/black-and-white/cable/satellite television)
der Fernsehfilm [-e] television film
die Fernsehserie [-n] television series
der Funk broadcasting; radio (**der Kinderfunk** children's programmes; **der Schulfunk** schools' broadcasting; **der Werbefunk** commercial radio)
der/die Hörer/in [-/-nen] listener
das Hörspiel [-e] radio play (**das Fernsehspiel** TV play)
das Interview [-s] interview
der Kanal [÷e] channel
die Kassette [-n] cassette
der/die Korrespondent/in [-en/-nen] correspondent
das Magazin [-e] magazine (programme)
die Medien *n pl* media (**die Massenmedien** mass media)
das Mikrofon [-e] microphone
der Moderator [G -s *pl* **-en]/die Moderatorin [-nen]** presenter
die Nachrichten *f pl*; [television only] **die Tagesschau** news (**die Nachrichten *kommen um** + A the news is at . . .)
der/die Produzent/in [-en/-nen] producer

das Programm [-e] channel; *sing* programmes
das Radio; **der Rundfunk**; **der Hörfunk** radio [broadcasting] (**das Radio** [-s] radio [set]; **das Transistorradio** transistor; **im Radio** on the radio)
der/die Regisseur/in [-e/-nen] director
die Satellitenschüssel [-n] satellite dish
die Seifenoper [-n] soap opera
der Sender [-] (radio/TV) station (**das (Sender)netz** network; **die Sendepanne** [-n] breakdown; **die Sendepause** [-n] intermission; **die Sendezeit** air-time)
die Sendung [-en] broadcast; programme (**die Dokumentarsendung** documentary; **die Live-Sendung** live/outside broadcast; **die Wiederholungssendung**; **die Wiederholung** [-en] repeat
der/die Sprecher/in [-/-nen]; **der/die Ansager/in** [-/-nen] announcer (**der/die Nachrichtensprecher/in** newscaster)
die Störung interference
das Studio [-s] studio
der Ton sound
der Transistor [G -s *pl* -en] transistor
der Videoclip [-s] video; video clip (**der Videorecorder** [-] video recorder; **die Videokamera** [-s] camcorder)
der Vorspann front credits (**der Nachspann** end credits)
der Walkman [-s] walkman®
die Welle [-n] wave(band) (**auf Kurz-/Lang-/Mittelwelle** on short/long/medium wave; **UKW** [= **die Ultrakurzwelle**] VHF; FM)
der Werbespot [-s] commercial (**die Werbung** advertising; commercial(s); **der/die Auftraggeber/in** [-/-nen] advertiser)
der/die Zuschauer/in [-/-nen] viewer

ab|spielen play [video, cassette]
***auf|nehmen** record
aus|schalten; **aus|machen** switch off
ein|schalten; **an|machen** switch on
ein|stellen tune in
***fern|sehen** watch television
hören listen to
lauter stellen turn up (**leiser stellen** turn down)

löschen wipe
schalten auf + A tune to
*sehen watch
senden broadcast (**live** live)
*über'tragen (im Fernsehen/Radio) televise/broadcast
um|schalten switch over; change channels/stations

Die Presse The press

der Artikel [-] article
die Auflage [-n] circulation
die Beilage [-n] supplement
die Briefkastentante [-n] agony aunt
der Druckfehler [-] misprint (**drucken** print)
der/die Herausgeber/in [-/-nen]; der/die Verleger/in [-/-nen]
  publisher (***heraus|bringen; ver'legen** publish)
die Illustrierte [-n] photo-magazine
das Inserat [-e] [newspaper] advertisement (**der Inseratenteil [-e]**
  advertising section; **die Kleinanzeige [-n]** small ad)
der/die Journalist/in [-en/-nen] journalist
der/die Kritiker/in [-/-nen] critic
der Leitartikel [-] leading article
der/die Leser/in [-/-nen] reader (**der Leserbrief [-e]** letter to the
  editor; ***lesen** read)
der/die Mitarbeiter/in [-/-nen] contributor
die Nachricht [-en] (piece of) news (**das Neueste** the latest news;
  die Nachrichten-/Presseagentur [-en] news agency)
die Presse press (**die Sensationspresse** gutter press; **eine gute/
  schlechte Presse *haben/*be'kommen** have/get a good/bad
  press)
die Presseabteilung [-en] publicity department
der/die Pressefotograf/in [-en/-nen] newpaper photographer
die Pressekonferenz [-en] press conference
der/die Redakteur/in [-e/-nen] editor (**der Redakteur für Politik**
  political editor; **der/die Chefredakteur/in** managing editor)
die Reportage [-n] report
der/die Reporter/in [-/-nen] reporter

die Rubrik [-en] column; section
die Schlagzeile [-n] headline (**Schlagzeilen machen** make headlines)
die Titelseite [-n] front page
die Zeitschrift [-en]; [newspaper supplement] **das Magazin** [-e] magazine (**die Wochen-/Monatsschrift** weekly/monthly)
die Zeitung [-en] newspaper (**die Tages-/Abend-/Sonntags-/Wochenzeitung** daily/evening/Sunday/weekly paper)

SEE ALSO: **Cinema and Photography; Music; Politics; Theatre**

34. Money Geld

der Abzug [ᵇe] deduction
die Aktie [-n] share [in company]
die Ausgabe [-n] item of expenditure; *pl* expenses
der Besitz [-e] property (**mein persönlicher Besitz** my assets)
der Betrag [ᵇe] amount (due)
die Bezahlung [-en] payment
die Bilanz [-en] balance sheet
die Brieftasche [-n] wallet
das Budget [-s]; **der Etat** [-s] budget (**der Haushaltsplan** [ᵇe]
  personal budget)
das Darlehen [-] loan (***auf|nehmen** raise)
das Depot [-s] safe-deposit
die Ersparnis [-se] saving(s)
der/die Fälscher/in [-/-nen] counterfeiter
der Gewinn [-e] profit
die Hypothek [-en] mortgage
die Inflation inflation (**mit Inflationsausgleich** inflation-proof)
die Investition [-en]; **die Anlage** [-n] investment
das Kapital capital
der Kauf [ᵇe] purchase
der Kredit [-e] credit; loan (**jm einen Kredit ge'währen** grant sb a
  loan)
die Lebensunterhaltungskosten *pl* cost of living (**der Lebens-
  standard** standard of living)
der Lieferschein [-e] invoice
die Lotterie [-n] lottery
der/die Millionär/in [-e/-nen] millionaire
das Portemonnaie [-s] purse
der Preis [-e] price (**hoch** high; **niedrig** low; **der Selbstkostenpreis**
  cost price; **die Preiserhöhung** [-en] price increase; **die
  Preisermäßigung** [-en] price reduction)
der Prozentsatz [ᵇe] percentage

die Quittung [-en] receipt
die Rate [-n] instalment (**auf Raten kaufen** buy on hire-purchase)
die Rechnung [-en] bill
die Schuld [-en] debt (**Schulden machen** get into debt; **1 000 Mark Schulden *haben** have debts of 1,000 marks)
die Schwankung [-en] fluctuation
die Steuer [-n] tax (**die Mehrwertsteuer** value added tax)
die Summe [-n] sum
der Verkauf [⁼e] sale
der Verlust [-e] loss
die Währung [-en] currency
der Wert value
der Wertverlust depreciation (**die Abschreibung** allowance for depreciation; write-down)
die Zahlung [-en] payment (**in Zahlung *nehmen** take in part-exchange; **die Barzahlung** cash payment)

*ab|heben withdraw
akzeptieren; *nehmen take [e.g. credit cards]
*aus|geben spend
*aus|kommen mit + D/**ohne** + A manage on/without
be'rechnen (+ D) charge (sb)
ein|lösen cash [cheque]
*ein|werfen insert [money in slot]
ein|zahlen pay in
sich [D] gönnen; sich [D] leisten treat oneself to
in Umlauf m ***bringen** put into circulation
kaufen buy
kosten cost
*leihen lend ((**sich [D]**) ***leihen** borrow)
machen come to (**das macht 30 Mark zusammen** that comes to DM 30 all together)
schulden owe
sparen save
ver'dienen earn
ver'kaufen sell
wechseln; um|tauschen (**in** + A) change (into)

wert *sein be worth (**soviel ist es nicht wert** it's not worth that much)

zahlen [money]; **be'zahlen** [person, debt, bill] pay (**bar/mit Scheck/mit Kreditkarte zahlen** pay cash/by cheque/by credit card)

arm poor
billig cheap
gefälscht forged
gültig valid
knapp bei Kasse short of cash
Kopf oder Zahl heads or tails
kostenlos free
pleite broke
preiswert good value
reich rich
teuer dear
wertvoll valuable

Währungen Currency

die Blüte [-n] dud/forged note
die Devisen *pl*; **die Valuta** [*pl* **Valuten**]; **die Sorten** *pl* foreign currency
die (D-)Mark; die deutsche Mark [-] (German) mark
der Dollar [*pl* - or -s] dollar
der Franken [-] (Swiss) franc (**der Franc** [-s] (French) franc)
das Geld [-er] money (**das Taschengeld** pocket money; **das Bargeld** cash)
der Groschen [-] (German) ten-pfennig coin; (Austrian) groschen [1/100 of a schilling]
der Hundertmarkschein [-e] hundred-mark note
das Markstück [-e] one-mark coin
die Münze [-n] coin; mint
der Pfennig [*pl* - or -e] pfennig [1/100 of a mark]
das Pfund [*pl* - or -e] pound
der Rappen [-] (Swiss) centime

der Schein/Geldschein [-e]; **die Banknote** [-n] banknote
der Schilling [*pl* - or -e] (Austrian) schilling
die Währung [-en] currency
das Wechselgeld change (given back) (**das Kleingeld** small
change)

Finanzanstalten Financial institutions

die Bank [-en] bank (**auf der Bank** in the bank; **der Schalter** [-]
counter; position; **die Kasse** [-n] cash counter; **der/die Kassierer/in**
[-/-nen] cashier; **der Geldautomat** [-en] cash dispenser)
die Börse [-n] stock exchange
die Sparkasse [-n] savings bank (**das Sparkassenbuch** [¨er]
savings book)
die Versicherungsgesellschaft [-en] insurance company (**die
Versicherung** insurance; **die Police** [-n] policy; **die Prämie** [-n]
premium)
die Wechselstube [-n] bureau de change (**der Wechselkurs** [-e]
rate of exchange)

Ihr Bankkonto Your bank account

die Abhebung [-en] withdrawal
das Darlehen [-]; **der Kredit** [-e] loan (**ge'währen** grant; **kündigen**
call in)
die Einzahlung [-en] deposit
die Ersparnisse *f pl* savings
die Gebühr [-en] commission
das Giro [-s] giro
die Hypothek [-en] mortgage (**die Anzahlung** [-en] payment)
das Konto [*pl* **Konten** or **Konti**] account (**das Giro-/Spar-/
Postgirokonto** current/deposit/Girobank® account; **gemeinsam**
joint; **er'öffnen** open)
der Kontoauszug [¨e] statement
die Kontoführungskosten *pl* bank charges
der Kontostand [¨e] balance (**das Guthaben** [-] credit balance)
die Kontoüberziehung overdraft

die **Überweisung** *no pl* (**an** + A/**auf** + A) transfer (to)
die **Zinsen** *m pl* (**auf** + A) interest (on) (**zu 10% Zinsen** at 10%
  interest; **der Zinssatz** [⸚e] interest rate)

ab|be'zahlen pay off
***ab|heben** withdraw
ein|lösen cash
ein|zahlen pay in; deposit (**auf ein Konto** into an account)
***gut|schreiben** credit (**einem Konto** to an account)
in den roten/schwarzen Zahlen *sein be in the red/black
***leihen** + D lend to ((**sich** [D]) ***leihen von** + D borrow from)
sparen save (**sparen für** + A/**auf** + A save up for)
***über'weisen** transfer
***über'ziehen** overdraw (**um DM 30 überzogen *sein** be over-
  drawn by DM 30)
zurück|zahlen pay back

Karten und Schecks Cards and cheques

der **Ausweis** [-e] identity card
die **Debetkarte** [-n] debit card
der **Eurocheque** [-s] Eurocheque
der **Giroscheck** [-s] giro check
die **Kontokarte** [-n] bank card
die **Kreditkarte** [-n] credit card
die **Postanweisung** [-en] = postal order
der **Reisescheck** [-s] traveller's cheque
der **Scheck** [-s] cheque (**über DM 30** for DM 30; **mit Scheck** by
  cheque; **faul** dud; **der Verrechnungs-/Blanko-/Barscheck**
  crossed/blank/open cheque)
das **Scheckheft** [-e] cheque-book
die **Scheckkarte** [-n] cheque card

SEE ALSO: **Crimes and Criminals; Numbers and Quantities; Shops
  and Shopping**

35. Music Musik

der **Dirigentenstab** [⁼e] baton
die **Disco** [-s] disco (**die rollende Disco** travelling disco)
der **Gesang** singing
das **Instrument** [-e] instrument
die **Juke-/Musikbox** [-en] juke-box
die **Kassette** [-n] cassette
der **Kassettenrecorder** [-] cassette recorder
das **Konzert** [-e] concert (**das Sinfonie-/Rock-/Solistenkonzert**
  symphony concert/rock concert/recital)
die **Konzerthalle** [-n] concert hall
das **Opernhaus** [⁼er]; **die Oper** [-n] opera house
die **Platte** [-n] record (**die CD-/Langspielplatte** CD/LP)
der **Plattenspieler** [-] record-player
die **Saite** [-n] string
der **Schlüssel** [-] clef
die **Taste** [-n] key [of instrument]
der **Videorecorder** [-] video recorder (**die Videokassette** [-n] video
  cassette)
die **Zugabe** [-n] encore (**Zugabe!** encore!)
der/die **Zuhörer/in** [-/-nen] listener (**die Zuhörer** *pl* audience)

Musiker Musicians

der **Alt** [-e] alto [singer]; contralto/alto [voice, part]; the
  contralto/alto section (**die Altistin** [-nen] contralto [singer])
der **Bariton** [-e] baritone; the baritone section (**die Baritonstimme**
  [-n] baritone [voice, part])
der **Baß** [⁼sse] bass; the bass section
der/die **Begleiter/in** [-/-nen] accompanist
der **Contratenor** [-s] counter-tenor
der/die **Dirigent/in** [-en/-nen] conductor
der/die **Komponist/in** [-en/-nen] composer
der/die **Konzertmeister/in** [-/-nen] leader [of orchestra]

der/die **Musiker/in** [-/-nen] musician
der/die **Sänger/in** [-/-nen] singer
die **Sinfoniker** *m pl* symphony orchestra
der/die **Solist/in** [-en/-nen] soloist
der **Sopran** [-e] soprano [singer, voice, part]; the soprano section
  (die **Sopranistin** [-nen] [also] soprano [singer])
der/die **Spieler/in** [-/-nen] player
der **Tenor** [≃e] tenor [singer, voice, part]; the tenor section

Musikkapellen Bands

der **Chor** [≃e] choir; chorus
das **Duett** [-e] [voices]; das **Duo** [-s] [instruments] duet
die **Gruppe** [-n] group (die **Rock-/Popgruppe** rock/pop group)
die **Kapelle/Musikkapelle** [-n] band (die **Blaskapelle** brass band)
das **Orchester** [-] orchestra
das **Quartett** [-e] quartet (das **Streichquartett** string quartet)
das **Streichorchester** [-] string orchestra
das **Trio** [-s] trio

Was sie spielen What they play

der **Akkord** [-e] chord
die **Arie** [-n] aria
die **Dissonanz** [-en] discord
die **Harmonie** [-n] harmony
die **Hitparade** [-n] hit parade
der **Jazz** jazz
das **Lied** [-er] song
die **Melodie** [-n] tune; melody
die **Musik** musik (die **Pop-/Volks-/Kammermusik** pop/folk/
  chamber music; **klassisch** classical)
die **Note** [-n] note [= the printed symbol] (die **Noten** *pl* sheet
  music)
die **Oper** [-n] opera
die **Operette** [-n] operetta
die **Ouvertüre** [-n] (+ G) overture (to)

die Partitur [-en] score
der Rock rock
der Schlager [-] hit; pop-song
die Sinfonie [-n] symphony
die Sonate [-n] sonata
das Stück [-e] piece
der Ton [ːe] note [sound]; (**die Taste** [-n] [key of piano] note (**der Mißton** wrong note)
die Tonleiter [-n] scale

Was sie tun What they do

auf]legen put on [record]
***blasen** blow
dirigieren conduct
interpretieren interpret
***schlagen** beat
***singen** sing (**richtig/falsch** in/out of tune)
spielen play
üben practise

Instrumente Instruments

Where not otherwise indicated the player of the instrument is **der/die** [instrument]**spieler/in** [-/-nen]

das Akkordeon [-s]; **die Ziehharmonika** [-s] accordeon (**der/die Akkordeonist/in** [-en/-nen] accordeon player)
die Becken *n pl* cymbals (**ein Beckenteller** *m* a cymbal)
das Blechinstrument [-e] brass instrument (**die Blechbläser** *m pl* the brass section)
die Blockflöte [-n] recorder (**der/die Blockflötenspieler/in** [-/-nen] recorder player)
das Bügelhorn [ːer] bugle
das Cello [*pl* -s or **Celli**] cello (**der/die Cellist/in** [-en/-nen] cellist)
das Cembalo [*pl* **Cembali**] harpsichord (**der/die Cembalist/in** [-en/-nen] harpsichordist)

der **Dudelsack** [ːe] (set of) bagpipes
das **Euphonium** [*pl* **Euphonien**] euphonium
das **Fagott** [-e] bassoon (**der/die Fagottist/in** [-en/-nen] bassoonist)
die **Flöte** [-n] flute (**der/die Flötist/in** [-en/-nen] flautist)
die **Geige** [-n] fiddle (**der/die Geigenspieler/in** [-/-nen] fiddler)
die **Gitarre** [-n] guitar (**der/die Gitarrist/in** [-en/-nen] guitarist)
die **Harfe** [-n] harp (**der/die Harfenist/in** [-en/-nen] harpist)
das **Harmonium** [*pl* **Harmonien**] harmonium
das **Holzblasinstrument** [-e] woodwind [instrument] (**die Holz-
bläser** *m pl* the woodwind section)
die **Kesselpauken** *f pl* timpani (**der/die Paukist/in** [-en/-nen]
timpanist)
das **Horn/Waldhorn** [ːer] French horn (**das Jagdhorn** hunting
horn; **das Englischhorn** cor anglais)
die **Klarinette** [-n] clarinet (**der/die Klarinettist/in** [-en/-nen]
clarinettist)
die **Klaviatur** [-en] keyboard
das **Klavier** [-e]; [grand] der **Flügel** [-] piano (**der/die Pianist/in**
[-en/-nen] pianist)
der **Kontrabaß** [ːsse] double bass (**der/die Bassist/in** [-en/-nen]
double-bass player)
die **Mundharmonika** [-s] mouth organ
die **Oboe** [-n] oboe (**der/die Oboist/in** [-en/-nen] oboist)
die **Orgel** [-n] organ (**der/die Organist/in** [-en/-nen] organist)
die **Posaune** [-n] trombone (**der/die Posaunist/in** [-en/-nen]
trombonist)
das **Saxophon** [-e] saxophone (**der/die Saxophonist/in** [-en/-nen]
saxophonist)
das **Schlagzeug** [-e] drums; drum-kit; the percussion section (**der/
die Schlagzeuger/in** [-/-nen] percussionist)
die **Streichinstrumente** *n pl* strings (**die Streicher** *m pl* the string
section)
das **Tamburin** [-e] tambourine
der **Triangel** [-] triangle
die **Trommel** [-n] drum (**die große Trommel** bass drum)
die **Trompete** [-n] trumpet (**der/die Trompeter/in** [-/-nen]
trumpeter)

die Violine [-n] violin (**der/die Violinist/in [-en/-nen]** violinist)
das Xylophon [-e] xylophone

Die Tonleiter The scale

das As A flat
das A A
das Ais A sharp
das B B flat
das H B
das C C
das Cis C sharp
das Des D flat
das D D
das Dis D sharp
das Es E flat
das E E
das F F
das Fis F sharp
das Ges G flat
das G G
das Gis G sharp

Die Tonarten The keys

A; **A-Dur** A major
a; **a-Moll** A minor
As; **As-Dur** A♯ minor
ais; **ais-Moll** A♭ minor etc.

SEE ALSO: **Leisure and Hobbies; The Media; The Senses; Theatre**

36. Nature Natur

Der Weltraum Space

der Asteroid [-en] asteroid
die Eklipse [-n] eclipse (die Sonnen-/Mondfinsternis [-se] eclipse
of the sun/moon)
die Erde Earth (die Erdkugel [-n] terrestrial globe)
die Ewigkeit eternity
das Fernrohr [-e]; das Teleskop [-e] telescope
die Galaxie [-n] galaxy (die Galaxis the [= our] Galaxy)
der Himmel sky (unter freiem Himmel; im Freien in the open air)
der Horizont [-e] horizon
der Komet [-en] comet
der Kontinent [-e]; der Erdteil [-e] continent
die Luft air
die Milchstraße Milky Way
der Mond [-e] moon (der Voll-/Neumond full/new moon; das
Mondlicht moonlight)
der Nebel [-] nebula
das Observatorium [*pl* -torien]; die Sternwarte [-n] observatory
der Planet [-en] planet
der Raum space (der Weltraum outer space; das Raumschiff [-e]
space ship; die Raumfähre [-n] space shuttle; der/die Raum-
fahrer/in [-/-nen] spaceman/-woman)
der Satellit [-en] satellite
die Sonne [-n] sun (der Sonnenaufgang/Sonnenuntergang [¨e]
sunrise/sunset; die Morgen-/Abenddämmerung dawn/dusk)
der Stern [-e] star (das Sternbild [-er] constellation)
die Welt [-en] world (die Weltkarte [-n] map of the world)
das Weltall; das Universum universe

blitzen twinkle
*zu|nehmen wax (*ab|nehmen wane)
*auf|gehen rise (*unter|gehen set)
sich drehen um + A revolve around

funkeln sparkle
*scheinen shine

Die Landschaft The countryside

der Abgrund [⏜e] precipice; abyss
der Abhang [⏜e] slope; incline
die Abkürzung [-en] short-cut
die Anhöhe [-n] knoll
der Bach [⏜e] stream (**der Sturzbach** torrent)
der Bauernhof [⏜e] farm (**das Bauernhaus** [⏜er] farmhouse; **der Bauer** [-n]/**die Bäuerin** [-nen]; **der/die Landwirt/in** [-e/-nen] farmer/farmer's wife)
der Baum [⏜e] tree (**der Wipfel** [-] tree-top)
der Berg [-e] hill; mountain (**die Bergkette** [-n] mountain chain; **der Gipfel** [-] mountain top; **die Spitze** [-n] summit)
der Boden [⏜] land; soil
die Brücke [-n] bridge (**die Hänge-/Drehbrücke** suspension/swing bridge; **der Steg** [-e] foot-bridge)
der Brunnen [-] well
der Busch [⏜e] bush
das Buschwerk *no pl* scrub (**das Buschland** [⏜er] scrubland)
das Delta [*pl* -s or **Delten**] delta
das Dorf [⏜er] village
der Dschungel [-] jungle
die Düne [-n] dune
die Ebene [-n] plain
die Erde earth; soil (**der Erdboden** earth; face of the earth)
das Feld [-er]; **der Acker** [⏜] (cultivated) field (**pflügen** plough; **den Acker be'stellen** till the field; **die Furche** [-n] furrow; **das Eisfeld** ice-field)
das Festland [⏜er] mainland; continent
das Flachland *no pl* lowlands
der Fluß [⏜sse]; [larger] **der Strom** [⏜e] river (**das Ufer** [-] bank; **das Bett** [-en] bed; **flußaufwarts/flußabwärts** upriver/downriver; **die Furt** [-en] ford; **der Damm/Staudamm** [⏜e] dam)

das **Gebirge** [-] (range of) mountains (**der Gebirgszug** [≈e]; **die Gebirgskette** [-n] mountain range)

der **Gletscher** [-] glacier

der **Graben** [≈] ditch

das **Grasland** [≈er]; **die Prärie** [-n] prairie

der **Grund** ground

das **Gut** [≈er] estate

der **Hang** [≈e] slope; hillside

die **Hecke** [-n] hedge

die **Heide** [-n] heath

der **Heuschober** [-]; **die Heudieme** [-n] haystack

die **Hochebene** [-n]; **das Plateau** [-s] plateau

das **Hochland** [≈er] highlands

die **Höhle** [-n] cave

der **Hügel** [-] hill

der **Kanal** [≈e] canal

die **Klamm** [-en]; **die Schlucht** [-en] ravine; gorge

das **Land** country (**auf dem Lande** in the country; **auf das Land** to the country; **über Land *fahren** go across country; **die Landschaft** [-en] countryside; landscape; region; **die Landwirtschaft** agriculture)

das **Landsträßchen** [-] (country) lane

die **Lichtung** [-en] clearing

der **Mast** [G -(e)s, *pl* -en or -e] pylon

das **Moor/Hochmoor** [-e] moor (**das Moorland** [≈er] moorland)

die **Mühle** [-n] mill (**die Windmühle** windmill)

die **Mündung** [-en] estuary; river mouth

der **Nationalpark** [-s] national park

der **Nebenfluß** [≈sse] tributary

die **Niederung** [-en] hollow

die **Oase** [-n] oasis

der **Obstgarten** [≈] orchard

der **Paß** [≈sse] pass

der **Pfad** [-e]; **der Weg/Fußweg** [-e] path (**der Wegweiser** [-] signpost)

die **Quelle** [-n] spring

die **Scheune** [-n] barn

der Schlamm mud
der Schuppen [-] shed
der See [-n] lake
der Stein [-e] stone; rock
der Steinbruch [ⁿe] quarry
die Steppe [-n] steppe
die Straße [-n] road (**die Haupt-/Landstraße** main/country road)
der Sumpf [ⁿe] marsh; swamp
das Tal [ⁿer] valley
der Teich [-e] pond
das Tor [-e]; **das Gatter** [-] gate
der Tümpel [-] pool
die Vogelscheuche [-n] scarecrow
der Vulkan [-e] volcano (**der Vulkanausbruch** [ⁿe] eruption; **die Lava** lava; **der Krater** [-] crater; **tätig** active; **untätig** dormant)
der Wald [ⁿer] wood; forest (**der Forst** [-e] commercially cultivated forest; **der Urwald** primeval forest; **der tropische Urwald** tropical rainforest)
der Wasserfall [ⁿe] waterfall
der Wasserlauf [ⁿe] watercourse
die Weide [-n] pasture; meadow
der Weiler [-] hamlet
der Weinberg [-e] vineyard
die Wiese [-n] meadow (**die Salzwiese** salt meadow)
die Wüste [-n] desert
der Zaun [ⁿe] fence

auf|ragen rise [mountain]
durch'waten ford
ein|dämmen dam
sich er'strecken stretch
*****fließen** flow
grenzen/an|grenzen an + A border
*****liegen** lie; be situated
*****stehen** stand
*****über|laufen** overflow
*****über'schwemmen** flood

um'ringen (mit + D) surround (with)

bergig mountainous
eben/uneben even/uneven
flach flat
fruchtbar/unfruchtbar fertile/infertile
glatt smooth
hüg(e)lig hilly
nackt bare
rauh rough
saftig lush
sandig sandy
schiffbar navigable
schroff precipitous
senkrecht vertical
staubig dusty
steil steep
steinig stony
üppig luxuriant
zackig jagged

Das Meer und die Küste The sea and the coast

die Boje [-n] buoy
die Brandung surf (**surfen** surf)
die Bucht [-en] bay
die Dünung swell
der Felsen [-] rock; cliff (**der Fels [G -en;** *no pl***]** rock [the material])
das Festland continent [as opposed to island]
das Gewässer [-] stretch of water
die Gezeiten *no sing* tides (**die Flut [-en]** (high) tide; **die Ebbe [-n]** low tide)
der Golf [-e] gulf
der Hafen [⸚] port; harbour
der Horizont [-e] horizon

die Insel [-n] island (**die Halbinsel** [-n] peninsula; **die Landenge** [-n] isthmus; **die Inselgruppe** [-n] archipelago)

der Kai [-s] quay

das Kap [-s] cape

der Kies shingle

der Kiesel [-]; **der Kieselstein** [-e] pebble

die Klippe [-n] cliff

die Korallenbank [¨e]; **das Korallenriff** [-e] reef

die Küste [-n] coast; seaside

die Landungsbrücke [-n] jetty

der Landungssteg [-e] landing-stage

der Leuchtturm [¨e] lighthouse

die Marina [-s]; **der Jachthafen** [¨e] marina

das Meer [-e]; **die See** sea (**ans Meer/an die See *fahren** go to the seaside; **das offene Meer**; **die offene See** the open sea; **aufgewühlt** rough; **ruhig** calm; **bewegt** choppy; **stürmisch** stormy; **der Meeresboden**; **der Meeresgrund** sea bed; **der Meeresspiegel** [-] sea-level)

die Mole/Hafenmole [-n] mole

die Mündung [-en] river-mouth; estuary

die Muschel [-n]; **die Muschelschale** [-n] sea shell

der Ozean [-e] ocean

der Pier [-s] pier; jetty

der Sand sand (**die Sandburg** [-en] sand-castle; **die Sandbank** [¨e] sandbank)

der Schaum foam

das Seebad [¨er] seaside resort

der Sprühnebel spray

der Stein [-e] stone; rock

der Strand [¨e] beach (**die Strandpromenade** [-n] promenade; **der/die Rettungsschwimmer/in** [-/-nen] life-guard; **der Liegestuhl** [¨e] deck-chair; **der Strandkorb** [¨e] beach basket-chair)

die Straße/Wasserstraße [-n] strait

die Strömung [-en]; **der Strom** [¨e] current (**gegen den Strom** against the current)

das Ufer/Seeufer [-] shore

die Untiefe [-n] shoal; shallows

das **Vorgebirge** [-] promontory
die **Welle** [-n] wave

Die Welt der Menschen The world of men

die **Antarktis** the Antarctic (**der südliche Polarkreis** [-e] Antarctic
 Circle)
der **Äquator** equator
die **Arktis** the Arctic (**der nördliche Polarkreis** [-e] Arctic Circle)
das **Ausland** foreign parts (**im/ins Ausland** abroad)
der **Bezirk** [-e] (larger) administrative district
die **Breite** [-n] latitude
das **Dorf** [∸er] village
das **Gebiet** [-e] region; territory
die **Gegend** [-en] district
die **Gemeinde** [-n] municipality; parish; community
der **Globus** [G - or -ses; *pl* -se or **Globen**] globe
die **Grafschaft** [-en] (British) county
die **Grenze** [-n] frontier; border
die **Halbkugel** [-n] hemisphere (**nördlich** northern; **südlich**
 southern)
die **Heimat** [-en] home (country/town/village) (**das Heimatland**
 [∸er] native land)
die **Karte/Landkarte** [-n] map
der **Kontinent** [-e]; **der Erdteil** [-e] continent
der **Kreis** [-e] (smaller) administrative district
das **Land** [∸er] country; (German) state (**das Entwicklungsland**
 [∸er] developing country)
die **Länge** [-n] longitude
die **Nation** [-en] nation
der **Pol** [-e] pole (**der Nord-/Südpol** North/South Pole)
die **Provinz** [-en] province (**aus der Provinz** [pejorative]
 provincial)
der **Staat** [-en] state (**die Staatsangehörigkeit** [-en] nationality)
die **Stadt** [∸e] town (**die Groß-/Hauptstadt** city/capital)
die **Tropen** *pl* the Tropics (**der Wendekreis** [-e] **des Krebses/
 Steinbocks** Tropic of Cancer/Capricorn)

das Volk [¨er] people
der Wahlkreis [-e] (electoral) ward
der Weiler [-] hamlet

SEE ALSO: **Animals; Disasters; Places, People, and Languages; Plants; Science; The Weather**

37. Numbers and Quantities
Zahlen und Mengen

---

der Bruch [∺e]; **die Bruchzahl** [-en] fraction
der Durchschnitt [-e] average
die Einheit [-en]; [maths] **der Einer** [-] unit
das Ganze *adj n* the whole
die Nummer [-n] [in series, street, telephone]; **die Zahl** [-en]
   [numeral]; **die Anzahl** [quantity] number (**eine gerade/ungerade/
   ganze Zahl** an even/odd/whole number)
das Rechnen; **die Arithmetik** arithmetic
der Rechner [-] calculator
der Teil [-e] part
die unendliche Menge infinity
der Unterschied [-e] difference
die Ziffer [-n] figure (**die arabischen/römischen Ziffern** arabic/
   roman numbers)

*ab|ziehen; subtrahieren (von + D from) subtract
auf|teilen share out
ge'nügen be enough
gleich *sein equal (**eins und eins sind gleich zwei** one and one are/
   is/equals two)
leeren empty
*mal|nehmen; multiplizieren (mit + D) multiply (by)
*messen measure
rechnen calculate
schätzen estimate
teilen; dividieren (durch + A) divide (by)
ver'doppeln double
ver'dreifachen triple
ver'teilen distribute
*wiegen weigh (**schwer** heavy; a lot)
zählen count
zusammen|zählen; addieren add

etwa about
fast almost
genau exactly; just
höchstens at most (**allerhöchstens** at the very most)
kaum scarcely
mehr oder weniger more or less
mindestens at least
nur only
ungefähr; zirka; circa approximately (**ca.** approx.)
völlig completely
wieder again

einzig only; sole
genau/ungenau exact/inexact
genug *inv*; **genügend** enough
gleich/ungleich equal/unequal
selten infrequent; rare
überflüssig superfluous
übermäßig excessive
sicher/unsicher definite/indefinite
zahllos; unzählig countless
zahlreich numerous

durch divided by
mal times
minus minus
plus plus
Prozent *n* per cent (**zehn Prozent** 10%; **in Prozenten aus|drücken** give as a percentage)
quadrieren square (**drei hoch zwei** three squared)

Die Kardinalzahlen The cardinal numbers

0 null	**5 fünf**
1 ein; eins	**6 sechs**
2 zwei; *colloq* **zwo**	**7 sieben**
3 drei	**8 acht**
4 vier	**9 neun**

10 zehn	28 achtundzwanzig
11 elf	29 neunundzwanzig
12 zwölf	30 dreißig
13 dreizehn	31 einunddreißig
14 vierzehn	40 vierzig
15 fünfzehn	50 fünfzig
16 sechzehn	60 sechzig
17 siebzehn	70 siebzig
18 achtzehn	80 achtzig
19 neunzehn	90 neunzig
20 zwanzig	100 (ein)hundert
21 einundzwanzig	101 (ein)hundert(und)eins
22 zweiundzwanzig	200 zweihundert
23 dreiundzwanzig	201 zweihundert(und)eins
24 vierundzwanzig	1000 (ein)tausend
25 fünfundzwanzig	1001 tausendeins
26 sechundzwanzig	1002 tausendzwei
27 siebenundzwanzig	2000 zweitausend

      1 000 000 **eine Million**
      1 200 000 **eine Million zweihunderttausend**
      2 000 000 **zwei Millionen**
  1 000 000 000 **eine Milliarde**
  2 000 000 000 **zwei Milliarden**
1 000 000 000 000 **eine Billion**

Ein has an **-s** when counting, in arithmetic, and when used after a noun (**Zimmer eins**, *room one*); otherwise it declines like the indefinite article. Unlike the indefinite article, **ein** = *one* is stressed in spoken German.

As well as their numerical-adjective forms above, **das Hundert** and **das Tausend** are also nouns (**viele Tausende von Menschen**, *many thousands of people*). **Die Million** and **die Milliarde** have only noun forms. Both take plural (**-(e)n**); this plural form is also used when counting.

Die Ordinalzahlen The ordinal numbers

erst- first

zweit-; *colloq* **zwot-** second

dritt- third

viert- fourth

fünft- fifth

sechst- sixth

siebt- seventh

acht- eighth

neunt- ninth

zehnt- tenth

elft- eleventh

zwölft- twelfth

dreizehnt- thirteenth

vierzehnt- fourteenth

fünfzehnt- fifteenth

sechzehnt- sixteenth

siebzehnt- seventeenth

achtzehnt- eighteenth

neunzehnt- nineteenth

zwanzigst- twentieth

einundzwanzigst- twenty-first

dreißigst- thirtieth

vierzigst- fortieth

fünfzigst- fiftieth

sechzigst- sixtieth

siebzigst- seventieth

achtzigst- eightieth

neunzigst- ninetieth

(ein)hundertst- hundredth

(ein)hundert(und)erst- hundred and first

zweihundertst- two hundredth

(ein)tausendst- thousandth

zweitausendst- two thousandth

millionst- millionth

milliardst- thousand millionth

billionst- billionth

letzt- last

erstens firstly

zweitens secondly

drittens thirdly

viertens fourthly

einmal once

zweimal twice

dreimal three times; thrice

viermal four times

x-mal umpteen times

einfach simple

zweifach; doppelt double

dreifach triple

vierfach fourfold

mehrfach multiple

Brüche Fractions

halb *adj*; **die Hälfte** half
ein drittel one/a third
ein viertel one/a quarter (**ein Viertel** *n* **Leberwurst** a quarter
  (pound) of liver sausage; **Viertel vor eins** a quarter to one;
  dreiviertel *inv adj and adv* three-quarters)
ein fünftel one/a fifth
drei siebtel three sevenths
ein achtel one/an eighth (**ein achtel Liter** an eighth of a litre)
ein zehntel one/a tenth
ein zwanzigstel one/a twentieth
ein hundertstel one/a hundredth

eineinviertel one and a quarter
anderthalb; ein(und)einhalb one and a half
zweieinhalb two and a half

eins Komma sieben null vier; einskommasiebennullvier (1,704)
  one point seven o four (1.704)

Mengenausdrücke Expressions of quantity

die meisten *pl* most
ein bißchen a bit (of)
eine Menge a lot (of) (**die Menge [-n]** crowd; **jede Menge** any
  amount)
einige some; a few
ein paar a few
ein wenig a little
etwas a little; some (**etwas Kleines** something small; **etwa** about)
genug enough
kein no
mehr more (**die meisten** most)
mehrere several
nichts nothing
viel much; a lot of (**viele** *pl* many; **zu viel/zu viele** too much/too
  many; **wieviel/wie viele** how much?/how many?; **so viel** as
  much; **recht viele** a fair number)

wenig little (**wenige** few; **weniger** less; fewer)

der Becher [-] (plastic) pot; [ice-cream] tub; glass

der Bissen [-] mouthful [food] (**der Schluck** [*pl* -e or ∺e] mouthful [drink])

die Büchse [-n]; **die Dose** [-n] tin; can

das Faß [∺sser] barrel; drum

die Flasche [-n] bottle

das Glas [∺er] glass; jar

die Handvoll [-] handful

der Haufen [-] heap (**ein Haufen . . .** a pile of; loads of)

die Herde [-n] herd; flock

die Kanne [-n] [coffee, tea] pot

der/das Knäuel [-] [wool, string] ball

der Löffel [-] spoon(ful)

das Paar [-e] pair (**ein paar** a few)

das Päckchen [-]; **das Paket** [-e] packet

die Packung [-en] [cigarettes] pack; [chocolates] box

die Portion [-en] portion; helping; serving

der Riegel [-]; [larger] **die Tafel** [-n] (chocolate) bar

die Rolle [-n] roll

die Schachtel [-n] box

die Scheibe [-n] slice

die Schüssel [-n] bowl; dish

der Stapel [-] pile; stack

das Stück [-e] piece; item (**zwei Stück, bitte** two of those, please)

die Tasse [-n] cup(ful)

der Teller [-] plate(ful)

die Tube [-n] tube

die Tüte [-n] bag

Maße und Gewichte Weights and measures

das Ampere [-] amp

das Gramm [*pl* - or -e] gram

der/das Hektar [*pl* - or -e] hectare

die **Kalorie** [-n] calorie
das **Kilogramm** [*pl* - or -e] kilogram (das **Kilo** [*pl* - or -s] kilo)
der **Kilometer** [-] kilometre
der/das **Liter** [-] litre
die **Meile** [-n] mile
der/das **Meter** [-] metre
der/das **Millimeter** [-] millimetre
das **Pfund** [*pl* - or -e] pound [half a kilo]
die **Tonne** [-n] (metric) ton; tonne [1,000 kg.]
die **Unze** [-n] ounce
das **Volt** [-] volt (die **Netzspannung** voltage)
das **Watt** [-] watt
der/das **Zentimeter** [-] centimetre
der **Zentner** [-] (metric) hundredweight [50 kg.]

Kubik- cubic
Quadrat- square

die **Breite** [-n] breadth; width
die **Dicke**; die **Stärke** thickness
die **Dimension** [-en]; die **Abmessung** [-en] dimension
die **Entfernung** [-en] distance
die **Fläche** [-n] (surface) area
das **Gewicht** [-e] weight
die **Größe** [-n] size; [person, animal, building] height
die **Höhe** [-n] height
die **Länge** [-n] length
das **Maß** [-e] measurement (bei jm **Maß/die Maße *nehmen** take
  sb's measurements)
der **Rauminhalt** [-e]; das **Volumen** [-] volume
die **Tiefe** [-n] depth

breit broad; wide
eng narrow
flach flat
groß large; tall
hoch; hoh- high
hohl hollow

klein small
kurz short
lang long
leicht light
niedrig low
schwer heavy
seicht shallow
sperrig bulky
tief deep

Dimensionen Dimensions

wie groß/breit/lang/hoch/tief ist es? how big/wide/long/high/deep
is it?
es ist drei Meter breit/lang/hoch/tief it's three metres wide/long/
high/deep
zwei (Meter) mal fünf Meter two metres by five

die Größe [-n] size in clothes (**welche Größe *haben/*tragen Sie?**
what size do you take?; **in Größe 40** in size 40; **wie groß sind
Sie?** what is your height?)
die Hüftweite/der Hüftumfang hip size (**die Hüfte [-n]** hip)
die Kragenweite collar size (**der Kragen [-]** collar)
die Oberweite bust size (**sie hat Oberweite 90** she has a 34-inch
bust)
die Schuhgröße; die Schuhnummer shoe size (**welche Schuhgröße/
Schuhnummer hast du?** what size shoes do you take?)
die Taillenweite waist measurement (**die Taille [-n]** waist)
die Weite [-n] width [clothing]

SEE ALSO: **Money; Post and Telephone; Time**

38. Places, People, and Languages
Orte, Völker und Sprachen

Ozeane, Meere, Seen Oceans, seas, lakes

die Adria Adriatic
der Atlantik/der Atlantische Ozean Atlantic
der Bodensee Lake Constance
der Genfer See Lake Geneva
der Indische Ozean Indian Ocean
die Irische See Irish Sea
der Kanal/Ärmelkanal English Channel
die Karibik Caribbean
das Mittelmeer Mediterranean
die Nordsee North Sea
die Ostsee Baltic
der Pazifik; der Pazifische Ozean; der Stille Ozean Pacific

Erdteile und ihre Einwohner
Continents and their inhabitants

(das) Afrika Africa   **afrikanisch; der/die Afrikaner/in [-/-nen]** African
(das) Amerika America **(Süd-/Mittel-/Nord-** South/Central/ North)   **amerikanisch; der/die Amerikaner/in [-/-nen]** American
die Antarktis Antarctica   **antarktisch** antarctic
(das) Asien Asia **(Kleinasien** Asia Minor)   **asiatisch; der/die Asiat/in [-en/-nen]** Asian
(das) Australien Australia   **australisch; der/die Australier/in [-/-nen]** Australian
(das) Europa Europe   **europäisch; der/die Europäer/in [-/-nen]** European

Flüsse und Berge Rivers and mountains

die Alpen Alps (**alpin**; **Alpen-** alpine)
die Donau Danube
die Mosel Moselle
die Pyrenäen *pl* Pyrenees
der Rhein Rhine (**rheinisch**; **Rhein-** Rhineland *adj*)
die Themse Thames
der Vesuv Vesuvius
die Vogesen *pl* Vosges
die Wolga Volga

Städte, Inseln, Gebiete Towns, islands, regions

Algier Algiers
die Antillen Antilles; West Indies
Antwerpen Antwerp
(das) Arabien Arabia (**arabisch** Arabian; **der/die Araber/in** [-/-nen] Arab)
Athen Athens
der Balkan the Balkans (**auf dem Balkan** in the Balkans)
Basel Basle (**der/die Bas(e)ler/in** [-/-nen] inhabitant of Basle)
(das) Bayern Bavaria (**bay(e)risch** Bavarian; **der/die Bayer/in** [-/-nen] Bavarian)
(das) Böhmen Bohemia (**böhmisch** Bohemian; **der Böhme** [-n]/**die Böhmin** [-nen] Bohemian)
die Bretagne Brittany
die Britischen Inseln *f pl* the British Isles (**Großbritannien** *n* Great Britain; **britisch** British; **der Brite** [-n]/**die Britin** [-nen] Briton; **Brit**; *pl* the British)
Brügge Bruges
Brüssel Brussels
das Burgund Burgundy
die dritte Welt the Third World
(das) Den Haag [also **(das) Haag** and **der Haag**] The Hague
Edinburg Edinburgh

(das) Elsaß Alsace (**elsässisch** Alsatian; **der/die Elsässer/in** [-/-nen]
  Alsatian)
die Europäische Gemeinschaft (EG) the European Community
  (EC)
die Ex-DDR [= **Deutsche Demokratische Republik**] former
  GDR [= German Democratic Republic]; eastern Germany
der Ferne Osten the Far East (**der Nahe Osten** the Middle East;
  fernöstlich Far Eastern; **nahöstlich** Middle Eastern)
(das) Flandern Flanders (**flämisch** Flemish; **der Flame** [-n]/**die
  Flamin/Flämin** [-nen] Fleming)
Genf Geneva
Gent Ghent
Genua Genoa
Hannover Hanover (**hannoversch**; **der/die Hannoveraner/in**
  [-/-nen] Hanoverian)
die Hebriden Hebrides
(das) Helgoland Heligoland
(das) Hessen Hesse (**hessisch** Hessian; **der Hesse** [-n]/**die Hessin**
  [-nen] Hessian)
Kairo Cairo
die Kanalinseln the Channel Islands
Köln Cologne
Kopenhagen Copenhagen
(das) Korsika Corsica
(das) Kreta Crete
die Krim Crimea
Lissabon Lisbon
(das) Lothringen Lorraine
Lüttich Liège
Mailand Milan
(das) Mallorca Majorca
Mekka Mecca
Moskau Moscow
München Munich (**der/die Münch(e)ner/in** [-/-nen] inhabitant of
  Munich)
Neapel Naples (**der/die Neapolitaner/in** [-/-nen] Neapolitan)

(das) Ostfriesland East Friesland (**ostfriesisch** East Frisian; **der Ostfriese [-n]/die Ostfriesin [-nen]** East Frisian)

der Orient Middle East and S.W. Asia (**der Orientale [-n]/die Orientalin [-nen]** Middle Easterner; **orientalisch** oriental)

Prag Prague

(das) Preußen Prussia (**preußisch** Prussian; **der Preuße [-n]/die Preußin [-nen]** Prussian)

das Rheinland Rhineland (**rheinisch** Rhenish; **Rhineland** *adj*; **der/die Rheinländer/in [-/-nen]** Rhinelander)

Rom Rome (**römisch** Roman; **der/die Römer/in [-/-nen]** Roman)

(das) Sachsen Saxony (**sächsisch** Saxon; **der Sachse [-n]/die Sächsin [-nen]** Saxon)

die Sahara Sahara

(das) Sardinien Sardinia

(das) Schwaben Swabia (**schwäbisch** Swabian; **der Schwabe [-n]/die Schwäbin [-nen]** Swabian)

der Schwarzwald the Black Forest (**Schwarzwälder** Black Forest [*as adj*])

(das) Sizilien Sicily (**sizilianisch** Sicilian)

(das) Skandinavien Scandinavia (**skandinavisch** Scandinavian; **der/die Skandinavier/in [-/-nen]** Scandinavian)

Tanger Tangiers

(das) Thüringen Thuringia (**thüringisch** Thuringian; **der/die Thüringer/in [-/-nen]** Thuringian)

(das) Tirol the Tyrol (**Tiroler** Tyrolean; **der/die Tiroler/in [-/-nen]** Tyrolean)

Tokio Tokyo

Venedig Venice (**venezianisch** Venetian; **der/die Venezianer/in [-/-nen]** Venetian)

die Vereinten Nationen United Nations

Wallonien Wallonia (**wallonisch** Walloon)

Warschau Warsaw

Westfalen Westphalia (**westfälisch** Westphalian; **der Westfale [-n]/die Westfälin [-nen]** Westphalian)

Wien Vienna (**wienerisch; Wiener** Viennese; **der/die Wiener/in [-/-nen]** Viennese)

Länder und ihre Einwohner
Countries and their inhabitants

(das) Ägypten Egypt **ägyptisch; der/die Ägypter/in [-/-nen]** Egyptian

(das) Algerien Algeria **algerisch; der/die Algerier/in [-/-nen]** Algerian

(das) Bangladesch Bangladesh **bangalisch; der/die Bangali [-s]** Bangladeshi

(das) Belgien Belgium **belgisch; der/die Belgier/in [-/-nen]** Belgian

(das) Brasilien Brazil **brasilianisch; der/die Brasilianer/in [-/-nen]** Brazilian

(das) Bulgarien Bulgaria **bulgarisch; der Bulgare [-n]/die Bulgarin [-nen]** Bulgarian

(das) Chile Chile **chilenisch; der Chilene [-n]/die Chilenin [-nen]** Chilean

(das) China China **chinesisch; der Chinese [-n]/die Chinesin [-nen]** Chinese

(das) Dänemark Denmark **dänisch** Danish; **der Däne [-n]/die Dänin [-nen]** Dane

(das) Deutschland Germany **(die Bundesrepublik** Federal Republic) **deutsch; der/die Deutsche** *adj n* German

(das) England England **englisch** English; **der/die Engländer/in [-/-nen]** Englishman/-woman

(das) Finnland Finland **finnisch** Finnish; **der Finne [-n]/die Finnin [-nen]** Finn

(das) Frankreich France **französisch** French; **der Franzose [-n]/die Französin [-nen]** Frenchman/-woman

(das) Griechenland Greece **griechisch; der Grieche [-n]/die Griechin [-nen]** Greek

(das) Holland Holland **(die Niederlande** *pl* the Netherlands) **holländisch** Dutch; **der/die Holländer/in [-/-nen]** Dutchman/-woman **(niederländisch** Netherlands [*as adj*]; **der/die Niederländer/in [-/-nen]** Netherlander)

(das) Indien India **indisch; der/die Inder/in [-/-nen]** Indian

(das) Irland Ireland **(Nordirland** Northern Ireland) **irisch** Irish;
der Ire [-n]/die Irin [-nen] Irishman/-woman

(das) Island Iceland **isländisch** Icelandic; **der/die Isländer/in
[-/-nen]** Icelander

(das) Israel Israel **israelisch; der/die Israeli** [*pl* - or **-s**] Israeli
(jüdisch Jewish; **der Jude [-n]/die Jüdin [-nen]** Jew)

(das) Italien Italy **italienisch; der/die Italiener/in [-/-nen]** Italian

(das) Japan Japan **japanisch; der/die Japaner/in [-/-nen]**
Japanese

(das) Kanada Canada **kanadisch; der/die Kanadier/in [-/-nen]**
Canadian

(das) Korea Korea **koreanisch; der/die Koreaner/in [-/-nen]**
Korean

(das) Kroatien Croatia **kroatisch; der Kroate [-n]/die Kroatin
[-nen]** Croat

(das) Kuba Cuba **kubanisch; der/die Kubaner/in [-/-nen]** Cuban

(das) Libyen Libya **libysch; der/die Libyer/in [-/-nen]** Lybian

(das) Luxemburg Luxemburg **luxemburgisch** Luxemburg [*as
adj*]; **der/die Luxemburger/in [-/-nen]** Luxemburger

(das) Malta Malta **maltesisch; der/die Malteser/in [-/-nen]**
Maltese

(das) Marokko Morocco **marokkanisch; der/die Marokkaner/in
[-/-nen]** Moroccan **(maurisch** Moorish; **der Maure [-n]/die Maurin
[-nen]** Moor)

(das) Mexiko Mexico **mexikanisch; der/die Mexikaner/in [-/-nen]**
Mexican

(das) Neuseeland New Zealand **neuseeländisch** New Zealand
[*as adj*]; **der/die Neuseeländer/in [-/-nen]** New Zealander

(das) Norwegen Norway **norwegisch; der/die Norweger/in [-/-nen]**
Norwegian

(das) Österreich Austria **österreichisch; der/die Österreicher/in
[-/-nen]** Austrian

(das) Pakistan Pakistan **pakistanisch; der/die Pakistaner/in
[-/-nen]; der/die Pakistani** [*pl* - or **-s**] Pakistani

(das) Palästina Palestine **palästinensisch; der/die Palästinenser/in
[-/-nen]** Palestinian

(das) Peru Peru **peruanisch; der/die Peruaner/in [-/-nen]**
Peruvian

(das) Polen Poland **polnisch** Polish; **der Pole [-n]/die Polin [-nen]**
Pole

(das) Portugal Portugal **portugiesisch; der Portugiese [-n]/die
Portugiesin [-nen]** Portuguese

(das) Rumänien Romania **rumänisch; der Rumäne [-n]/die
Rumänin [-nen]** Romanian

(das) Rußland Russia **(die ehemalige Sowjetunion** former Soviet
Union) **russisch; der Russe [-n]/die Russin [-nen]** Russian

(das) Schottland Scotland **schottisch** Scottish; **der Schotte [-n]/
die Schottin [-nen]** Scotsman/-woman; Scot

(das) Schweden Sweden **schwedisch** Swedish; **der Schwede [-n]/
die Schwedin [-nen]** Swede

die Schweiz Switzerland **schweizerisch; der/die Schweizer/in
[-/-nen]** Swiss

(das) Serbien Serbia **serbisch; der Serbe [-n]/die Serbin [-nen]**
Serbian; Serb

die Slowakei Slovakia **slowakisch; der Slowake [-n]/die
Slowakin [-nen]** Slovak

(das) Slowenien Slovenia **slowenisch; der Slowene [-n]/die
Slowenin [-nen]** Slovenian

(das) Spanien Spain **spanisch** Spanish; **der/die Spanier/in [-/-nen]**
Spaniard

(das) Südafrika South Africa **südafrikanisch; der/die Südafri-
kaner/in [-/-nen]** South African

die Tschechische Republik the Czech Republic **tschechisch; der
Tscheche [-n]/die Tschechin [-nen]** Czech

die Türkei Turkey **türkisch** Turkish; **der Türke [-n]/die Türkin
[-nen]** Turk

(das) Ungarn Hungary **ungarisch; der/die Ungar/in [-n/-nen]**
Hungarian

das Vereinigte Königreich United Kingdom

die Vereinigten Staaten *m pl* **(von Amerika)** (the) United States
(of America) **(die USA** *pl* the USA) **amerikanisch; der/die
Amerikaner/in [-/-nen]** American

(das) Vietnam Vietnam **vietnamesisch; der Vietnamese [-n]/die Vietnamesin [-nen]** Vietnamese

(das) Wales Wales **walisisch** Welsh; **der/die Waliser/in [-/-nen]** Welshman/-woman

die Westindischen Inseln West Indies **westindisch; der/die Westinder/in [-/-nen]** West Indian

Sprachen Languages

(das) Deutsch German (**auf deutsch** in German; **ins Deutsche** into German)

[and similarly all other languages that correspond to adjectives in the 'Countries' list above]

der Akzent [-e] accent
(das) Altgriechisch classical Greek
die Aussprache [-n] pronunciation; accent
der/die Deutschsprachige *adj n* German speaker
der Dialekt [-e]; die Mundart [-en] dialect
(das) Gälisch Gaelic
die Grammatik grammar
(das) Latein(isch) Latin
die Linguistik; die Sprachwissenschaft linguistics
die Phonetik phonetics
(das) Schweizerdeutsch Swiss German
die Sprache [-n] language (**die Muttersprache** mother tongue; **die Fremdsprache** foreign language; **neuere/tote Sprachen** modern/dead languages; **das Sprachgefühl** feeling for languages)
der Wortschatz [ːe]; das Vokabular [-e] vocabulary

sich aus|drücken express oneself
*aus|sprechen pronounce
lernen learn
meinen [= intend to convey]; **be'deuten** [= signify] mean (**was willst du damit sagen?** what do you mean by that?)

*sprechen speak (**fließend** fluently)
über'setzen translate
*ver'stehen understand

SEE ALSO: **Identity; Nature; Towns**

39. Plants Pflanzen

die Abholzung; die Entwaldung deforestation (**die Wiederauf-forstung** reafforestation)

der Ast [≃e] (large) branch (**der Zweig [-e]** small branch; twig)

der Baum [≃e] tree (**der Weihnachts-/Christbaum** Christmas tree; **der Obstbaum** fruit tree; **der Laubbaum** broad-leafed/deciduous tree; **der Nadelbaum** conifer)

die Baumschule [-n] tree nursery

die Beere [-n] berry

das Blatt [≃er] leaf

die Blume [-n] flower (**das Blumenbeet [-e]** flower-bed; **der (Blumen)strauß [≃e]** bunch of flowers; bouquet)

die Blüte [-n] blossom (**in voller Blüte** in full flower)

das Blütenblatt [≃er] petal

die Borke; die Rinde bark

der Busch [≃e] bush

das Dickicht [-e] thicket

der Dorn [-en]; der Stachel [-] thorn

der Duft [≃e] scent

die Ernte [-n] harvest

der Forst [-e] forest

die Frucht [≃e] fruit

die Gärtnerei [-en] nursery; gardening

das Geäst *no pl* branches

das Gebüsch [-e] bushes; clump of bushes

das Gemüse [-] vegetable(s)

die Girlande [-n] garland

der Halm [-e]; der Stiel [-e] stalk

die Hecke [-n] hedge

der Kern [-e] pip

die Knospe [-n] bud

der Kranz [≃e] wreath

das Laub *no pl* leaves; foliage

die Lichtung [-en] clearing

der **Obstgarten** [⸚] orchard
die **Pflanze** [-n] plant (**wildwachsend** wild)
die **Plantage** [-n] plantation
der **Pollen** [-]; der **Blütenstaub** *no pl* pollen
der **Rasen** [-] lawn; turf
der **Saft** [⸚e] sap
der **Samen** [-]; das **Samenkorn** [⸚er] seed
der **Stamm** [⸚e] trunk
der **Stein** [-e] stone [of fruit]
der **Strauch** [⸚er] shrub
der **Stumpf** [⸚e] tree-stump
der **Trieb** [-e]; der **Sproß** [-ssen] shoot
das **Unkraut** weed(s)
das **Unterholz** undergrowth
der **Wald** [⸚er] wood; forest (der **Urwald** primeval forest)
das **Wäldchen** [-] copse
der **Weinberg** [-e]; der **Weingarten** [⸚] vineyard
der **Wipfel** [-] tree-top
die **Wurzel** [-n] root

aus|dünnen thin out
***aus|reißen** uproot
***aus|treiben** shoot
***be'gießen** water
blühen blossom
ernten harvest
fällen fell
***graben** [hole]; ***um|graben** [garden] dig
harken rake
jäten weed
klettern auf + A climb
kultivieren; be'bauen cultivate
pflanzen; an|bauen plant
pflücken pick
pflügen plough
pfropfen graft
reifen ripen (**reif** ripe)

roden clear
säen; aus|säen sow
***schneiden** trim
um|pflanzen transplant
um'zäunen fence in (**der Zaun** [≈e] fence)
ver'faulen rot
ver'welken fade; wither
***wachsen;** [flowers, crops] **züchten/an|pflanzen** grow
***zurück|schneiden** prune

Wald- und Zierbäume, Sträucher
Forest and ornamental trees, shrubs

der Ahorn [-e] maple
der Bambus [-se] bamboo
die Birke [-n] birch (**die Weißbirke** silver birch)
die Buche [-n] beech (**die Blutbuche** copper beech)
der Buchsbaum [≈e] box (tree)
die Eibe [-n] yew
die Eiche [-n] oak (**die Eichel** [-n] acorn)
die Erle [-n] alder
die Esche [-n] ash
die Espe [-n] aspen
die Fichte [-n] spruce
der Flieder [-] lilac [also its flower]
das Geißblatt *no pl*; **das Jelängerjelieber** [-] honeysuckle
der Goldregen [-] laburnum
die Hainbuche [-n]; **der Hornbaum** [≈e] hornbeam
der Holunder [-] elder
die Hortensie [-n] hydrangea
der Jasmin [-e] jasmine
die Kamelie [-n] camellia
die Kiefer [-n] pine (**der Kiefernzapfen** [-] pine-cone; **die Kiefernnadel** [-n] pine-needle)
der Lavendel [-] lavender
der Liguster [-] privet

die **Linde** [-n] lime
die **Lorbeerkirsche** [-n] laurel
die **Magnolie** [-n] magnolia
der **Mahagonibaum** [ˉe] mahogany tree (**das Mahagoni** mahogany [wood])
die **Myrte** [-n] myrtle
die **Pappel** [-n] poplar
die **Pinie** [-n] (umbrella) pine
die **Platane** [-n] plane tree
der/das **Rhododendron** [*pl* **-dren**] rhododendron
die **Roßkastanie** [-n] horse-chestnut
die **Stechpalme** [-n] holly
die **Tanne** [-n]; der **Tannenbaum** [ˉe] fir
die **Ulme** [-n] elm
die **Weide** [-n] willow (die **Trauerweide** weeping willow)
der **Weißdorn** [-e] hawthorn (der **Rotdorn** red hawthorn)
die **Zeder** [-n] cedar
die **Zypresse** [-n] cypress

Obst- und Nußbäume Fruit and nut trees

der **Apfelbaum** [ˉe] apple tree
die **Aprikose** [-n] apricot tree
die **Bananenstaude** [-n] banana palm
der **Birnbaum** [ˉe] pear tree
der **Brombeerstrauch** [ˉer] blackberry bush
die **Dattelpalme** [-n] date palm
der **Feigenbaum** [ˉe] fig tree
der **Granat(apfel)baum** [ˉe] pomegranate tree
der **Hazelnußstrauch** [ˉer] hazel
die **Kastanie/Edelkastanie** [-n] (sweet) chestnut
der **Kirschbaum** [ˉe] cherry tree
die **Kokospalme** [-n] coconut palm
der **Mandelbaum** [ˉe] almond tree
der **Nußbaum/Walnußbaum** [ˉe] walnut tree
der **Ölbaum** [ˉe]; der **Olivenbaum** [ˉe] olive tree

der **Orangenbaum** [ːe] orange tree
der **Pfirsichbaum** [ːe] peach tree
der **Pflaumenbaum** [ːe] plum tree
die **Weinrebe** [-n]; der **Weinstock** [ːe] vine
der **Zitronenbaum** [ːe] lemon tree

Blumen Flowers

die **Anemone** [-n] anemone
die **Aster** [-n] aster
die **Butterblume** [-n] buttercup
die **Chrysantheme** [-n] chrysanthemum
die **Dahlie** [-n] dahlia
das **Edelweiß** [-e] edelweiss
der **Fingerhut** [ːe] foxglove
das **Gänseblümchen** [-] daisy
die **Geranie** [-n] geranium
der **Goldlack** wallflower(s)
die **Hyazinthe** [-n] hyacinth (die **Sternhyazinthe** bluebell)
das **Immergrün** [-] periwinkle
die **Iris** [-] iris
der **Jasmin** [-e] jasmine
die **Kornblume** [-n] cornflower
der **Krokus** [*pl* -se or -] crocus
die **Levkoje** [-n] stock
die **Lilie** [-n] lily
der **Löwenzahn** dandelion(s)
das **Maiglöckchen** [-] lily of the valley
die **Margerite** [-n] ox-eye daisy
der **Mohn** [plant]; die **Mohnblume** [-n] [flower] poppy
die **Narzisse** [-n] narcissus (die **gelbe Narzisse**; die **Osterglocke** [-n] daffodil)
die **Nelke** [-n] carnation
die **Orchidee** [-n] orchid
die **Petunie** [-n] petunia
die **Pfingstrose** [-n] peony

die **Primel** [-n] primrose
die **Rose** [-n] rose (der **Rosenstrauch** [⸚er] rose-bush)
die **Schlüsselblume** [-n] cowslip
das **Schneeglöckchen** [-] snowdrop
die **Seerose** [-n] water-lily
die **Sonnenblume** [-n] sunflower
das **Stiefmütterchen** [-] pansy
die **Tulpe** [-n] tulip
das **Veilchen** [-] violet
das **Vergißmeinnicht** [*pl* -e or -] forget-me-not
die **Wicke** [-n] sweet pea

Wildwachsende Pflanzen Wild plants

die **Distel** [-n] thistle
der **Efeu** *no pl* ivy
der **Farn** [-e] fern
der **Ginster** [-] broom (der **Stechginster** gorse)
das **Gras** [⸚er] grass (die **Quecke** couch-grass)
das **Heidekraut** *no pl* heather
der **Klee** *no pl* clover
die **Mistel** [-n] mistletoe (der **Mistelzweig** piece of mistletoe)
das **Moos** [-e] moss
die **Nessel/Brennessel** [-n] nettle (die **Taubnessel** dead nettle)
das **Schilf** [-e] reed(s)
der **Tang/Seetang** [-e] seaweed
das **Unkraut** [⸚er] weed(s)

Getreidearten Grains

die **Gerste** barley
das **Getreide** *no pl* grain; cereals
der **Hafer** *no pl* oats
das **Heu** hay
das **Korn** [⸚er] corn; grain of corn
der **Mais** maize

der Roggen rye
der Weizen wheat

SEE ALSO: **Cooking and Eating** (for herbs); **Food** (for fruits, vegetables, nuts); **Nature**

40. Politics Politik

die **Abstimmung** [-en] poll
der **Adel** nobility
die **Arbeiterklasse** *no pl* working class (**an|ge'hören** + D be a
  member of)
die **Aristokratie** aristocracy
der **Aufstand** [ˌe] riot; rebellion
die **Barrikade** [-n] barricade
die **Brüderlichkeit** fraternity
das **Budget** [-s]; der **Etat** [-s] budget
der **Coup** [-s] coup (der **Staatsstreich** [-e] *coup d'état*)
die **Debatte** [-n] debate
die **Demonstration** [-en] demonstration
die **Diskussion** [-en] discussion
die **Einheit** unity
der **Erlaß** [-sse] decree
die **Fahne** [-n]; [national] die **Flagge** [-n] flag
der **Fortschritt** [-e] step forward; [*often pl*] progress
die **Freiheit** [-en] freedom; liberty
das **Gesetz** [-e] law; act (der **Gesetzentwurf** [ˌe] bill; die **Debatte** [-n]
  debate)
die **Gleichheit** equality
die **Heimat** [-en] homeland
die **Inflation** inflation
die **Krise** [-n] crisis
die **Krönung** [-en] coronation (die **Krone** [-n] crown)
das **Land** [ˌer] country (das **Land**; das **Bundesland** (German)
  Federal Land)
die **Linke** the left (die **Rechte** the right)
die **Macht** [ˌe] power (**an die Macht *kommen** take power)
die **Mehrheit** [-en] majority (**knapp** narrow; **überwiegend** great)
die **Meinungsumfrage** [-n] opinion poll (die **Meinung** [-en]
  opinion; die **öffentliche Meinung** public opinion)
die **Menge** [-n] crowd

das Menschenrecht [-e] human right
die Minderheit [-en] minority
die Mitte the centre (**rechts von der Mitte** right of centre)
der Mittelstand *no pl* middle class(es)
der Mob *no pl*; **der Pöbel** *no pl* the mob
die Neutralität neutrality
die Oberschicht [-en] upper class
die Opposition opposition (**der/die Oppositionsführer/in [-/-nen]**
  Leader of the Opposition)
die Partei [-en] party
die Pflicht [-en] duty
die Politik [-en] politics; policy
das Recht [-e] right; law
das Referendum [*pl* **-den** or **-da**] referendum
das Regime [-] regime
die Revolution [-en] revolution
der Sitz [-e]; das Mandat [-e] seat [in parliament]
die Solidarität solidarity
die Staatsangehörigkeit [-en] nationality
die Steuer [-n] tax (**die Besteuerung** taxation)
die Tagung [-en] conference
die Verantwortung responsibility
die Vereinigung union
die Verfassung [-en] constitution
die Versammlung [-en] rally
die Verwaltung administration
das Volk [-̈er] the people
die Wahl [-en] election (**das Wahlrecht** *no pl* right to vote;
  franchise; **die Wählerschaft [-en]** electorate; **der Wahlkampf [-̈e]**
  election campaign; **der Wahlkreis [-e]** constituency; **die
  Wahlurne [-n]** ballot-box; **die Stimme [-n]** vote; **eine Abstimmung** a vote [= act of voting]; **der Stimmzettel [-]** ballot-paper)
die Wiedervereinigung reunification (**die Wende** the turnaround
  [pre-unification political U-turn in E. Germany])
die Wirtschaft [-en] economy
die Zusammenarbeit co-operation
ab|lehnen reject

ab|schaffen abolish
auf|lösen dissolve
be'steuern tax
demonstrieren demonstrate
*er'nennen appoint
gültig *werden come into effect
herrschen rule
nationalisieren; ver'staatlichen nationalize
organisieren organize
privatisieren privatize
regieren govern; rule
revoltieren revolt
stimmen vote (**mit Ja/Nein stimmen** vote in favour/against)
unter'drücken repress
unter'stützen support
ver'abschieden pass [bill]
*ver'treten represent
wählen elect; choose; vote for [party]
zentralisieren centralize (**dezentralisieren** decentralize)
*zurück|treten resign

autonom autonomous
einstimmig unanimous
extremistisch extremist
gemäßigt moderate
links left(-wing) (**rechts** right(-wing))
linksextrem; links-radikal extreme left(-wing) (**rechtsextrem; rechtsradikal** extreme right(-wing))
politisch political

Die Institutionen The institutions

der Bundesrat Federal Upper House
der Bundestag Federal Lower House
die EG the EC (**die Europäische Gemeinschaft** European Community; **der Gemeinsame Markt** Common Market)
das Kabinett [-e] Cabinet

die Monarchie [-n] monarchy
die Nation [-en] nation
das Parlament [-e] parliament
die Regierung [-en] government
die Republik [-en] republic (**die Bundesrepublik (Deutschland)** (German) Federal Republic)
der Stadtrat [ᵉe] town council
der Staat [-en] state (**der Wohlfahrtsstaat** Welfare State)
die UNO the UN (**die Vereinten Nationen** United Nations)
die Verfassung [-en] constitution

Die Männer und Frauen The men and women

der/die Abgeordnete *adj n* MP (**der/die Bundesabgeordnete** Member of the Federal Parliament)
der/die Botschafter/in [-/-nen] ambassador (**die Botschaft [-en]** embassy)
der Bundeskanzler Federal Chancellor; [Swiss] Chancellor of the Federation
der/die Bundespräsident/in Federal President; [Swiss] President of the Confederation
der/die Bürger/in [-/-nen] citizen
der/die Bürgermeister/in [-/-nen] mayor
der/die Demokrat/in [-en/-nen] democrat
der Diktator [G -s *pl* **-en]** dictator
der/die Fürst/in [-en/-nen] prince/princess; ruler
der Kaiser [-] emperor (**die Kaiserin [-nen]** empress; **das Kaiserreich [-e]** empire)
der/die Kandidat/in [-en/-nen] candidate
der Kanzler [-] chancellor
der König [-e] king (**die Königin [-nen]** queen; **das Königreich [-e]** kingdom; **der Thron [-e]** throne; **die Königinmutter** queen mother)
der/die Minister/in [-/-nen] (government) minister (**der Staatsminister** minister of state; **der Außen-/Finanzminister** foreign minister/Chancellor of the Exchequer)

der/die Ministerpräsident/in [-en/-nen] prime minister; minister-president [of a German Land]
der/die Mitbürger/in [-/-nen] compatriot; fellow citizen
der/die Politiker/in [-/-nen] politician
der/die Präsident/in [-en/-nen] president
der/die Premierminister/in [-/-nen] prime minister
der Prinz [-en] prince (**die Prinzessin** [-nen] princess)
der/die Regierungschef/in [-s/-nen] head of government
der Souverän [-e] sovereign
der Staatsbeamte *adj n*/**die Staatsbeamtin** [-nen] civil servant
der Staatsmann [¨er] statesman
das Staatsoberhaupt [¨er] Head of State

Ideologien Ideologies

der Anarchismus anarchism (**die Anarchie** anarchy)   **anarchistisch** anarchistic (**anarchisch** anarchic)
der Antisemitismus anti-Semitism   **antisemitisch** anti-Semitic
der Chauvinismus chauvinism   **chauvinistisch** chauvinist
die Demokratie [-n] democracy   **demokratisch** democratic
die Diktatur [-en] dictatorship   **diktatorisch** dictatorial
der Faschismus Fascism   **faschistisch** Fascist
die Ideologie [-n] ideology   **ideologisch** ideological
der Imperialismus imperialism   **imperialistisch** imperialist (**kaiserlich** imperial)
der Internationalismus internationalism   **international** international
der Kapitalismus capitalism   **kapitalistisch** capitalist
der Kommunismus Communism (**der Marxismus** Marxism)   **kommunistisch** Communist (**marxistisch** Marxist)
der Konservatismus conservatism   **konservativ** conservative
der Liberalismus liberalism   **liberal** liberal
der Monarchismus monarchism (**die Monarchie** monarchy)   **monarchisch** monarchical (**königlich** royal)
der Nationalismus nationalism   **nationalistisch** nationalistic (**national** national)
der Patriotismus patriotism   **patriotisch** patriotic

der Pazifismus pacifism   **pazifistisch** pacifist
der Radikalismus radicalism   **radikal** radical
der Rassismus racism   **rassistisch** racist
der Republikanismus republicanism   **republikanisch** republican
die Sozialdemokratie social democracy   **sozialdemokratisch**
  social democratic
der Sozialismus socialism   **sozialistisch** socialist
die Tyrannei tyranny (**der Tyrann** [**-en**] tyrant)   **tyrannisch**
  tyrannical

SEE ALSO: **Arguments For and Against; History; Justice and Law; The Media; War, Peace, and the Armed Services**

41. Post and Telephone
Post und Telefon

Die Post The post

der/die Absender/in [-/-nen] sender (**Abs.** from [on back of envelope])

die Adresse [-n]; **die Anschrift** [-en] address

die Anlage [-n] enclosure

der Brief [-e] letter (**die Antwort** [-en] reply)

der Briefkasten [⸗] post-box (**der Schlitz** [-e] slot)

die Briefmarke [-n]; [official language] **das Postwertzeichen** [-] (postage) stamp (**eine Briefmarke zu . . .** [+ D] a . . . stamp; **der Satz** [⸗e] set; **die Sondermarke** commemorative stamp)

der Briefmarkenautomat [-en] stamp-machine

der/die Briefträger/in [-/-nen] postman/-woman (**zu|stellen** deliver; **ab|holen** collect; **die Zustelltasche** [-n] post-bag; **der Geldbriefträger** special postman for letters containing money)

der Briefwechsel [-] correspondence

die Drucksache [-n] (item of) printed matter

der Eilbrief [-e] express letter

der Einschreibebrief [-e] registered letter (**per Einschreiben** by registered post)

der/die Empfänger/in [-/-nen] addressee

das Formular [-e] form (**aus|füllen** fill in)

die Geld-/Postanweisung [-en] = postal order

die Karte [-n] card (**die Post-/Ansichts-/Geburtstags-/Weihnachtskarte** post-/picture post-/birthday/Christmas card)

der Kartenbrief [-e] letter-card

die Leerung [-en] collection

die Luftpost airmail (**der Luftpostbrief** [-e] airmail letter)

das Paket [-e] parcel (**die Paketpost** parcel post; **der Inhalt** contents; **das Packpapier** brown paper)

das Porto postage (**die Nachgebühr** postage due; **die Portomarke** [-n] postage-due stamp)

die Post post (**mit der Post** by post; **mit getrennter Post** under separate cover; **postlagernd** poste restante)

das Postamt [≃er] post office (**der Schalter** [-] counter; position; **der Postbeamte** *adj n*/**die Postbeamtin** [-nen] counter clerk)

das Postfach [≃er] PO box

die Postleitzahl [-en] post-code

der Poststempel [-] postmark (**Datum** *n* **des Poststempels** date as postmarked)

das Siegel [-] seal

das Streifband [≃er] wrapper

das Telegramm [-e] telegram

der Umschlag/Briefumschlag [≃e] envelope

die Waage [-n] scales (**die Briefwaage** letter scales)

der Werbeprospekt [-e] (advertising) circular

die Zollerklärung [-en] customs declaration

die Zustellung [-en] (postal) delivery

adressieren address

*auf|geben; auf die Post *geben; *ab|senden; *ein|werfen post

be'antworten [letter]; **antworten auf** + A [invitation, question] answer; reply to

bei|legen enclose

*ein|schreiben register (**eingeschrieben *ver'senden** send by registered post)

*ent'halten contain

*er'halten receive

frei|machen; frankieren frank (**mit 0,50 DM freimachen** put a 50-pfennig stamp on; (**un**)**frankiert** (un)stamped)

kleben stick

lesbar/unlesbar *sein; leserlich/unleserlich *sein be legible/illegible

nach|schicken forward (**bitte nachschicken!** please forward)

schicken; *senden send (**ab|schicken; *ab|senden** send off)

siegeln [with wax]; **zu|kleben** [stick down] seal (**der Siegellack** sealing wax)

sortieren sort

*wiegen weigh

zurück|schicken send back

abgestempelt in + D postmarked . . .
als Eilsache *f* express
bei . . . ; per Adresse . . . care of . . .
beigeheftet attached
dringend urgent
per Luftpost by airmail
per Post postal
postwendend by return of post
siehe Rückseite see overleaf

Das Telefon The telephone

das Amt/Fernmeldeamt [⸚er] (telephone) exchange
das Amts-/Freizeichen [-]; **der Wählton** [⸚e] dialling tone
der Anrufbeantworter [-] answering machine (**der Signalton** [⸚e]
 tone)
die Auskunft/Fernsprechauskunft directory enquiries
das Autotelefon [-e] car-phone
das Besetztzeichen [-] engaged tone
das Ferngespräch [-e] long-distance call
der Fernsprechkunde [-n]/**die Fernsprechkundin** [-nen] subscriber
die gelben Seiten *f pl*; **das Branchenverzeichnis** [-se] Yellow Pages
das Gesprach/Telefongespräch [-e]; **der Anruf** [-e] (phone) call
 (**ein Telefongespräch führen/*er'halten** make/receive a call; **das**
 Gespräch mit Voranmeldung personal call)
der Hörer [-] receiver (**den Hörer *ab|nehmen/auf|legen** pick up/
 put down the receiver)
der Nebenanschluß [⸚sse] extension (**Apparat 7** extension 7)
der Notruf [-e] emergency call/number (**die Notrufsäule** [-n]
 emergency telephone)
die Nummer/Telefonnummer [-n]; **die Rufnummer** [-n] phone
 number (**die falsche Nummer** wrong number)
das Ortsgespräch [-e] local call
das R-Gespräch [-e] reverse-charge call (**an|melden** make)
das Rufzeichen [-] ringing tone

das Telefon [-e]; **der Fernsprecher** [-] telephone (**das Tastentelefon** push-button phone; **die Taste** [-n] button; **drahtlos** cordless; **der Münzfernsprecher** payphone)
das Telefonbuch [¨er] telephone directory
die Telefonkarte [-n] phonecard
die Telefonleitung [-en] telephone line (**eine schlechte Verbindung** a bad line; **die Verbindung** [-en] connection)
die Telefonzelle [-n] call-box
das Telegramm [-e] telegram
die Vermittlung *no pl* operator (**der/die Telefonist/in** [-en/-nen] switchboard operator)
die Vorwahl [-en] dialling code
die Wählscheibe [-n] dial [of phone]
die Zeitansage speaking clock
die Zentrale [-n] switchboard

***an|rufen**; **telefonieren mit** + D (tele)phone; call
antworten answer
auf|legen hang up
besetzt/außer Betrieb *sein be engaged/out of order
***durch|kommen** get through
***ein|werfen** insert
läuten; **klingeln** ring
sich melden answer
telefonisch er'reichen reach by phone
***ver'binden mit** + D connect with (**falsch verbunden *sein** have a wrong number)
wählen dial (**durch|wählen** dial direct; **sich ver'wählen** dial the wrong number)
***zurück|rufen** call back

Was man sagt und hört
What you say and hear

am Apparat! speaking!
auf Wiederhören goodbye [on phone]
bleiben Sie am Apparat! hold the line!

danke für den Anruf thanks for calling

der Anschluß/die Nummer ist besetzt/außer Betrieb/antwortet nicht the number is engaged/out of order/does not answer (**der Betrieb** operation)

es ist eine sehr schlechte Verbindung it's a very bad line

es ist jemand in der Leitung we've got a crossed line

es ist niemand da there's no one there

hallo! hello

hier (ist) X this is X; X speaking

ich habe mich verwählt I've dialled the wrong number

ich möchte (mit) X sprechen; [politer] **ich hätte gern mit X gesprochen** I'd like to speak to X

ich rufe (Sie) zurück I'll call (you) back

ich verbinde (Sie) (mit + D) I'm putting you through (to)

meine Nummer ist zwoundzwanzig null sieben neunundneunzig my number is 220799

Moment mal; Augenblick mal just a moment

niemand meldet sich there's no answer

Sie sind durch you're through

Sie sind/ich bin falsch verbunden you've/I've got the wrong number

soll ich/würden Sie etwas ausrichten? can I take/may I leave a message?

Vermittlung! operator!

wer ist am Apparat, bitte?; wer spricht, bitte? who's speaking please?

wir sind unterbrochen worden we've been cut off

Buchstabiertabelle Spelling Code

A wie [as in] Anton	G wie Gustav
Ä wie Ärger	H wie Heinrich
B wie Berta	I wie Ida
C wie Cäsar	J wie Julius
D wie Dora	K wie Konrad
E wie Emil	L wie Ludwig
F wie Friedrich	M wie Martin

N wie Nordpol	U wie Ulrich
O wie Otto	Ü wie Übel
Ö wie Ökonom	V wie Viktor
P wie Paula	W wie Wilhelm
Q wie Quelle	X wie Xanten
R wie Richard	Y (Ypsilon)
S wie Siegfried	Z wie Zeppelin
T wie Theodor	

SEE ALSO: **Greetings and Replies; Reading and Writing**

42. Reading and Writing
Lesen und Schreiben

Die Leute, die es tun People who do it

der Antiquar [-e] second-hand bookseller
der Autor [G -s *pl* **-en]/die Autorin [-nen]; der/die Schriftsteller/in [-/-nen]** author
der/die Biograph/in [-en/-nen] biographer
der/die Brieffreund/in [-e/-nen] pen-friend
der/die Buchhändler/in [-/-nen] bookseller (**die Buchhandlung [-en]** bookshop)
der/die Dichter/in [-/-nen] poet
der/die Journalist/in [-en/-nen] journalist
der/die Leser/in [-/-nen] reader
der/die Romanautor [G -s *pl* **-en]/die Romanautorin [-nen]** novelist
der/die Verleger/in [-/-nen] publisher

Was sie tun What they do

aus|füllen fill in
be'antworten answer
*be'schreiben describe
dichten write [especially poetry]
drucken print
*er'finden invent
faxen fax
korrespondieren correspond
kritzeln scribble
*lesen read
*nach|senden forward
notieren note down
reimen rhyme
*schaffen create

schmökern browse
*schreiben write
tippen; *maschine|schreiben [*inf and past part.* only] type (**mit der Maschine geschrieben; maschinegeschrieben** typed)
*unter'halten entertain
*unter'schreiben sign
*unter'streichen underline
ver'öffentlichen publish
zitieren quote

Was sie gebrauchen What they use

der Absatz [ˣe] paragraph
der Aktendeckel [-] folder
die Anlage [-n] enclosure
der Ausdruck [ˣe] expression
der Auszug [ˣe] extract
die Beschreibung [-en] description
die Bibliothek [-en] library
der Bleistift [-e] pencil (**der Drehbleistift** propelling pencil; **der Bunt-/Filzstift** crayon/felt-tip pen)
der Bleistiftspitzer [-] pencil-sharpener
der Blockbuchstabe [-n] block capital (**in Druckschrift** *f sing* in block letters)
die Büroklammer [-n] paper-clip
der Computer [-] computer (**die Diskette** [-n] floppy disc; **die Magnet-/Festplatte** [-n] hard disc; **die Datei** [-en] file; **der Datenbestand** [ˣe] database; **das Text(verarbeitungs)system** [-e] word processor; **der (Laser-/Matrix)drucker** [-] (laser/dot-matrix) printer; **die Maus** [ˣe] mouse)
das Etikett [G -s; *pl* **-en** or **-e**] label (**selbstklebend** adhesive)
das Fax [*pl* **-** or **-e**]; **die Fernkopie** [-n] fax (**das Fax; der Fernkopierer** [-] fax machine; **die Faxnummer** [-n] fax number)
das Fotokopiergerät [-e] photocopier (**die Fotokopie** [-n] photocopy)
der Füller [-]; **der Füllhalter** [-] (fountain) pen

der Großbuchstabe [-n] capital letter (**der Kleinbuchstabe** small letter; **groß/klein geschrieben** written with a capital/small letter)

der Gummi/Radiergummi [-s] rubber; eraser

die Handlung [-en] plot

die Handschrift handwriting (**leserlich/unleserlich** legible/illegible)

das Heft [-e] exercise book

der Hefter [-] stapler (**die Heftklammer [-n]** staple)

die Illustration [-en] illustration

der Kugelschreiber [-]; der Kuli [-s] ball-point

der Leim; der Klebstoff glue

das Lineal [-e] ruler

die Linie [-n] line

das Notizbuch [ᵁer] notebook (**die Notiz [-en]** note)

das Papier paper (**das Umweltpapier** recycled paper; **das Schreib-/Briefpapier** writing-paper)

die Patrone [-n] [ink] cartridge

der Rand [ᵁer] margin

der Reim [-e] rhyme

die Reißzwecke [-n] drawing-pin

der Rhythmus [*pl* Rhythmen] rhythm

der Satz [ᵁe] sentence

der Schreibblock [*pl* ᵁe or -s] writing-pad

die Schreibmaschine [-n] typewriter (**das Farbband [ᵁer]** ribbon)

die Schreibwarenhandlung [-en] stationer's

der Stil style

der Tesafilm℗ sellotape℗

die Tinte [-n] ink

der Umschlag [ᵁe] envelope

das Wort [*pl* -e = continuous words, **ᵁer** = individual words] word

der Zettel note

das Zitat [-e] (aus + D) quotation (from)

Ihre Werke Their products

die Ausgabe [-n] edition (**die Erstausgabe** first edition)

die Autobiographie [-n] autobiography

die Ballade [-n] ballad

der Band [ᵘe] volume

die Biographie [-n] biography

der Brief [-e] letter (**das Briefchen [-]** note)

das Buch [ᵘer] book (**die Hard-cover-Ausgabe [-n]** hardback; **das Paperback [-s]**; **das Taschenbuch** paperback)

der Comicstrip [-s] strip cartoon

die Dichtung poetry

das Gedicht [-e] poem

die Geschichte [-n] story (**die Kurzgeschichte** short story)

die Gespenstergeschichte [-n] ghost story (**der Geist [-er]**; **das Gespenst [-er]** ghost; **das Skelett [-e]** skeleton; **der Vampir [-e]** vampire; **das Ungeheuer [-e]** monster; **spuken in + D** haunt)

das Handbuch [ᵘer] handbook

das Kapitel [-] chapter

die Karte [-n] card; map (**die Gruß-/Ansichtskarte** greetings card/ picture postcard)

der Katalog [-e] catalogue

das Konzept [-e] rough draft

der Krimi [*pl* - or -s] crime thriller

das Lesen reading

das Lied [-er] song

die Literatur literature

das Märchen [-] fairytale (**die Magie**; **der Zauber** magic; **die Fee [-n]** fairy; **der Kobold [-e]** goblin; **die Hexe [-n]** witch; **der Zauberer [-]** magician; wizard; **der Zauberstab [ᵘe]** magic wand; **der Zwerg [-e]** dwarf; **der Riese [-n]** giant)

das Meisterwerk [-e] masterpiece

das Nachschlagewerk [-e] reference book

die Ode [-n] (an + A) ode (to)

die Postkarte [-n] postcard

die Prosa prose

der Reiseführer [-] guidebook

der Roman [-e] novel

die Sage [-n] myth; legend

die Sammlung [-en] collection

das Schreiben [-] (formal) letter (**Betreff** re; **in der Anlage** enclosed; **(mit Bezug) auf Ihr Schreiben . . .** in reply to your letter . . .)

die Science-fiction science fiction (**das außerirdische Wesen [-]** extra-terrestrial being; **das Raumschiff [-e]** spaceship; **das Ufo [-s]** [= **unbekanntes fliegendes Objekt**] UFO)

das Sonett [-e] sonnet

die Strophe [-n] verse

das Tagebuch [̈er] diary

der Text [-e] text

der Titel [-] title

die Unterschrift [-en] signature

das Wörterbuch [̈er] dictionary

die Zeitschrift [-en]; das Magazin [-e] magazine

die Zeitung [-en] newspaper

Anreden und Grußformeln
Beginnings and endings to letters

Lieber/Liebe X; Hallo X Dear X [informal]

Lieber Herr X; Liebe Frau X Dear Mr/Mrs X [moderately formal]

Sehr geehrte(r) Frau/Herr X Dear Mrs/Mr X [formal]

Sehr geehrte Damen und Herren Dear Sir or Madam [to a firm]

Alles Liebe All the best

Bis bald See you soon

Dein(e) X Yours, X

Herzliche Grüße Ever

Hochachtungsvoll Yours truly [very formal]

Mit besten Empfehlungen Yours faithfully [formal]

Mit freundlichen Grüßen Yours sincerely [moderately formal]

Mit herzlichen Grüßen Best wishes [moderately informal]

Tschüs Cheers

Viele liebe Grüße With love from

SEE ALSO: **Arguments For and Against; Education; The Media; Post and Telephone**

43. Relationships
Verwandschaftsverhältnisse

das Au-Pair-Mädchen [-] au pair
das Baby [-s] baby (**der Säugling [-e]** infant)
der/die Bekannte *adj n* acquaintance
die Braut [⸚e] bride; fiancée (**der Bräutigam [-e]** bridegroom; fiancé)
der/die Erwachsene *adj n* grown-up (**erwachsen** adult)
die Familie [-n] family (**das Familienmitglied [-er]** member of the family; **der Familienkreis** family circle; **Familie Schmidt** the Schmidt family)
der Freund [-e] boyfriend (**die Freundin [-nen]** girlfriend)
der Junggeselle [-n] bachelor (**eingefleischt** confirmed)
die Junggesellin [-nen] single girl
der/die Kamerad/in [-en/-nen] companion; comrade; friend
das Kind [-er] child (**das Einzelkind** only child)
der Kollege [-n]/die Kollegin [-nen] colleague
der Kumpel [-] pal; mate
der/die Liebhaber/in [-/-nen]; der/die Geliebte *adj n* lover
der/die Nachbar/in [-n/-nen] neighbour
der Nachkomme [-n] descendant
der Stammbaum [⸚e] family tree
der/die Verwandte *adj n* relative; relation (**meine Verwandtschaft** *sing* my relatives; **nah(e)-** near; **entfernt** distant)
der Vorfahr [-en] ancestor
die Waise [-n]; das Waisenkind [-er] orphan [male or female]
die Witwe [-n] widow (**der Witwer [-]** widower)
der Zwilling [-e] twin (**der Zwillingsbruder [⸚]** twin brother; **die Zwillingsschwester [-n]** twin sister)

adoptiert adopted
minderjährig under age (**der/die Minderjährige** *adj n* minor)
mütterlicherseits on mother's side (**väterlicherseits** on father's side)
verwandt mit + D related to

Die Familie The family

der Bruder [≟] brother (**der Halbbruder** half-brother; **brüderlich** fraternal)

der/die Cousin/e [-s/-n] cousin (**der Vetter** [G -s *pl* -n] (male) cousin; **die Kusine** [-n] (female) cousin; **der/die Cousin/e zweiten Grades** second cousin)

das Ehepaar married couple (**die (Ehe)frau** [-en] wife; **der (Ehe)mann** [≟er] husband)

die Eltern *no sing* parents (**der Elternteil** [formal] parent)

der Enkel [-] grandson (**die Enkelin** [-nen] granddaughter; **die Enkel** *pl* [also] grandchildren; **das Enkelkind** [-er] grandchild; **der/die Urenkel/in** great-grandson/-granddaughter)

das Geschwister [-] sibling; [*in pl*] brothers and sisters

die Großeltern *no sing* grandparents (**die Großmutter** [≟] grandmother; **der Großvater** [≟] grandfather; **die Oma** [-s] granny; **der Opa** [-s] grandpa)

das Kind [-er] child (**das Adoptivkind** adopted child)

die Mutter [≟] mother (**Mutti** *f* mum)

der Neffe [-n] nephew (**der Großneffe** great-nephew)

die Nichte [-n] niece (**die Großnichte** great-niece)

der Onkel [-] uncle (**der Großonkel** great-uncle)

der Pate/Taufpate [-n]; **der Patenonkel** [-] godfather (**die Patin/Taufpatin** [-nen]; **die Patentante** [-n] godmother; **die Taufpaten** *pl* [also] godparents)

das Patenkind [-er] godchild (**der Patensohn** [≟e] godson; **die Patentochter** [≟] goddaughter)

der Schwager [≟] brother-in-law (**die Schwägerin** [-nen] sister-in-law)

die Schwester [-n] sister (**die Halbschwester** half-sister)

die Schwiegereltern *no sing* parents-in-law (**die Schwiegermutter** [≟]/**der Schwiegervater** [≟]/**der Schwiegersohn** [≟e]/**die Schwiegertochter** [≟] mother-/father-/son-/daughter-in-law)

der Sohn [≟e] son (**der Adoptivsohn** adopted son)

die Stiefmutter [≟]/**der Stiefvater** [≟]/**der Stiefsohn** [≟e]/**die Stieftochter** [≟] stepmother/-father/-son/-daughter

die Tante [-n] aunt (**die Großtante** great-aunt)

die Tochter [=] daughter (**die Adoptivtochter** adopted daughter)
die Urgroßeltern *no sing* great-grandparents (**der/die Urgroß-
vater** [=]/**Urgroßmutter** [=] great-grandfather/-grandmother)
Urur- great-great-
der Vater [=] father (**Vati** *m* dad)
der/die Verlobte *adj n* fiancé/fiancée

SEE ALSO: **Birth, Marriage, and Death**

44. Religion Religion

der Allmächtige *adj n* the Almighty
(der) Buddha Buddha
Jesus [G Jesu] **Christ** Jesus Christ (**der Christus** [G Christi]
  Christ; **das Christkind** the Christ-child)
(der) Mohammed Mohammed
(der) Mose(s) Moses

das Abendmahl [protestant]; **die Kommunion** [Catholic] Com-
  munion
die Absolution absolution (**er'teilen** give)
der Apostel [-] apostle
die Blasphemie [-n]; **die Gotteslästerung** [-en] blasphemy
der Dämon [G -s *pl* -en] demon
der Engel [-] angel
die Erlösung salvation
die Erschaffung; **die Schöpfung** creation
das Fegefeuer purgatory
der Geist [-er] spirit; ghost
der Glaube(n) [G -ns] (**an** + A) faith; belief (in)
der Gott [ˉer] god (**die Göttin** [-nen] goddess)
der Gottesdienst [-e] service (**der Familiengottesdienst** family
  service)
der Götze [-n] idol (**die Götzenverehrung** idolatry)
der Heide [-n]/**die Heidin** [-nen] heathen; pagan
der/die Heilige *adj n* saint
die Hexerei witchcraft (**die Hexe** [-n] witch; **der Hexer** [-]
  sorcerer)
der Himmel [-] heaven
die Hölle [-n] hell
die Hymne [-n]; **das Kirchenlied** [-er] hymn (**die Nationalhymne**
  national anthem)
der Jünger [-] disciple
der/die Ketzer/in [-/-nen] heretic (**die Ketzerei** [-en] heresy)

die Konversion [-en] conversion
die Lehre [-n] doctrine
die Magie magic (der/die Magier/in [-/-nen]; der/die Zauberer/in
  [-/-nen] magician)
der/die Märtyrer/in [-/-nen] martyr
die Messe [-n] mass
das Paradies paradise (auf Erden earthly)
der/die Pilger/in [-/-nen]; der/die Wallfahrer/in [-/-nen] pilgrim
  (die Pilger-/Wallfahrt [-en] pilgrimage)
die Predigt [-en] sermon
der Prophet [-en] prophet (die Prophetin [-nen] prophetess; die
  Prophezeiung [-en] prophecy)
das Schicksal fate
die Sekte [-n] sect
die Sünde [-n] sin (der/die Sünder/in [-/-nen] sinner)
der Teufel [-] devil
die Versuchung [-en] [act]; die Verlockung [-en] [thing] tempta-
  tion
die Vorsehung providence
das Wunder [-] miracle (Wunder wirken work miracles)

*be'gehen commit
beichten confess
be'reuen repent of
beten pray
glauben an + A believe in
konvertieren be converted
kreuzigen crucify
predigen preach
segnen bless (der Segen [-] blessing)
sündigen sin
ver'dammen damn
wiedergut'machen [ich mache wieder gut] atone for

Was man glaubt What you believe

abergläubisch susperstitious (**der Aberglaube** [G **-ns**; *no pl*] superstition)

agnostizistisch agnostic (**der Agnostizismus** agnosticsm; **der/die Agnostiker/in** [-/-nen] agnostic)

anglikanisch Anglican; Church of England (**der Anglikanismus** Anglicanism; **der/die Anglikaner/in** [-/-nen] Anglican)

atheistisch atheist (**der Atheismus** atheism; **der/die Atheist/in** [-en/-nen] atheist)

buddhistisch Buddhist (**der Buddhismus** Buddhism; **der/die Buddhist/in** [-en/-nen] Buddhist)

christlich Christian (**das Christentum** Christianity; **der/die Christ/in** [-en/-nen] Christian; **die Bibel** the Bible; **das Alte/Neue Testament** [-e] the Old/New Testament; **das Kreuz** the Cross; **die Kreuzigung** the Crucifixion)

evangelisch; protestantisch Protestant (**der Protestantismus** Protestantism; **der/die Protestant/in** [-en/-nen]; **der/die Evangelische** *adj n* Protestant)

fromm pious (**die Frömmigkeit** piety)

heilig holy; blessèd (**die Heiligkeit** holiness)

jüdisch Jewish (**das Judentum**; **der Judaismus** Judaism; **der Jude** [-n]/**die Jüdin** [-nen] Jew)

katholisch Catholic (**der Katholizismus** Catholicism; **der/die Katholik/in** [-en/-nen] Catholic)

konvertiert converted (**der/die Konvertit/in** [-en/-nen] convert)

moslemisch; muslimisch Moslem (**der Islam** Islam; **der Moslem** [-s]/**die Moslime** [-n] Moslem; **der Koran** the Koran)

puritanisch puritanic (**der Puritanismus** Puritanism; **der/die Puritaner/in** [-/-nen] Puritan)

skeptisch sceptical (**die Skepsis**; **die Skeptizismus** scepticism; **der/die Skeptiker/in** [-/-nen] sceptic)

Bauten und Geistliche
Buildings and clergy

der Abt [≃e] abbott (**die Äbtin [-nen]** abbess)
die Abtei [-en] abbey
der Bischof [≃e] bishop (**der Erzbischof** archbishop)
der Dom [-e]; das Münster [-] cathedral
der/die Geistliche *adj n* minister; clergyman
der Kardinal [≃e] cardinal
die Kirche [-n] church
der Kurat [-en] curate
der Mönch [-e] monk
die Moschee [-n] mosque
der Muezzin [-s] muezzin
die Nonne [-n] nun
der Papst [≃e] Pope
der/die Pfarrer/in [-/-nen] vicar; minister
der Priester [-] priest (**die Priesterin [-nen]** priestess)
der Rabbi [*pl* Rabbinen]; der Rabbiner [-] rabbi (**der Oberrabbiner** Chief Rabbi)
die Synagoge [-n] synagogue

SEE ALSO: **Art and Architecture; Birth, Marriage, and Death; History**

45. Science Naturwissenschaften

das **Ammoniak** ammonia
das **Atom** [-e] atom
die **Chemikalie** [-n] chemical
das **Chlor** chlorine
der **Druck** pressure
die **Elektrizität** electricity (der **Strom** current)
das **Element** [-e]; der **Grundstoff** [-e] element
die **Erfindung** [-en] invention (der/die **Erfinder/in** [-/-nen]
  inventor; das **Patent** [-e] patent)
das **Experiment** [-e]; der **Versuch** [-e] (an + D) experiment (on)
die **Formel** [-n] formula
die **Forschung** [-en] research
der **Gefrierpunkt** [-e] freezing-point (der **Siedepunkt** boiling-
  point)
die **Gleichung** [-en] equation
das **Jod** iodine
der **Kohlenstoff** carbon (das **Kohlenmonoxid** carbon monoxide;
  das **Kohlendioxid** carbon dioxide)
die **Kraft** [⁼e] force
das **Labor** [*pl* -s or -e]; das **Laboratorium** [*pl* **Laboratorien**]
  laboratory
das **Licht** light
der **Magnetismus** magnetism (der **Magnet** [-e] magnet)
das **Mikroskop** [-e] microscope
das **Molekül** [-e] molecule
die **Reaktion** [-en] reaction
die **Reibung** friction
der **Sauerstoff** oxygen
die **Säure** [-n] acid
der **Schall** sound
der **Schwefel** sulphur (die **Schwefelsäure** sulphuric acid)
die **Schwerkraft**; die **Gravitation** gravity (der **Schwerpunkt** [⁼e]
  centre of gravity)

der Stickstoff nitrogen (**das Distickstoffmonoxid** nitrous oxide)
der Strahl [-en] ray (**der Röntgenstrahl** X-ray)
die Strahlung radiation
die Technik; die Technologie technology (**der Technologe [-n]/die Technologin [-nen]** technologist)
das Teleskop [-e] telescope (**die Linse [-n]** lens)
die Wärme heat
der Wasserstoff hydrogen
die Welle [-n] wave (**die Licht-/Schallwelle** light/sound wave)
die Wissenschaft [-en] science (**angewandt** applied; **rein** pure; **die Natur-/Sozialwissenschaften** *pl* physical/social science)
der/die Wissenschaftler/in [-/-nen] scientist

Namen von Naturwissenschaften
Names of Sciences

die Akustik acoustics
die Algebra algebra
die Anthropologie anthropology
die Archäologie archaeology
die Arithmetik arithmetic
die Astronomie astronomy
die Biologie biology (**die Molekularbiologie** molecular biology)
die Botanik botany
die Chemie chemistry (**organisch/anorganisch** organic/inorganic)
die Differentialrechnung differential calculus
die Elektronik electronics (**die Mikroelektronik** micro-electronics)
die Geologie geology
die Geometrie geometry
die Optik optics
die Mathematik mathematics
die Mechanik mechanics
die Metallurgie metallurgy
die Mineralogie mineralogy

die Physik physics (**die Atom-/Quantenphysik** atomic/quantum physics)

das Programmieren computer programming (**der Computer** [-] computer)

die Psychologie psychology

die Soziologie sociology

die Trigonometrie trigonometry

die Zoologie zoology

Naturwissenschaftler Scientists

der Anthropologe [-n]/**die Anthropologin** [-nen] anthropologist

der Archäologe [-n]/**die Archäologin** [-nen] archaeologist

der/die Astronom/in [-en/-nen] astronomer

der Biologe [-n]/**die Biologin** [-nen] biologist

der/die Botaniker/in [-/-nen] botanist

der/die Chemiker/in [-/-nen] chemist (**der/die (An)organiker/in** [-/-nen]/ (in)organic chemist)

der/die Elektroniker/in [-/-nen] electronics engineer

der Geologe [-n]/**die Geologin** [-nen] geologist

der/die Mathematiker/in [-/-nen] mathematician

der/die Metallurg/in [-en/-nen] metallurgist

der Mineraloge [-n]/**die Mineralogin** [-nen] mineralogist

der/die Physiker/in [-/-nen] physicist

der/die Programmierer/in [-/-nen] computer programmer

der Psychologe [-n]/**die Psychologin** [-nen] psychologist

der Soziologe [-n]/**die Soziologin** [-nen] sociologist

der Zoologe [-n]/**die Zoologin** [-nen] zoologist

SEE ALSO: **Animals; Art and Architecture; Education; Health and Sickness; The Human Body; Materials; Nature; Numbers and Quantities; Plants; The Senses**

46. The Senses Die Sinne

Gesichtssinn Sight

das Aufleuchten flash(ing)

das Auge [-n] eye (**sich [D] die Augen *ver'derben** spoil one's eyesight; **die Augen *auf|-/nieder|schlagen** look up/down; **aus den Augen *ver'lieren** lose sight of; **einäugig** one-eyed)

der Blick [-e] look [glance] (**der Seitenblick** sidelong look; **auf den ersten Blick** at first sight; **einen (kurzen) Blick *werfen auf + A** glance at; **das Aussehen** look [appearance])

das Blinzeln blink

die Brille [-n] (pair of) spectacles (**die Sonnenbrille** sunglasses; **das Monokel [-]** monocle)

die Dunkelheit; die Finsternis darkness (**dunkel; finster** dark)

die Farbe [-n] colour

das Fernglas [ëer]; das Binokular [-e] (pair of) binoculars

der Gesichtssinn [visual faculty]; **der Anblick [-e]** [thing seen]; **das Sehvermögen** [ability to see] sight (**jn vom Sehen** *n* ***kennen** know sb by sight)

die Helligkeit brightness

das Licht [-er] light

die Lupe [-n]; das Vergrößerungsglas [ëer] magnifiying glass

das Mikroskop [-e] microscope

der Schein *no pl* gleam

der Schimmer *no pl* glimmer; shimmer

die Sehkraft vision (**das Sehfeld** field of vision; **die Sichtweite** range of vision)

die Sicht [-en] visibility; view (**in Sicht** in sight)

das Teleskop [-e] telescope

das Zwinkern wink

auf|leuchten flash
*auf|sehen look up (***nach|schlagen** look up [in sth])
aus|machen make out
*aus|sehen wie look like

be'merken notice
be'obachten observe; watch
be'trachten look at; contemplate
blenden dazzle (**blendend** dazzling; **geblendet** dazzled)
blicken look (**zur Seite blicken** look away)
blinzeln blink
er'blicken catch sight of
er'leuchten illuminate
*__er'scheinen__ appear (**wieder auf|tauchen** reappear)
glitzern sparkle
gucken peep
schielen squint
*__sehen__ see; look (**sich um|sehen** look back; **wieder|sehen** see
  again; **nichts zu sehen** nothing to be seen)
starren auf + A stare at
suchen look for
unter'suchen (**auf** + A) examine (for)
*__ver'schwinden__ disappear
*__wahr|nehmen__ discern; perceive
zwinkern wink (**zu|zwinkern** + D wink at)

blind blind (**die Blindenschrift** Braille; **verblendet** blinded)
düster gloomy
farblos colourless
hell bright; light
kurzsichtig short-sighted (**weitsichtig** long-sighted)
sichtbar/unsichtbar visible/invisible

SEE ALSO: **Health and Sickness** (At the optician's)

Gehör Hearing

das Echo [-s] echo
die Explosion [-en] explosion
das Flüstern *no pl* whisper(ing)
das Gehör hearing
das Geräusch [-e] sound; noise

die Hörweite earshot (**in/außer Hörweite** within/out of earshot)
das Klingeln ring(ing)
das Knarren creak(ing)
das Knistern crackle; crackling
der Kopfhörer [-] (pair of) headphones
das Krachen crash(ing)
\\der Lärm *no pl* noise; din
das Läuten ringing; tolling
der Lautsprecher [-] loudspeaker (**die Lautsprecheranlage [-n]** PA system)
das Lied [-er] song
das Ohr [-en] ear (**die Ohren spitzen** prick up one's ears)
das Radio [-s]; **der Rund-/Hörfunk** *no pl* radio (**im Rundfunk** on the radio)
das Rascheln rustle; rustling
der Schall [-e] sound
der Schrei [-e] cry
das Singen singing
die Sirene [-n] siren
die Sprechanlage [-n] intercom
die Stimme [-n] voice
das Summen buzzing
die Taubheit deafness (**das Hörgerät [-e]** hearing-aid)
der Ton [ẍe] tone; note; sound [film, TV]
der Walkman [-s] walkman℗

brummen buzz; drone
donnern thunder
dröhnen throb
flüstern whisper
hören hear (**hörbar/unhörbar** audible/inaudible)
klingen sound
knarren creak
knistern crackle
läuten [church bell, phone]; **klingeln** [doorbell, alarm, phone] ring
***pfeifen** whistle

rascheln rustle
rauschen roar [waterfall]; swish [silk]; rustle [leaves]
*schallen ring out; resound (**die Schallmauer** the sound barrier)
*singen sing
summen hum
surren whirr
wider|hallen echo
zu|hören + D listen to

durchdringend piercing
laut loud
leise soft
matt faint
ohrenbetäubend deafening
schalldicht soundproof
schrill shrill; sharp
schwach faint
schwerhörig hard of hearing
still silent
taub deaf (**taubstumm** deaf and dumb)

Tastsinn Touch

die Berührung [-en] touch (**der Tastsinn** touch [the sense])
das Gefühl [-e] feeling (**das Fingerspitzengefühl** *no pl* (**für** + A)
  special feeling (for); **die Fingerspitze** [-n] fingertip)
der Händedruck [ⸯe] handshake
die Hitze heat (**die Wärme** warmth; heat)
die Kälte cold
die Liebkosung [-en] caress
der Schlag [ⸯe] blow
der Stoß [ⸯe] bump; kick; punch
das Streicheln *no pl* stroke; stroking

be'fingern finger
be'rühren touch
*er'fahren experience

fühlen feel (**sich weich/hart an|fühlen** feel soft/hard; **tasten
  nach** + D feel for)
*greifen grip; grab
kitzeln tickle
klopfen (an + A) knock (against)
kratzen scratch
*reiben rub
*schlagen hit
*stoßen (gegen + A) bump (into)
streicheln stroke

glatt smooth
hart hard
heiß hot
kalt cold
rauh rough
warm warm
weich soft

Geruchssinn Smell

das Aroma [_pl_ **Aromen]** aroma [also flavour; taste]
der Duft [⸚e] scent; [pleasant] smell
der Geruch [⸚e] (nach + D) smell (of) (**der Geruchssinn** smell
  [= sense])
der Gestank _no pl_ stench
die Nase [-n] nose (**das Nasenloch [⸚er]** nostril)
das Parfüm/Parfum [-s] perfume
der Rauch smoke

auf|spüren smell out
parfümieren perfume (**parfümiert** fragrant)
*riechen (gut/schlecht/nach + D) smell (nice/nasty/of)
schnüffeln sniff
*stinken stink (**stinkend** stinking)
wittern scent; detect

geruchlos odourless
muffig musty

rauchig smoky; smelling of smoke
stickig stuffy
stinkend stinking
streng strong; pungent

Geschmackssinn Taste

der Geschmack [¨e] taste [also = discernment]; flavour (**der Geschmack(ssinn)** taste [the sense]; **die Geschmacksrichtung** [-en] [individual's] taste; **die Geschmacksknospe** [-n] taste-bud)
der Mund [¨er] mouth (**die Zunge** [-n] tongue)
der Speichel saliva (**die Speicheldrüse** [-n] salivary gland)

*essen eat
*ge'nießen enjoy; savour
kauen chew
kosten (A or **von** + D) taste; try; sample
lecken lick
pfeffern pepper (**stark gepfeffert** peppery)
probieren try; taste
salzen salt
schlucken swallow
schlürfen slurp up; sip (**nippen an** + D sip at/from)
schmecken nach + D taste of
süßen sweeten (**ungesüßt** unsweetened)
*trinken drink
*ver'schlingen gobble up
würzen spice
zuckern sugar

appetitlich; **appetitanregend** savoury; appetizing
bissig acid
bitter bitter
fade insipid
geschmackvoll in good taste (**geschmacklos** tasteless; in bad taste)
herb sharp; dry [wine]
köstlich delicious

lecker tasty
pikant piquant
ranzig rancid
salzig salty
sauer sour
scharf hot [= spicy]; pungent
süß sweet
zuckrig sugary

SEE ALSO: **Adornment** (for perfume); **Cooking and Eating**; **Drinks**; **Health and Sickness**; **The Human Body**; **Music**; **Tobacco and Drugs**

47. Shops and Shopping
Geschäfte und Einkaufen

die **Abteilung** [-en] department
der **Artikel** [-] article
die **Auswahl** range
die **Besorgung** [-en] errand (**Besorgungen machen** go shopping)
die **Bestellung** [-en] order
der **Betrieb** [-e] business (**Betriebsruhe** *f* **montags** closed on Mondays)
die **Bude** [-n] stall
der **Einkauf** [ᵉe] purchase
das **Einkaufen** shopping
der **Einkaufskorb** [ᵉe] shopping basket
die **Einkaufstasche** [-n] shopping bag
der **Einkaufswagen** [-] (supermarket) trolley
das **Einkaufszentrum** [*pl* -zentren] shopping centre
das **Erzeugnis** [-se] product (**deutsches Erzeugnis** made in Germany)
die **Filiale** [-n] branch
das **Flaschenpfand** [ᵉer] deposit [on bottle]
die **Garantie** [-n] guarantee
das **Geld** money (**das Wechselgeld** change [returned]; **das Kleingeld** (small) change)
der **Gelegenheitskauf** [ᵉe] bargain
das **Geschäft** [-e] shop; business
der/die **Geschäftsführer/in** [-/-nen] manager (**der/die Filialleiter/in** [-/-nen] branch manager)
die **Geschäftszeit(en)** *f sing* or *pl* opening hours
das **Geschenkpapier** gift wrap(ping) (**als Geschenk** *n* **ein|packen** gift-wrap)
die **Größe** [-n] size
der **Großmarkt** [ᵉe] superstore
der **Gutschein** [-e] coupon (**der Geschenkgutschein** gift voucher)

der Handel trade

der/die Händler/in [-/-nen] dealer; trader

die Herabsetzung [-en] reduction (**herabgesetzt** reduced; cut-price)

die Kasse [-n] till; check-out

der Kassenzettel [-] receipt

der/die Käufer/in [-/-nen] buyer

das Kaufhaus [⸚er]; **das Warenhaus** [⸚er] department store

der Kaufmann [*pl* -leute] merchant

der Kiosk [-e] kiosk

die Kreditkarte [-n] credit card (**die Debetkarte** debit card)

der Kunde [-n]/**die Kundin** [-nen] customer

der Kundendienst after-sales service

der Laden [⸚]; **die Handlung** [-en] shop (**der/die Ladenbesitzer/in** [-/-nen] shopkeeper)

das Ladenfenster [-] shop window

der Ladentisch [-e] counter

die Lieferung [-en] delivery

der Markt [⸚e] market (**der Flohmarkt** flea market; **der Trödelmarkt**; **der Wohltätigkeitsbazar** [-e] jumble sale; **die Markthalle** [-n] market hall; **der Markttag** [-e] market day; **der Stand** [⸚e] stall)

die Mietung; **die Pachtung** rental (**der Autoverleih** car-rental)

das Mindesthaltbarkeitsdatum use-by date (**mindest haltbar bis . . .** use by . . .)

das Muster [-] sample

die Packung [-en] packet

die Plastiktüte [-en] plastic bag

der Preis [-e] price (**der Einkaufs-/Verkaufs-/Sonderpreis** whole-sale/retail/special price)

das Produkt [-e] product

die Quittung [-en] receipt

die Rechnung [-en] bill

die Rückzahlung [-en] refund

der Schalter [-] counter; service point

das Schaufenster [-] shop window (**einen Schaufensterbummel** [-] **machen** go window-shopping)

der Scheck [-s] cheque (**die Scheckkarte** [-n] cheque card)
die Schlange [-n] queue (***an|stehen** queue up)
die Selbstbedienung self-service
das Sonderangebot [-e] special offer (**im Sonderangebot** on offer)
der Supermarkt [ːe] supermarket
die Theke [-n] bar-counter
der Umtausch [-e] exchange
der/die Verbraucher/in [-/-nen]; **der/die Konsument/in** [-en/-nen]
  consumer (**die Konsumgüter** *n pl* consumer goods)
der Verkauf [ːe] sale (**der Aus-/Schluß-/Sommerschluß-/Winter-**
  schlußverkauf clearance/end-of-season/summer/winter sale)
der/die Verkäufer/in [-/-nen] shop assistant
die Versteigerung [-en]; **die Auktion** [-en] auction (**der Abschlag** [ːe]
  Dutch auction)
die Ware [-n] article; *pl* goods
das Wechselgeld change

*an|bieten offer
*an|nehmen take delivery of
*aus|geben spend
be'stellen order
be'zahlen [bill, etc.]; **zahlen** [hand over money] pay (**bar**
  (be)zahlen pay cash; **mit Scheck** *m*/**Kreditkarte** *f* by cheque/
  credit card)
ein|kaufen shop (**einkaufen *gehen**; **Einkäufe** *m pl* **machen** go
  shopping)
feilschen haggle
garantieren guarantee
kaufen buy
kosten cost (**drei Mark das Stück** three marks apiece)
liefern deliver
machen come to (**was macht das?** what does it come to?)
*mit|nehmen take with one (**zum Mitnehmen** to go; to take
  away)
reparieren *lassen have repaired
um|tauschen exchange
ver'kaufen sell

ver'steigern auction
wählen choose (aus|wählen choose [from a selection])
*zurück|geben return [goods]

ausverkauft sold out; out of stock
billig cheap
erhältlich (bei + D) available (at)
gebraucht second-hand; used
geöffnet; auf open
geschlossen; zu closed (wir haben montags zu we're closed on
  Mondays)
günstig/preisgünstig very reasonably priced
kostenlos *adj*; gratis *adj* free
preiswert good value
reduziert; herabgesetzt reduced
teuer dear
umsonst for nothing

Geschäfte und ihre Besitzer
Shops and shopkeepers

das Antiquariat [-e] second-hand bookshop (das moderne
  Antiquariat remaindered bookshop; der Antiquar [-e] second-
  hand book dealer)
der Antiquitätenladen antiques shop (die Antiquität antique; der/
  die Antiquitätenhändler/in [-/-nen] antique-dealer)
die Apotheke dispensing chemist's; pharmacy (der/die Apothe-
  ker/in [-/-nen] dispensing chemist; pharmacist)
die Bäckerei [-en] baker's (der/die Bäcker/in [-/-nen] baker)
die Bank [-en] bank (die Sparkasse [-n] savings bank; der/die
  Bankangestellte *adj n* bank clerk)
die Bibiothek [-en]; die Bücherei [-en] library (der/die Bibliothe-
  kar/in [-e/-nen] librarian)
die Blumenhandlung [-en] florist's (der/die Blumenhändler/in
  [-/-nen] florist)
die Boutique [-n] boutique

die Buchhandlung [-en] bookshop (**der/die Buchhändler/in** [-/-nen] bookseller)

die Drogerie chemist's (**der/die Drogist/in** [-en/-nen] chemist)

das Eisenwarengeschäft [-e] ironmonger's (**der/die Eisenwarenhändler/in** [-/-nen] ironmonger)

der Feinkostladen [≟] delicatessen

das Fischgeschäft [-e] fishmonger's (**der/die Fischhändler/in** [-/-nen] fishmonger)

die Fleischerei [-en]; **die Metzgerei** [-en] butcher's (**der/die Fleischer/in** [-/-nen]; **der/die Metzger/in** [-/-nen] butcher)

das Fotogeschäft [-e] camera shop (**der/die Fotograf/in** [-en/-nen] photographer)

der Friseursalon [-s] hairdresser's (**der Friseur** [-e]/**die Friseuse** [-n] hairdresser)

die Gemüsehandlung [-en] greengrocer's (**der/die Gemüsehändler/in** [-/-nen] greengrocer)

das Haushaltswarengeschäft [-e] household-goods/hardware shop

der Herrenausstatter [-] gentlemen's outfitter

das Hutgeschäft [-e] milliner's (**der/die Putzmacher/in** [-/-nen] milliner)

das Juweliergeschäft [-e] jeweller's shop (**der Juwelier** [-e] jeweller)

die Konditorei [-en] cake shop (**der/die Konditor/in** [G -s *pl* -en/-nen] pastry-cook)

das Lebensmittelgeschäft [-e] grocer's (**der/die Lebensmittelhändler/in** [-/-nen] grocer)

die Lederwarenhandlung [-en] leather-goods shop

die Maklerfirma [*pl* -firmen] estate agency (**der/die Grundstücksmakler/in** [-/-nen] estate agent)

das Möbelgeschäft [-e] furniture shop

das Modegeschäft [-e]; **das Modehaus** [≟er] fashion store

die Obsthandlung [-en] fruiterer's (**der/die Obsthändler/in** [-/-nen] fruiterer)

die Parfümerie [-n] perfume shop; cosmetics store

das Platten-/Schallplattengeschäft [-e] record shop (**das Musikgeschäft** music shop)

das Porzellangeschäft [-e] china shop

die Post [-en]; das Postamt [̈er] post office (**der Postbeamte** *adj n*/**die Postbeamtin [-nen]** counter clerk)

das Reformhaus [̈er] health-food shop

die Reinigung [-en] dry cleaner's; dry-cleaning

das Reisebüro [-s] travel agency (**der Reisebürokaufmann** [*pl* **-leute**]/**die Reisebürokauffrau [-en]** travel agent)

die Schneiderei [-en] tailor's; dressmaker's (**der/die Schneider/in [-/-nen]** tailor; dressmaker)

der Schönheitssalon [-s] beauty salon (**der/die Kosmetiker/in [-/-nen]** beautician)

das Schreibwarengeschäft [-e] stationer's (**der/die Schreibwarenhändler/in [-/-nen]** stationer)

das Schuhgeschäft [-e] shoe-shop (**der/die Schuhhändler/in [-/-nen]** shoe salesman/woman; **der/die Schuster/in [-/-nen]** shoe-repairer; cobbler)

der Selbstbedienungsladen [̈] self-service shop

der Souvenirladen [̈] souvenir shop

das Spielwarengeschäft [-e] toyshop

das Sportwarengeschäft [-e] sport's shop

der Supermarkt [̈e] supermarket (**die Kassendame [-n]**/**der Kassenjunge [-n]** check-out assistant)

das Süßwarengeschäft [-e] sweet-shop (**der/die Süßwarenhändler/in [-/-nen]** sweet-shop keeper)

der Tabakladen [̈]; die Tabakwarenhandlung [-en] tobacconist's (**der/die Tabak(waren)händler/in [-/-nen]** tobacconist)

das Textilgeschäft [-e] draper's (**der Textilkaufmann** [*pl* **-leute**]/**die Textilkauffrau [-en]** draper)

die Tierhandlung [-en] pet shop (**der/die Tierhändler/in [-/-nen]** pet-shopkeeper)

das Waren-/Kaufhaus [̈er] department store (**der/die Verkäufer/in [-/-nen]** sales assistant)

die Wäscherei [-en] laundry (**der Waschsalon [-s]** launderette; **der/die Wäscher/in [-/-nen]** laundryman/woman)

der Wein- und Sprituosenladen [̈] = off-licence (**der/die Weinhändler/in [-/-nen]** wine-merchant)

das Zeitungsgeschäft [-e]/der Zeitungskiosk [-e] newspaper shop/
kiosk (**der/die Zeitungshändler/in [-/-nen]** newsagent; news-
vendor)

Was der Ladenbesitzer sagt
What the shopkeeper says

das macht zusammen . . . that comes to . . .
haben Sie Kleingeld? do you have change?
ich kann auf einen Hundertmarkschein nicht herausgeben I
  haven't got change for a hundred-mark note
könnten Sie mir das Geld passend geben? could you give me the
  exact money?
soll ich es als Geschenk verpacken? shall I gift-wrap it?
(und) sonst noch etwas? anything else?
was darf es sein? can I help you?
wir haben es leider nicht vorrätig I'm afraid it isn't in stock
wollen Sie es mitnehmen? will you take it with you?

Was Sie sagen What you say

darf ich es anprobieren? may I try it on?
das ist alles that's all
es gefällt mir (nicht) I (don't) like it
es ist genau/nicht das, was ich suche it's exactly/not what I'm
  looking for
es ist im Schaufenster it's in the window
ich hätte gern . . . ; ich möchte . . . I should like . . .
ich möchte das umtauschen/zurückgeben I want to exchange/
  return this
ich will mich nur umsehen I'm only looking
kann ich mit (einem) Scheck bezahlen? can I pay by cheque?
können Sie es mir bestellen? can you order it for me?
können Sie mir eine Quittung/noch einen Plastikbeutel geben
  bitte? could I have a receipt/another plastic bag please?
können Sie mir helfen? can you help me?

können Sie mir mein Geld zurückerstatten? can you refund my money?
legen Sie es für mich zurück, bitte please put it aside for me
nehmen Sie Kreditkarten? do you take credit cards?
was kostet . . . ? how much does . . . cost?
wieviel macht das? what does that come to?

SEE ALSO: **Adornment; Cinema and Photography; Clothing; Drinks; Food; Hair; Health and Sickness; Leisure and Hobbies; The Media; Money; Music; Numbers and Quantities; Post and Telephone; Sport and Games; Tobacco and Drugs; Towns**

48. Sports and Games
Sport und Spiele

der **Amateur** [-e] amateur
der/die **Anfänger/in** [-/-nen] beginner
der **Angriff** [-e] attack (der/die **Angreifer/in** [-/-nen] attacker)
der/die **Anhänger/in** [-/-nen] supporter
der **Anstoß** [⸚e] kick-off (der **Anpfiff** whistle for the start of play)
der **Aufschlag** [⸚e] service; serve
das **Aus**; [rugby, also] die **Mark** touch (im **Aus** in touch)
der **Einstand** deuce [tennis]
das **Endspiel** [-e] final
das **Ergebnis** [-se] result (eins zu null one-nil)
die **Etappe** [-n] stage; leg
der **Fan** [-s] [male or female] fan
das **Feld** [-er] [running, cycling] pack
das **Finale** [*pl* - or -s]; das **Endspiel** [-e] final (das Viertel-/
  Halbfinale quarter-/semi-final)
das **Foul** [-s] foul
der **Freistoß** [⸚e] free kick
die **Führung**; die **Spitze** lead (in Führung *gehen/*liegen go into/
  be in the lead)
das **Gedränge** scrum
der/die **Gegner/in** [-/-nen] opponent; competitor
die **Halbzeit** half-time; half [of match]
das **Herreneinzel** men's singles (das Dameneinzel women's
  singles; das Herren-/Damendoppel men's/women's doubles; das
  gemischte Doppel mixed doubles)
die **Laufwettbewerbe** *m pl* track events (die technischen
  Disziplinen field events)
die **Leistung** [-en] performance
der **Libero** [-s] sweeper [football]
die **Liga** [*pl* Ligen] league; division (die Bundesliga [German]
  football league)

los! go! (**auf die Plätze, fertig, los!** on your marks, get set, go!;
  Achtung, fertig, los! ready, steady, go!)
die Mannschaft [-en]; das Team [-s]; [football, also] **die Elf [-en]**
  team
der Marathonlauf [ᵜe] marathon
die Medaille [-n] medal
der/die Meister/in [-/-nen] champion
die Meisterschaft [-en] championship (**die Weltmeisterschaft**
  world cup)
der/die Mittelfeldspieler/in [-/-nen] midfield player
die Niederlage [-n] defeat
die Olympischen Spiele Olympic Games
der Paß [ᵜsse]; die Abgabe [-n] pass (**der Vorpaß** forward pass)
der Pokal [-e] cup
der Profi [-s] professional
die Rallye [-s] [motor] rally
der Rechtsaußen [-] outside right (**der Linksaußen** outside left)
die Regatta [*pl* **Regatten**] regatta
der Rekord [-e] record (**auf|stellen** set; ***inne|haben** hold;
  *brechen break)
das Rennen [-] race (**das tote Rennen** dead heat)
der Renntag [-e] race-meeting
die Runde [-n] round; lap
der Satz [ᵜe] set [tennis]
der/die Schiedsrichter/in [-/-nen] referee; umpire (**der Ring-/
  Kampfrichter** boxing/wrestling referee)
der Schuß [ᵜsse] (auf + A) shot (at)
der Sieg [-e] victory (**auf Sieg spielen** go for a win)
der/die Sieger/in [-/-nen] winner
das Spiel [-e] match; game ([football, tennis, also] **das/der Match**
  [*pl* **-s** or **-e**] match; **der Kampf [ᵜe]** (boxing) match)
der/die Spieler/in [-/-nen] player
der Spielstand [ᵜe] score (**der Halbzeit-/Endstand** half-time/final
  score; **die Punktzahl [-en]** (personal) score)
der Sport [*no pl*: *use* **die Sportarten** types of sport] sport
der/die Sportler/in [-] sportsman/woman
der Sprint [-s] sprint

der Sprung [≃e] jump (**der Hoch-/Weitsprung** high/long jump)

der Spurt [*pl* -s or -e] spurt (**der Endspurt** final spurt)

der Stoß [≃e] kick; [swimming, rowing] stroke

der Strafstoß [≃e]; **der Elfmeter** [-] penalty [football] (**der Straftritt** penalty [rugby]; **das Elfmeterschießen** [-] penalty shoot-out)

der/die Stürmer/in [-/-nen] striker

die Tabelle [-n] (league) table (**die Tabelle an|führen** be at the top of the table)

der/die Titelhalter/in [-/-nen] title holder

das Tor [-e] goal (**der Torpfosten** [-] goal-post; **die Querlatte** [-n] crossbar; **das Netz** [-e] net; **der Torwart** [-e] goal-keeper)

der/die Trainer/in [-/-nen] coach; trainer

das Training training (**im Training *sein** be in training)

das Treffen [-] meeting (**das Rennen** [-] race-meeting)

die Tribüne [-n] stand

die Turnhalle [-n] gymnasium

das Turnier [-e] tournament

das Unentschieden [-]; [chess] **das Remis** [*pl* - or -en] draw (**mit einem Unentschieden enden** end in a draw)

die Verlängerung injury/extra time (**nach Verlängerung** after extra time)

der/die Verlierer/in [-/-nen] loser

der Versuch [-e] try [rugby] (**er'zielen; legen** score)

die Verteidigung defence (**der/die Verteidiger/in** [-/-nen] defender)

der Vorlauf [≃e] heat

der Wettkampf [≃e]; **der Wettbewerb** [-e] competition (**der/die Wettkämpfer/in** [-/-nen]; **der/die Wettbewerber/in** [-/-nen] competitor)

das Wettrennen [-]; **der Wettlauf** [≃e] race (**einen Wettlauf machen** run a race)

das Wettschwimmen [-] swimming competition

der Wintersport *no pl* winter sports

der/die Zeitnehmer/in [-/-nen] timekeeper (**die Stoppuhr** [-en] stop-watch)

das Ziel [-e] finish (**der Zielpfosten** [-] winning-post)

die Ziel-/Schießscheibe [-n] target

der/die Zuschauer/in [-/-nen] spectator

*ab|geben pass
*auf|schlagen serve (***zurück|schlagen** return)
aus|buhen boo (sb)
*aus|gehen end; result
er'zielen score (**einen Punkt erzielen** score a point)
führen lead; be ahead (**nach Punkten** on points; **in Führung
  *liegen** be in the lead; **die Führung *über'nehmen** take the lead)
galoppieren gallop
*ge'winnen; siegen win
jagen hunt
*schießen shoot
*schlagen beat
spielen play
Sport *m* ***treiben** go in for sport
*springen bounce
*teil|nehmen an + D take part in
traben trot
trainieren train
sich trimmen get into shape
üben practise
*ver'lieren lose
wetten (auf + A) bet (on) (**die Odds** *pl* odds)
zählen keep score
zischen hiss
zu|jubeln (+ D) cheer (sb)

Sportarten Sports

das Aerobic aerobics
das Angeln fishing
der Autorennsport motor racing
der Basketball basketball
das Bergsteigen mountaineering
das Bogenschießen archery
das Bowling (ten-pin) bowling

das Boxen boxing
der Crosslauf; der Querfeldeinlauf cross-country running
das Diskuswerfen discus-throwing
das Drachenfliegen hang-gliding (**das Ultraleichtflugzeug [-e]** microlight)
das Eishockey ice hockey
der Eiskunstlauf figure-skating
das Fallschirmspringen parachuting
das Fechten fencing
der Federball badminton
der Fußball football
das Gewichtheben weight-lifting
das Golf golf
der Handball handball
das Hockey hockey
das Jagen; die Jagd shooting; hunting (**die Fuchsjagd** fox-hunting)
das Jogging jogging
das Judo judo
der Kanusport canoeing
das Karate karate
das Kegelschieben skittles; ninepins
das Klettern/Felsklettern (rock-)climbing
das Kricket cricket
das Krocket croquet
das Kugelstoßen shot-putting
das Laufen running; walking
die Leichtathletik (track and field) athletics
der Netzball netball
der Radsport cycling
der Reitsport; das Reiten (horse-)riding
das Rennen running; racing; race (**das Kirchturmrennen** point-to-point)
der Rennsport racing (**die Wette [-n]** bet; **wetten** bet)
das Ringen wrestling (**das Freistilringen** all-in wrestling)
das Rodeln tobogganing
das Rollschuhlaufen roller-skating

der Rudersport; das Rudern rowing
das Rugby rugby
das Schießen shooting
das Schlittschuhlaufen skating
das Schwimmen swimming (**das Kraulen** crawl; **das Brust-
schwimmen** breast-stroke; **das Kunstspringen** diving)
das Segelbootrennen yacht racing
das Segelfliegen gliding
das Segeln sailing
das Skateboardfahren skateboarding
der Skilauf; das Skilaufen; der Skisport skiing (**der (Ski)langlauf**
cross-country skiing)
das Spazierengehen walking
das Speerwerfen javelin-throwing
das Squash squash
der Stabhochsprung pole-vaulting
die Stierkämpfe *m pl* bull-fighting (**der Stierkampf** bullfight)
das Strandsegeln sand-yachting
das Surfbrettfahren surf-boarding (**das Surfen** surfing)
das Tauchen (skin-)diving
das Tauziehen tug-of-war
das Trabrennen trotting
das Tennis tennis (**das Tischtennis** table tennis)
das Tontaubenschießen clay-pigeon shooting
das Turnen; die Gymnastik gymnastics
der Volleyball volley ball
das Wandern hiking
der Wasserball water polo
das Wasserskilaufen water-skiing
das Windhundrennen greyhound-racing
das Windsurfen windsurfing; sailboarding
der Wintersport winter sports

Sportsleute Sportspeople

der/die Angler/in [-/-nen] angler
der/die Athlet/in [-en/-nen]; der/die Sportler/in [-/-nen] athlete

der/die **Bergsteiger/in** [-/-nen] mountaineer

der **Bogenschütze** [-n] archer

der **Boxer** [-] boxer

der/die **Drachenflieger/in** [-/-nen] hang-glider

der/die **Eisläufer/in** [-/-nen] skater (der/die **Rollschuhläufer/in**
roller-skater; der/die **Eiskunstläufer/in** figure skater)

der/die **Fallschirmspringer/in** [-/-nen] parachutist

der/die **Fechter/in** [-/-nen] fencer

der/die **Fußballspieler/in** [-/-nen] footballer

der/die **Gewichtheber/in** [-/-nen] weight-lifter

der/die **Golfer/in** [-/-nen] golfer

der/die **Hochspringer/in** [-/-nen] high-jumper

der/die **Jäger/in** [-/-nen] hunter; marksman

der **Jockey** [-s]; der **Jockei** [-s] jockey

der/die **Jogger/in** [-/-nen] jogger

der/die **Kletterer/in** [-/-nen] climber

der/die **Läufer/in** [-/-nen] runner

der/die **Leichtathlet/in** [-en/-nen] athlete

der/die **Radfahrer/in** [-/-nen] cyclist (der/die **Radrennfahrer/in**
racing cyclist)

der/die **Reiter/in** [-/-nen] rider

der/die **Ringer/in** [-/-nen] wrestler

der/die **Rodler/in** [-/-nen] tobogganer; luger

der **Ruderer** [-] oarsman (die **Ruderin** [-nen] oarswoman)

der/die **Schlittschuhläufer/in** [-/-nen] skater

der/die **Schwimmer/in** [-/-nen] swimmer

der/die **Skiläufer/in** [-/-nen] skier

der/die **Spaziergänger/in** [-/-nen] walker (dcr/die **Geher/in** [-/-nen]
walker [in race])

der/die **Sportler/in** [-/-nen] sportsman/-woman

der/die **Surfer/in** [-/-nen] surfer

der/die **Taucher/in** [-/-nen] diver

der/die **Tennisspieler/in** [-/-nen] tennis-player

der/die **Turner/in** [-/-nen] gymnast

der/die **Windsurfer/in** [-/-nen] windsurfer

Was sie tun What they do

angeln fish

***berg|steigen** [*inf and past part. only*] go mountaineering/
  mountain climbing

boxen box

***gehen; *spazieren|gehen** walk

***heben** lift

***hoch|springen** [*inf and past part. only*] do the high jump

jagen hunt; shoot (**auf die Jagd *gehen** go hunting/shooting)

joggen jog

klettern climb

***laufen** run

***rad|fahren** cycle (**ich fahre Rad** I cycle)

***reiten** ride [horseback] (**traben** trot; **galoppieren** gallop)

***ringen** wrestle

rodeln toboggan

Rollschuh *m* ***laufen** roller-skate

rudern row

***schießen** shoot (**ein Tor schießen** score a goal)

Schlittschuh *laufen/*fahren skate

schwimmen** swim (treiben** float)

segeln sail

Ski *laufen/*fahren ski

***springen** jump

surfen surf

tauchen dive

Wasserski *laufen water-ski

***weit|springen** [*inf and past part. only*] do the long jump

***werfen** throw

Ausrüstung Equipment

die Angel [-n]; **die Angelrute** [-n] fishing-rod (**die Schnur** [ˮe] line;
  der Köder [-] bait; **der Schwimmer** [-] float)

der Badeanzug [ˮe] swimsuit

die Bahn [-en] track (**die Renn-/Radrennbahn** race-/cycle-track)

der Ball [**¨e**] ball (**die Kugel** [**-n**] ball [croquet, billiards]; bowl; bullet)
der Barren *sing* parallel bars
der Billiardstock [**¨e**]; **das Queue** [**-s**] cue
der Bogen [**-**] bow (**der Pfeil** [**-e**] arrow)
die Bowlingbahn [**-en**] (tenpin) bowling alley
der Boxhandschuh [**-e**] boxing-glove
die Eisbahn [**-en**] ice-rink
das Fahrrad [**¨er**] bicycle
der Federball [**¨e**] shuttlecock
das Gewehr [**-e**] gun
der Golfschläger [**-**] golf-club
der Hockeystock [**¨e**] hockey stick
die Kegelbahn [**-en**] skittle alley
das Kanu [**-s**] canoe
das Netz [**-e**] net
der Platz [**¨e**] court; ground (**der Tennis-/Golf-/Sportplatz** tennis-court/golf course/playing-field)
die Rennstrecke [**-n**] race-track; (race) distance
der Ring [**-e**] ring
der Rodelschlitten [**-**] toboggan
der Rollschuh [**-e**] roller-skate
das Ruderboot [**-e**] rowing-boat
der Sattel [**-**] saddle (**die Zügel** *m pl* reins)
der Schläger [**-**] racket; bat (**der Golfschläger** club)
der Schlitten [**-**] sledge
der Schlittschuh [**-e**] skate
die Schlittschuhbahn [**-en**] ice-rink
der Schnorchel [**-**] snorkel
das Schwimmbad [**¨er**] swimming-pool (**das Frei-/Hallenbad** open-air/indoor pool; **das Sprungbrett** [**-er**] diving-board)
die Schwimmflosse [**-n**] flipper
das Segelboot [**-e**] sailing-boat (**das Ding(h)i** [**-s**] dinghy)
das Skateboard [**-s**] skateboard
der Ski [*pl* **-er** or **-**] ski (**der Skistock** [**¨e**] ski pole; **der Skistiefel** [**-**] ski boot; **der Skilift** [*pl* **-e** or **-s**] ski-lift; **die Skipiste** [**-n**] ski-run; **der Wasserski** water-ski)

der Speer [-e] javelin
das Spielfeld [-er] field; pitch
das Sportfeld [-er]; **das Sportplatz** [ˮe] sports ground; sports
  stadium
das Stadion [*pl* **Stadien**] stadium (**die Tribüne** [-n] stand; **der**
  Umkleideraum [ˮe] dressing-room)
die Stoppuhr [-en] stop-watch
der Sturzhelm [-e] crash-helmet
das Surfbrett [-er] surf-board
der Tauch-/Naßanzug [ˮe] wetsuit
die Taucherbrille [-n] (pair of) diving-goggles
der Tennisschläger [-] tennis-racket
das Trikot [-s]; **das Jersey** [-s] jersey

Spiele Games

das Billiard(spiel) billiards (**eine Partie Billiard** a game of
  billiards)
das Bingo bingo
das Bowlspiel; **das Bowls** bowls
das Brettspiel [-e] board game (**der Würfel** [-] die [*pl* dice]; **der**
  Stein [-e] piece; **das Feld** [-er] square)
das Computerspiel [-e] computer game
die Dame *f sing* draughts (**Dame spielen** play draughts; **der Stein**
  [-e] draughtsman)
das Domino dominoes (**Domino spielen** play dominoes; **der Stein**
  [-e] domino [the piece])
der Flipperautomat [-en] pinball machine
das Kartenspielen card-playing (**die (Spiel)karte** [-n] playing-
  card; **das Kartenspiel** [-e] pack of cards; **der Kartentisch** [-e]
  card-table; **Karten spielen** play cards; **das Bridge** bridge; **der**
  Skat skat)
das Kreuzworträtsel [-] crossword
das Puzzle [-s]; **das Puzzlespiel** [-e] jigsaw (**der Teil** [-e] piece)
das Quartett happy families
das Schach chess (**Schach spielen** play chess; **das Schachbrett**
  [-er] chessboard; **die Schachfigur** [-en] chessman)

(das) Schnippschnapp(schnurr) snap
das Spiel [-e] game; pack (**das Glücksspiel** game of chance; **das
  Gesellschaftsspiel** party game)

SEE ALSO: **Leisure and Hobbies; Nature**

49. Theatre Theater

der Abgang [¨e] (actor's) exit
die Arie [-n] aria
die Aufführung [-en] performance; production (**zur Aufführung**
   *bringen put on)
der Auftritt [-e] entrance; scene (**seinen Auftritt *haben** make
   one's entrance; **2. Auftritt** scene 2)
der Beifall applause
die Karte/Theaterkarte [-n] ticket
die Kartenvorverkaufsstelle [-n] ticket agency
die Kritik [-en] review (**der/die Kritiker/in** [-/-nen] reviewer)
das Laientheater amateur dramatics
das Lampenfieber stage fright
die Nachmittagsvorstellung [-en] matinée
die Nummer [-n] number; turn
das Opernglas [¨er] (pair of) opera-glasses
die Pause [-n] interval
das Programm [-e]; **das Programmheft** [-e] programme
die Reservierung [-en] reservation; booking
die Show [-s] show
die Szene [-n] scene (**hinter der Szene** backstage; **in Szene setzen**
   stage)
der Text [-e] script
das Theater [-] theatre (**beim Theater *sein** work in the theatre;
   zum Theater *gehen go on the stage; **ins Theater *gehen** go to
   the theatre; **Theater spielen** act; **theatralisch** theatrical)
das Theaterplakat [-e] playbill; poster
die Tournee [*pl* -s or -n] tour (**auf Tournee** on tour)
die Vorstellung [-en] (actor's) performance; performance of play
   (**schwach** weak; **stark** strong; **die zweite Vorstellung** second
   house)
die Zugabe [-n] encore (**Zugabe!** encore!)

*ab|gehen exit (**Faust ab** exit Faust)
applaudieren applaud
auf|führen put on; stage; perform
*auf|treten enter (**Auftritt Faust** enter Faust)
aus|ver'kaufen sell out (**ausverkauft** house full)
buhen boo (**aus|buhen** boo (at sb))
inszenieren put on
klatschen; Beifall klatschen clap
proben rehearse
reservieren *lassen; **vor|be'stellen** book (in advance)
spielen act (**eine Rolle spielen** play a part)
tanzen dance
sich ver'beugen bow
zischen hiss
zurück|zahlen refund (**das Eintrittsgeld zurückzahlen** refund
  entrance)

Shows Shows

das Ballett [-e] ballet (**das Ballettabend** [-e] (evening of) ballet)
das Drama [*pl* **Dramen**] drama
die Komödie [-n]; **das Lustspiel** [-e] comedy
das Melodram(a) [*pl* **Melodramen**] melodrama
das Musical [-s] musical
die Oper [-n] opera [also, opera house]
die Operette [-n] operetta
die Posse [-n]; **die Farce** [-n] farce
das Puppen-/Marionettenspiel [-e] puppet-show
das Stück/Theaterstück [-e]; **das Schauspiel** [-e] play (**der Akt** [-e]
  act; **der Einakter** [-] one-act play; *geben put on)
der Tanz [≃e] dance
der Thriller [-] thriller
die Tragödie [-n]; **das Trauerspiel** [-e] tragedy
das Varieté [-s] variety-show
der Zirkus [-se] circus

Theaterleute Theatre people

die Besetzung [-en] cast (**die zweite Besetzung** understudy)

der/die Bühnenarbeiter/in [-/-nen] scene-shifter

der/die Bühnenbildner/in [-/-nen] designer

der Dramatiker [-] dramatist

der/die Dramaturg/in [-en/-nen] literary and artistic director

der Gewandmeister [-] wardrobe-master (**die Gewandmeisterin [-nen]** wardrobe-mistress)

der/die Inspizient/in [-en/-nen] stage-manager

der/die Intendant/in [-en/-nen] theatre director

die Platzanweiserin [-nen] usherette (**der Platzanweiser [-]** usher; attendant)

das Publikum audience

der/die Regisseur/in [-e/-nen] director

der Schauspieler [-] actor (**die Schauspielerin [-nen]** actress; ***auf|treten als** appear as)

der Souffleur [-e]/die Souffleuse [-n] prompter (**der Souffleurkasten** prompt-box)

der Star [-s] star [male or female]

der/die Tänzer/in [-/-nen] dancer

der/die Theaterbesucher/in [-/-nen] theatre-goer

die Truppe [-n] troupe; company

der/die Verfasser/in [-/-nen] author

der/die Zuschauer/in [-/-nen] member of the audience (**die Zuschauer** *pl* audience)

Das Haus The theatre building

der Ausgang [ːe] exit (door) (**der Notausgang** emergency exit)

der Balkon [*pl* -s or -e]; **der Rang [ːe]** circle (**erster/zweiter/dritter Rang** dress circle/upper circle/gallery; **der Olymp** the gods)

die Bühne [-n] stage

der Eingang [ːe] entrance (door)

das Foyer [-s] foyer

die Garderobe [-n] cloakroom

die Kasse [-n] box-office (**an der Kasse** at the box-office)

die Kulisse [-n] wing; flat; *pl* scenery (**der Kulissenwechsel** [-]
  scene-change; **hinter den Kulissen** behind the scenes)
das Haus [⸚er] theatre; house (**ausverkauftes Haus** full
  house)
die Loge [-n] box
der Orchestergraben [⸚] orchestra pit
das Parkett stalls
der Platz [⸚e] seat [place] (**der Sitz** [-e] seat [the physical
  object])
das Rampenlicht [-er] footlight; (light from the) footlights
die Reihe [-n] row
der Saal [*pl* **Säle**] auditorium
der Scheinwerfer [-] spotlight
die Vorführung [-en] performance; house
der Vorhang [⸚e] curtain (**der eiserne Vorhang** safety curtain;
  eisern iron; ***auf|gehen** rise; ***fallen** fall)
die Vorverkaufskasse [-n] advance-booking office (**der Vorverkauf** advance booking; **Karten im Vorverkauf be'sorgen** book
  tickets in advance)

Das Schauspiel The play

die Beleuchtung lighting (**an|strahlen** light)
das Bühnenbild [-er] set
die Dekoration [-en] scenery
die Handlung [-en] plot
die Inszenierung [-en] staging; production
das Kostüm [-e] costume
die Maske (theatrical) make-up
die Personen *f pl* cast; dramatis personae
die Premiere [-n] first night
die Probe [-n] rehearsal (**die Generalprobe** dress rehearsal)
die Regie direction (**Regie führen bei** + D direct)
das Requisit [G -s *pl* -en] prop(erty)
die Rolle [-n] role; part (**die Haupt-/Nebenrolle** leading/
  supporting role)

das Spiel acting (**tragisch** tragic; **komisch** comic; **dramatisch**
 dramatic)
der Text [-e] text; script; lines

SEE ALSO: **Adornment; Cinema and Photography; Leisure and
Hobbies; The Media; Music**

50. Time Zeit

das Datum [*pl* Daten] date
die Dauer duration
die Ewigkeit eternity
der Geburtstag [-e] birthday
die Hundertjahrfeier [-n] centenary
der Kalender [-] calendar
der Namenstag [-e] name-day; saint's day
die Periode [-n]; das Zeitalter [-] period
die Uhr clock time; time o'clock
die Verspätung [-en] delay
die Zeit [-en] time (die Sommerzeit Summer Time; die Zeit
  *ver'bringen/ver'schwenden/ver'geuden/*tot'schlagen spend/
  waste/fritter away/kill time)
die Zeitzone [-n] time zone (der Zeitunterschied [-e] time
  difference)

Die Uhr The clock

die Armbanduhr [-en] watch
die Glocke [-n] bell (der Glockenturm [¨e] belfry)
das Pendel [-] pendulum
die Uhr [-en] clock; watch (die Quarz-/Digitaluhr quartz/digital
  clock/watch; die Stoppuhr stop-watch; die Sonnenuhr sundial;
  die Schaltuhr timer; die Stand-/Kuckucksuhr grandfather/
  cuckoo clock; die Sanduhr hourglass; die Eieruhr egg-timer)
der Wecker [-] alarm clock (der Reise-/Küchenwecker travel
  alarm/kitchen timer)
der Zeiger [-] hand [of clock] (der Sekunden-/Minuten-/
  Stundenzeiger second/minute/hour hand)
die Zeitansage speaking clock
das Zifferblatt [¨er] dial; face

*auf|ziehen wind up
*schlagen strike
stellen nach + D set by
*vor|gehen be fast (***nach|gehen** be slow; **richtig *gehen** be right)

Uhrzeit Clock time

wieviel Uhr ist es?; wie spät ist es? what time is it?
haben Sie die richtige Uhrzeit? do you have the right time?

es ist . . .
  ein Uhr one o'clock
  zwei Uhr two o'clock
  fünf (Minuten) nach drei five past three
  Viertel nach vier quarter past four
  halb fünf half past four
  fünfundzwanzig (Minuten) vor sechs; fünf nach halb sechs
    twenty-five to six
  Viertel vor sieben quarter to seven
  Mittag/Mitternacht twelve o'clock (**der Mittag [-e]** noon; **die**
    Mitternacht *no pl* midnight)

  zwölf Uhr 12.00
  dreizehn Uhr zehn 13.10
  vierzehn Uhr fünfzehn 14.15
  fünfzehn Uhr dreißig 15.30
  vierundzwanzig Uhr 24.00
  null Uhr eins 00.01

abends in the evening [= p.m.]
morgens; vormittags in the morning [= a.m.]
nachmittags in the afternoon [= p.m.]
nachts at night [= a.m.]

erst um + A not until
gegen + A; **etwa um** + A at about
nach + D after
um + A at (**um wieviel Uhr . . . ?** at what time . . . ?; **genau**
  um . . . at exactly . . .)

vor + D before
während + G during

bei Einbruch *m* **der Dunkelheit** at nightfall
bei Sonnenaufgang *m* at sunrise (**bei Sonnenuntergang** *m* at
  sunset)
bei Tagesanbruch *m* at daybreak
im Morgengrauen *n* at dawn
in der Abenddämmerung at dusk
mittags at noon (**mitternachts** at midnight)

Zeiteinheiten Units of time

der Abend [-e] evening
der Augenblick [-e]; der Moment [-e] moment
die Epoche [-n] epoch
das Jahr [-e] year (**im Jahr X** in X; **das Schaltjahr** leap year; **das
  Halbjahr** (school) term)
die Jahreszeit [-en] season
das Jahrhundert [-e] century
das Jahrtausend [-e] millennium; thousand years
das Jahrzehnt [-e] decade
das Mal [-e] time [occasion] (**zum zweiten Mal** for the second
  time)
die Minute [-n] minute
der Monat [-e] month
der Morgen [-]; der Vormittag [-e] morning
der Nachmittag [-e] afternoon
die Nacht [≃e] night (**letzte/diese Nacht** last night/tonight)
die Sekunde [-n] second
die Stunde [-n] hour (**eine halbe Stunde** half an hour; **eine
  Viertelstunde** quarter of an hour; **eine Dreiviertelstunde** three-
  quarters of an hour; **anderthalb Stunden** an hour and a half)
der Tag [-e] day (**vierzehn Tage** a fortnight)
die Woche [-n] week (**das Wochenende [-n]** weekend; **heute in/vor
  einer Woche** a week today/a week ago today; **diese/nächste
  Woche** this/next week; **letzte/vorige Woche** last week)

jährlich yearly
monatlich monthly
täglich daily
wöchentlich weekly (**zweiwöchentlich** fortnightly)

Das Datum The date

der Wievielte ist heute?; was für ein Datum/welches Datum/den Wievielten haben wir heute? what is the date?

heute ist der erste/zweite/dritte Mai neunzehnhundertneunund-neunzig; heute ist der 1./2./3. Mai 1999 today is the first/second/third of May 1999

am 1. Mai on the first of May
stammen aus + D date from

Die Tage der Woche The days of the week

was ist heute für ein Tag?; welchen Tag haben wir heute? what day is it today?

heute ist Sonntag today's Sunday

der Sonntag [-e] Sunday (**am Sonntag; sonntags** on Sunday(s); **sonntags morgens** on Sunday mornings; **am folgenden Sonntag** the following Sunday; **letzten/nächsten/jeden Sonntag** last/next/every Sunday; **Sonntag in/vor einer Woche** a week on/ago Sunday; **der Sonntagmorgen/der Sonntagnachmittag** Sunday morning/afternoon)
der Montag [-e] Monday
der Dienstag [-e] Tuesday
der Mittwoch [-e] Wednesday
der Donnerstag [-e] Thursday
der Freitag [-e] Friday
der Sonnabend [-e] [N. Germany, E. Germany]; **der Samstag [-e]** [S. Germany, Austria, Switzerland] Saturday

Die Jahreszeiten The seasons

der Frühling [-e]; das Frühjahr [-e] spring (**im Frühling** in spring;
(**im**) **Frühling vergangenen/nächsten Jahres** last/next spring)
der Sommer [-] summer
der Herbst [-e] autumn
der Winter [-] winter

Die Monate The months

der Januar [-e] January (**im Januar** in January; **Anfang/Ende
Januar** at the beginning/end of January; **Mitte Januar** in mid-
January; **vor/nach Januar** before/after January)
der Februar [-e] February
der März [-e] March
der April [-e] (**der Aprilscherz** April-fool trick; **jn in den April
schicken** make an April fool of sb)
der Mai [-e] May (**der Maibaum [⸚e]** maypole; May-tree)
der Juni [-s] June
der Juli [-s] July
der August [-e] August
der September [-] September
der Oktober [-] October
der November [-] November
der Dezember [-] December

Wann geschieht es? When does it happen?

ab und zu now and then
alle drei Tage/Stunden etc. every three days/hours etc.
am nächsten/folgenden Tag/Abend etc. (on) the next/following
day/evening etc.
am übernächsten Tag two days later (**drei Tage später** three days
later)
am vorigen Tag/Abend etc. (on) the previous day/evening etc.
bald soon
dann [next]; **damals** [at that time] then

dann und wann now and then

früh early (**zu früh *kommen** be too early)

früher formerly

gerade just (now)

gestern yesterday (**gestern morgen/nachmittag** yesterday morning/afternoon; **gestern abend** last night)

gleichzeitig at the same time; simultaneously

häufig frequently

heute today (**heute vormittag/morgen** this morning; **heute nachmittag** this afternoon; **heute abend** tonight; **heute nacht** last night; tonight)

heutzutage nowadays

im Jahre 1900; 1900 in 1900 (**Anfang** *m*/**Mitte** *f*/**Ende** *n* **1970** at the beginning/in the middle/at the end of 1970)

immer always

im Moment *m*/**Augenblick** *m* at the moment

im zwanzigsten Jahrhundert in the twentieth century

in den sechziger Jahren in the sixties

in der Zukunft in future

in der Zwischenzeit in the meantime

in zwei Tagen in two days (**innerhalb von zwei Tagen** within two days)

jährlich yearly (**halbjährlich** biannual(ly); **zweijährlich** biennial(ly))

jede Minute any minute (now)

jeden Tag every day

jetzt now

längere Zeit for a long time

manchmal sometimes

morgen tomorrow (**morgen früh/nachmittag/abend** tomorrow morning/afternoon/night)

nachts; in der Nacht at night (**diese/letzte Nacht** tonight/last night)

nie; [stronger] niemals never

oft often
plötzlich suddenly
Punkt . . . . . . on the dot
pünktlich punctually
rechtzeitig on time
schließlich [last in a sequence]; **endlich** [at last; after all this time]
  finally)
schon already
seitdem since
selten seldom
sofort; (so)gleich immediately
spät [at an advanced hour]; **verspätet** [after the proper time] late
  (**du kommst so spät heute** you're so late today; **verspätet**
  *an|kommen arrive late; **X Minuten Verspätung** *f* ***haben** be X
  minutes late; **spätestens** at the latest)
stündlich hourly
tagsüber; am Tag(e) during the day (**am hellichten Tag(e)** in
  broad daylight)
übermorgen the day after tomorrow
um diese Tageszeit [-en] at this time of day (**zu jeder Tages- und**
  Nachtzeit at any time of the day or night)
von nun an from now on
von Zeit zu Zeit from time to time (**von Stunde zu Stunde** from
  hour to hour; **von morgens bis abends** from morning to night)
vor einer Woche etc. a week etc. ago
vorgestern the day before yesterday
vor kurzem; kürzlich; neulich recently; a short time ago
vor kurzer/langer Zeit a short/long time ago (**lange Zeit** for a
  long time)
währenddessen meanwhile
wieder; nochmals again
zuerst first
zu meiner Zeit in my day
zur Zeit at the moment (**zu der Zeit** at that time)

Feiertage und Feste
Public holidays and festivals

feiern celebrate

(das) Allerheiligen All Saints' Day/All Hallows

(das) Allerseelen All Souls' Day

(der) Aschermittwoch Ash Wednesday (**(der)Rosenmontag** Monday before Ash Wednesday)

(der) Buß- und Bettag Penitence Day [Wednesday 11 days before Advent]

Himmelfahrt/Christi Himmelfahrt *f* Ascension Day (**Mariä Himmelfahrt** Assumption)

Dreikönige *n* Epiphany; Twelfth Night (**zu/an Dreikönige** on Twelfth Night)

der erste April April Fools' Day (**April! April!** April fool!)

der Fasching [*pl* **-e** or **-s**] (pre-Lent) Carnival

die Fasten *f pl*; **die Fastenzeit** *sing* Lent

(der) Fastnachtsdienstag; **(die) Fastnacht** Shrove Tuesday

der Feiertag [**-e**]; **der Festtag** [**-e**] holiday (**der gesetzliche/ kirchliche Feiertag** public/religious holiday)

das Fest [**-e**] festival; celebration

das Festival [**-s**] festival

der Geburtstag [**-e**] birthday (**ich habe Geburtstag** it's my birthday)

(der) Gründonnerstag Maundy Thursday

(der) Karfreitag Good Friday

der Maifeiertag May Day

der Namenstag [**-e**] saint's day

(das) Neujahr New Year's Day (**ein gutes neues Jahr!** happy New Year!)

der Nikolaus St Nicolas' day

(das) Ostern Easter (**zu Ostern** at Easter; **nächste Ostern** *pl* next Easter; **fröhliche Ostern** *pl* happy Easter)

(der) Ostersonntag Easter Day

(der) Palmsonntag Palm Sunday

(das) Pfingsten Whitsuntide (**zu Pfingsten** at Whitsun) (der) **Pfingstmontag** Whit Monday

(der/das) **Silvester**; **der Neujahrsabend** New Year's Eve (**Silvester feiern** see the New Year in)

der Tag der deutschen Einheit Day of German Unity [3 October]

der Valentinstag St Valentine's day

(das) **Weihnachten** Christmas (**zu Weihnachten** at Christmas; **frohe/fröhliche Weihnachten** *pl* Merry Christmas; **der erste/ zweite Weihnachtstag** Christmas Day/Boxing Day; **der Heiligabend** Christmas Eve; **die Bescherung** distribution of presents)

SEE ALSO: **Birth; Marriage, and Death; History; Numbers and Quantities**

51. Tobacco and Drugs
Tabak und Drogen

Tabak Tobacco

der Aschenbecher [-] ashtray (**die Asche** ash)

das Feuerzeug [-e] lighter (**der Feuerstein [-e]** flint; **der Docht [-e]** wick; **die Patrone [-n]** refill)

der Lungenkrebs cancer of the lung

die Pfeife [-n] pipe (**der Pfeifenreiniger [-]** pipe-cleaner)

der Rauch smoke

der/die Raucher/in [-/nen] smoker (**der/die Nichtraucher/in** non-smoker)

der Schnupftabak snuff (**eine Prise [-n] schnupfen** take a pinch of snuff)

das Streichholz [ɛer] match (**die Schachtel [-n]** box)

der Tabak tobacco (**der Pfeifentabak** pipe tobacco; **der Tabak(s)beutel [-]** tobacco pouch)

das Verbot [-e] ban (**Rauchverbot; Rauchen** *n* **verboten** no smoking)

die Zigarette [-n] cigarette (**eine Schachtel [-n] Zigaretten** a packet of cigarettes; **die Stange [-n]** ten-packet carton; **die Filterzigarette** filter-tip cigarette; **der Filter [-]** filter-tip)

das Zigaretten-/Zigarrenetui [-s] cigarette-/cigar-case

die Zigarettenspitze [-n] cigarette-holder

der Zigarettenstummel [-] cigarette-end (**die Kippe [-n]** *colloq* fag-end)

die Zigarre [-n] cigar

an|zünden light up
*auf|geben give up
aus|drücken stub out
rauchen smoke
um Feuer *n* ***bitten** ask for a light (**jm Feuer *geben** give sb a light; **haben Sie Feuer?** have you got a match?)

Drogen Drugs

die **Behandlung** cure
das **Betäubungsmittel** [-] narcotic
die **Droge** [-n]; das **Rauschgift** *no pl* drug (**unter Drogen *stehen**;
  Rauschgift *nehmen be on drugs)
die **Drogeneinnahme** drug taking
der **Drogenhandel** drug trafficking
der/die **Drogenhändler/in** [-/-nen]; der/die **Dealer/in** [-/-nen] drug
  trafficker
das/der **Haschisch** hashish (**das Hasch** hash)
das **Heroin** heroin
das **Kokain** cocaine
die **Nadel** [-n] needle
der/die **Pusher/in** [-/-nen] drug pusher
die **Sucht** [ː̈e] (**nach** + D) addiction (to) (**süchtig** addicted; **der/
  die Süchtige** *adj n* addict)
die **Überdosis** overdose
die **Wiedereingliederung** rehabilitation [into society]

be'schlagnahmen confiscate
*nehmen take
sich [D] **et spritzen** inject oneself with sth

SEE ALSO: **Crimes and Criminals; Drinks; Health and Sickness**

52. Tools Werkzeuge

der Bastler DIY enthusiast (**basteln** make things)
der Werkzeugkasten [╌] tool-box

die Beißzange [-n] pincers ***heraus|ziehen** pull out
der Besen [-] broom **kehren** sweep
der Bohrer [-] drill **bohren** drill
das Bügel-/Plätteisen [-] iron **bügeln; plätten** iron
die Drahtzange wire-cutters (**der Draht** [╌e] wire)
  ***durch|schneiden** cut (through)
die Drehbank [╌e] lathe **drehen** turn
die Esse [-n] [hearth]; **die Schmiede** [blacksmith's shop] forge
  (**der Amboß** [-sse] anvil) **schmieden** forge
die Feile [-n] file **ab|feilen** file down
die Gabel [-n] (pitch)fork **gabeln** fork
die Gießkanne [-n] watering-can ***gießen; *be'gießen** water
das Gerüst [-e] scaffolding **bauen** build
die Hacke [-n] hoe **hacken** hoe
der Hammer [╌] hammer (**der Nagel** [╌] nail) **hämmern/**
  ***schlagen in** + A hammer into
die Harke [-n] rake **harken** rake (**zusammen|harken** rake up)
der Hobel [-] plane **hobeln** plane
der Holzhammer [╌]; **der Schlegel** [-] mallet ***schlagen** hit
die Leiter [-n] ladder (**die Stehleiter** step-ladder) ***steigen**
  auf + A climb up
der Lötkolben [-] soldering-iron (**das Lot** solder) **löten** solder
der Mähdrescher [-] combine harvester **ernten** harvest
die Maschine [-n] machine **be'nutzen** use
der Meißel [-] chisel **meißeln** chisel
die Nadel [-n] needle (**der Faden** [╌] thread; **der Fingerhut** [╌e]
  thimble) **flicken; aus|bessern** mend; **stopfen** darn
die Nähmaschine [-n] sewing-machine (**der Stich** [-e] stitch [in
  sewing]) **nähen** sew
die Pflanzkelle [-n] garden trowel ***aus|graben** dig up
der Pflug [╌e] plough **pflügen** plough

der Pinsel [-] paintbrush ***an|streichen** [houses]; **malen** [pictures] paint

der Preßluftbohrer [-] pneumatic drill ***auf|brechen** break up

der Rasenmäher [-] lawn-mower **mähen** mow

die Reißzwecke [-n] drawing-pin ***an|schlagen** pin up

die Säge [-n] saw **sägen** saw (**durch|-/um|sägen** saw in two/down)

das Sandpapier sandpaper **schmirgeln** sand down

die Schaufel [-n] shovel **schaufeln** shovel

die Schere [-n] (pair of) scissors (**die Heckenschere** garden shears) ***schneiden** cut; clip

der Schlauch [¨e] garden hose **be'spritzen** spray

der Schraubenschlüssel [-] spanner (**die Schraube** [-n] [threaded] bolt; **die Mutter** [¨n] nut) **lösen** loosen; ***an|ziehen** tighten

der Schraubenzieher [-] screwdriver (**die Schraube** [-n] screw) **schrauben** (**an** + A) screw (to) (**ab|-/los|schrauben** unscrew)

der Schraubstock [¨e] vice ***halten** hold

der Schubkarren [-] wheelbarrow ***tragen** carry

die Sense [-n] scythe **mähen; ab|mähen** mow

die Sichel [-n] sickle ***schneiden** cut; reap

der Spaten spade ***graben** dig

die Spitzhacke [-n] pick ***auf|brechen** break up

das Stemmeisen [-] (wood) chisel **stemmen** chisel [wood]

die Stricknadel [-n] knitting-needle (**die Masche** [-n] stitch [in knitting]; **der/das Knäuel** [-] ball [of wool]; **die Wolle** wool) **stricken** knit

der Trichter funnel ***aus|gießen** pour out

der Wagenheber [-] jack **auf|bocken** jack up

die Wasserwaage [-n]; **die Libelle** [-n] spirit-level **gerade machen** straighten

der Webstuhl [¨e] loom ***weben** weave

das Werkzeug [-e] tool **reparieren** repair

die Zange [-n] (pair of) pliers; (pair of) tongs ***biegen** bend

SEE ALSO: **Cooking and Eating** (for kitchen equipment); **Health and Sickness** (for medical equipment); **The Home** (for household equipment); **Jobs; Materials**

53. Towns Städte

Siedlungen Settlements

der Bezirk [-e] district; area
das Dorf [:er] village
die Großstadt [:e] city (**die Kleinstadt** small town)
die Hafenstadt [:e]; der Hafen [:] port
die Hauptstadt [:e] capital
die Metropole [-n] metropolis
das Nest [-er] tiny little place
der Ort [-e] place (**der Marktort** market town)
die Stadt [:e] town; city (**in die Stadt** to town; **in der Stadt** in town)
der Stadtteil [-e]; das (Stadt)viertel [-] district; part of town
die Vorstadt [:e] suburb (**in der Vorstadt** in the suburbs)
der Weiler [-] hamlet
das Wohngebiet [-e]; die Wohngegend [-en] residential area (**das Industriegebiet [-e]** industrial zone)

In der Stadt In town

der Abwasserkanal [:e] sewer
die Allee [-n] avenue
der botanische Garten [:] botanical gardens
die Brücke [-n] bridge
der Bürgersteig [-e] pavement
die Bushaltestelle [-n] bus-stop
das Denkmal [:er] monument (**das Kriegerdenkmal** war memorial)
die Einkaufspassage [-n] shopping arcade
das Einkaufszentrum [*pl* -zentren] shopping mall
die Fahrbahn [-en] carriageway
der Festplatz [:e] fairground (**der Jahrmarkt [:e]** fair)
der Flughafen [:e] airport

der Friedhof [≃e] cemetery (**das Grab** [≃er] grave)
der Fußgängerüberweg [-e] pedestrian crossing
die Fußgängerzone [-n] pedestrian precinct
die Gasse [-n] lane; narrow street
die Geschäftsstraße [-n] shopping street
die Grünanlagen *f pl* gardens
der Hafen [≃] harbour
das Hochschulgelände [-] university campus
die Kreuzung [-en] crossroads
die Lichtreklame [-n] neon sign
der Markt [≃e] market (**der Marktplatz** [≃e] market-place; **der
  Stand** [≃e] stall; **die Markthalle** [-n] market hall)
das Messegelände [-] exhibition centre/site
die öffentliche Anlage [-n] public garden; park
die öffentliche Toilette [-n]; **die Bedürfnisanstalt** [-en] public
  convenience
der Park [-s] park
der Parkplatz [≃e] car-park; parking-space (**die Parkuhr** [-en]
  parking-meter; **die Parkscheibe** [-n] parking-disc; **die Park-
  kralle** [-n] wheel-clamp)
das Pflaster road surface (**das Kopfsteinpflaster** cobble-stones)
das Plakat [-e] poster
der Platz [≃e] square
der Radweg [-e] cycle-track
die Ringstraße [-n] ring road (**die Umgehungsstraße** bypass)
der Rinnstein [-e] gutter
die Ruinen *f pl* ruins
die Sackgasse [-n] dead-end street; cul-de-sac
das Schwimmbad [≃er] swimming-pool
die Sehenswürdigkeit [-en] place of interest; *pl* the sights
der Springbrunnen [-] fountain
die Stadtautobahn [-en] urban motorway
die Stadtbahn [-en] urban railway
die Stadtmauer [-n] town wall(s)
die Stadtmitte [-n]; **das (Stadt)zentrum** [*pl* -zentren]; **die
  Innenstadt; die City** town/city centre (**die Altstadt** the old town;

der **Stadtrand** *sing*; die **Außenbezirke** *m pl* the outskirts; die
Umgebung [-en] surrounding area)
der **Stadtplan** [ẍe] street map
das **Stadttor** [-e] town gate
die **Statue** [-n] statue
die **Straße** [-n] street; road (die **Hauptstraße** high street; main
road; die **Einbahn-/Einkaufs-/Fußgängerstraße** one-way/shop-
ping/pedestrian street)
die **Straßenbahnhaltestelle** [-n] tram stop
die **Straßenecke** [-n] street corner
die **Straßenlampe** [-n]; die **Straßenlaterne** [-n] street lamp
die **Straßenüberführung** [-en] footbridge (die **Straßenunter-
führung** subway)
der **Taxistand** [ẍe] taxi-rank
die **U-Bahn-Station** [-en]; der **U-Bahnhof** underground station
der **Umzug** [ẍe] procession; demonstration
der **Verkehr** traffic (die **Verkehrsstockung** [-en] traffic jam; die
Verkehrsampel [-n] traffic-light; die **Verkehrsinsel** [-n] traffic
island; das **Verkehrszeichen** [-]; das **Straßenschild** [-er] road
sign; der **Wegweiser** [-] signpost)
der **Wall** [ẍe] rampart(s)
das **Wartehäuschen** [-] bus-shelter
der **Zoo** [-s] zoo

Stadtbauten Town buildings

die **Abtei** [-en] abbey
das **Arbeitsamt** [ẍer] job centre
der **Bahnhof** [ẍe] railway-station (der **Hauptbahnhof** main
railway station; der **Busbahnhof** bus/coach station)
die **Börse** [-n] stock exchange
die **Botschaft** [-en] embassy
die **Bücherei** [-en] library (**öffentlich** public)
das **Bürogebäude** [-] office-block
der **Dom** [-e]; das **Münster** [-] cathedral
die **Fabrik** [-en] factory
die **Feuerwache** [-n] fire station (die **Feuerwehr** [-en] fire brigade)

das Gebäude [-]; **der Bau** [*pl* **Bauten**] building

das Gefängnis [-se] prison

der Gerichtshof law courts

das Haus [﹖er] house; building (**das Hochhaus** high-rise building; tower block)

das Hotel [-s] hotel

das Jugendzentrum [*pl* -zentren] youth centre

die Kaserne [-n] barracks

das Kaufhaus [﹖er] department store

das Kino [-s] cinema

der Kiosk [-e] kiosk

die Kirche [-n] church; [Nonconformist] chapel (**der Kirchturm** [﹖e] tower; steeple)

das Konsulat [-e] consulate

die Konzerthalle [-n] concert hall

das Krankenhaus [﹖er]; **die Klinik** [-en] hospital

die Kunstgalerie [-n] art gallery (**die Malerei** [art of] painting; **die Bildhauerei** [art of] sculpture)

die Moschee [-n] mosque

das Museum [*pl* **Museen**] museum

das Nonnenkloster [﹖] convent (**die Nonne** [-n] nun; **das Kloster** monastery; **der Mönch** [-e] monk)

die Oper [-n]; **das Opernhaus** [﹖er] opera-house

der Palast [﹖e] palace

das Parkhaus [﹖er] multi-storey car-park (**die Tiefgarage** [-n] underground car-park)

das Planetarium [*pl* **Planetarien**] planetarium

die Polizeiwache [-n]; **das Polizeirevier** [-e] police station (**das Polizeipräsidium** police headquarters)

die Post [-en]; **das Postamt** [﹖er] post office

das Rathaus [﹖er] town hall (**der Stadtrat** [﹖e] town council(lor))

der Schlachthof [﹖e] abattoir

das Schloß [﹖sser] castle; mansion; palace (**die Burg** [-en] [fortified] castle)

der soziale Wohnungsbau council housing (**die Sozialwohnung** [-en] council flat)

die Spielhalle [-n] amusement arcade

das Stadion [*pl* **Stadien**] stadium
die Synagoge [**-n**] synagogue
das Theater [**-**] theatre (**das Theaterstück** [**-e**] play)
der Turm [ˬe] tower
das Verkehrsamt [ˬer]; **das (Fremden)verkehrsbüro** [**-s**] tourist
  information office
der Wohnblock [*pl* ˬe or **-s**] block of flats (**der Wohnkomplex** [**-e**]
  housing complex; **die Wohnsiedlung** [**-en**] housing estate)
der Wolkenkratzer [**-**] skyscraper

Die Einwohner The inhabitants

der/die Autofahrer/in [**-/-nen**] car-driver
der/die Berliner/in [**-/-nen**] etc. Berliner etc.
die Bevölkerung population
der/die Bürger/in [**-/-nen**] citizen (**der/die Staatsbürger/in** citizen
  of a country; national)
der/die Bürgermeister/in [**-/-nen**] mayor
der/die Dorfbewohner/in [**-/-nen**] villager
der/die Einwohner/in [**-/-nen**] inhabitant
der/die Fußgänger/in [**-/-nen**] pedestrian
der/die Großstädter/in [**-/-nen**] city-dweller
der/die Kleinstädter/in [**-/-nen**] small-town dweller
der/die Passant/in [**-en/-nen**] passer-by
der/die Stadtbewohner/in [**-/-nen**]; **der/die Städter/in** [**-/-nen**]
  town-/city-dweller
der/die Stadtstreicher/in [**-/-nen**] tramp; down-and-out
der/die Tourist/in [**-en/-nen**] tourist
der/die Vorstädter/in [**-/-nen**] suburbanite

Was man dort tut What you do there

als Fremdenführer/in dienen act as guide
beeindruckt *sein be impressed
be'suchen visit
bummeln stroll about (**einen Stadt-/Fensterbummel machen** take
  a stroll round town; go window-shopping)

die Sehenswürdigkeiten be'sichtigen see the sights
eine Stadtrundfahrt machen take a tour of the city
sich ver'irren; sich *ver'laufen [on foot]; **sich *ver'fahren** [in car]
  get lost
***vorbei|gehen an** + D go past
über'queren cross
wohnen live
zeigen show

SEE ALSO: **Art and Architecture; Cooking and Eating; Places,
  People, and Languages; Post and Telephone; Shops and
  Shopping; Transport**

54. Transport Verkehrsmittel

der Fahrgast [ːe]; **der Passagier** [-e] passenger
die Fahrt [-en] trip; journey
das Fahrzeug [-e] vehicle (**das Motorfahrzeug; das Kraftfahrzeug**
  motor vehicle)
die Reise [-n] journey (**eine Reise machen** go on a journey)
der/die Reisende *adj n* traveller; passenger
das Reiseziel [-e] destination
das Verkehrsmittel [-] (means of) transport (**die öffentlichen
  Verkehrsmittel** public transport)

*fahren; reisen travel (**links/rechts fahren** drive on the left/right;
  sich *ver'fahren go the wrong way; **Schritt fahren!** dead slow!)

Verkehrsmittel der Straße Road transport

AUTOS CARS
der Anhänger [-] trailer
das Auto [-s]; **der Wagen** [-] car (**mit dem Auto** by car; **die
  Automarke** [-n] make of car; **der/die Autofahrer/in** [-/-nen]
  motorist)
der Campingbus [-se]; **das Wohnmobil** [-e] camper
der Firmenwagen [-] company car
der Führerschein [-e] driving-licence (**die Fahrprüfung** [-en]
  driving test; **die Fahrschule** [-n] driving school; **die Fahrstunde**
  [-n] driving lesson)
der Gebrauchtwagen [-] used car
das Kabrio [-s]; **das Kabriolett** [-s] convertible
die Klapperkiste [-n] banger
der Kombi [-s]; **der Kombiwagen** [-] estate car
die Limousine [-n] saloon car
der Miet-/Leihwagen [-] hire-car
das Modell [-e] model (**die Marke** [-n]; **das Fabrikat** [-e] make)

der Pkw; der PKW [G and *pl* - or -s] [= **Personenkraftwagen**]
(private) car
der Rennwagen [-] racing car
der Sportwagen [-] sports car
das Taxi [-s]; **die Taxe** [-n] taxi
der Wohnwagen [-]; **der Wohnanhänger** [-]; **der Caravan** [-s]
caravan

MOTOR- UND FAHRRÄDER
MOTOR CYCLES AND BICYCLES

der Beiwagen [-] side-car
das Fahrrad [¨er]; **das Rad** [¨er] bicycle (**mit dem Rad** by bike;
der/die Radfahrer/in [-/-nen] cyclist)
das Mofa [-s] (low-powered) moped
das Moped [-s] moped
das Motorrad [¨er] motor cycle (**der/die Motorradfahrer/in** [-/-nen]
motor-cyclist; **der Beifahrer-/Soziussitz** [-e] pillion)
das Radfahren; der Radsport cycling
die Radtour [-en] cycle ride
der Radweg [-e] cycle-track
der Roller/Motorroller [-] (motor) scooter

auf das Rad *auf|steigen get on
auf|pumpen pump up
ein Loch flicken mend a puncture
im Freilauf *fahren freewheel
klingeln ring the bell
radeln; *rad|fahren cycle
vom Rad *ab|steigen get off

LASTWAGEN USW. LORRIES ETC.
der Abschleppwagen [-] breakdown lorry
der Anhänger [-] trailer
der Bulldozer [-]; **die Planierraupe** [-n] bulldozer
das Feuerwehrauto [-s] fire-engine
der Jeep® [-s] jeep®
der Karren [-] cart

der Kinderwagen [-] pram
der Krankenwagen [-] ambulance
der Lastwagen [-]; **der LKW**; **der Lkw** [G and *pl* - or -s]
 [= **Lastkraftwagen**] lorry (**der Schwerlastwagen** heavy goods
 vehicle; **der Lastzug** [≈e] lorry with trailer(s))
der Lieferwagen [-] van
der Möbelwagen [-] removal van
der Sattelschlepper [-] articulated lorry
der Tankwagen [-] tanker
der Traktor [G -s *pl* -en] tractor
der Transporter [-] goods vehicle

DIE TEILE EINES FAHRZEUGS
THE PARTS OF A VEHICLE

die Achse [-n] axle
der Anlasser [-]; **der Starter** [-] starter (***an|springen** start)
die Antenne [-n] aerial
das Armaturenbrett [-er] dashboard
der Auspuff *no pl* exhaust (**das Auspuffrohr** [-e] exhaust-pipe; **der
 Auspufftopf** [≈e]; **der Schalldämpfer** [-] silencer)
der Außenspiegel [-] wing mirror
das Autoradio [-s] car radio
die Batterie [-n] battery (**leer** flat)
der Benzinkanister [-] petrol can
die Benzinuhr [-en] fuel gauge
die Birne/Glühbirne [-n] bulb
der Blinker [-]; **der Richtungsanzeiger** [-] indicator (**blinken**
 indicate)
die Bremse [-n] brake (**die Scheibenbremse** disc brake; **die
 Handbremse** handbrake; **der Bremsbelag** [≈e] brake lining; **die
 Bremsflüssigkeit** brake fluid)
das Chassis [-]; **das Fahrgestell** [-e] chassis
der Choke [-s] choke
der Dachgepäckträger [-] roof-rack
das Ersatzteil [-e] spare (part)
die Federung suspension

das Fenster [-] window

der Feuerlöscher [-] fire-extinguisher

der Gang [ⁿe] gear (**einen Gang ein|legen** engage a gear; **der Rückwärtsgang** reverse; **der Leerlauf** neutral; **der Schalthebel** [-] gear-lever)

das Getriebe [-] transmission (**das Schalt-/Automatikgetriebe** manual/automatic transmission; **der Getriebekasten** [ⁿ] gear-box)

das Heck [*pl* -e or -s] back (of the car) (**der Heckmotor** [G -s *pl* -en] rear engine; **die Heckscheibe** [-n] rear window; **die Heckklappe** [-n] hatchback)

die Heizung heating

die Hupe [-n] horn (**die Lichthupe** headlight flasher; **die Lichthupe be'tätigen** flash)

die Karosserie bodywork

der Keilriemen [-] fan-belt

der Kilometerzähler [-]; **der Wegmesser** [-] milometer

der Kofferraum [ⁿe] boot

der Kotflügel [-] wing

der Kühler [-] radiator (**leck** leaking)

die Kupplung [-en] clutch

das Lenk-/Steuerrad [ⁿer] steering-wheel

das Licht [-er] light (**ein|-/aus|schalten** switch on/off)

die Lichtmaschine [-n] alternator

die Linkssteuerung left-hand drive (**die Rechtssteuerung** right-hand drive)

der Luftfilter [-] air filter (**der Ölfilter** oil filter)

der Meßstab [ⁿe] dip-stick

der Motor [G -s *pl* -en] engine (**der Motorraum** engine compartment; **die Motorhaube** [-n] bonnet; **der Motorlärm** engine noise; **der Motorschaden** engine trouble)

das Nummernschild [-er] number-plate

der Öl(stands)anzeiger [-] oil-gauge

das Pedal [-e] pedal (**das Gaspedal** accelerator)

das Rad [ⁿer] wheel (**das Vorder-/Hinter-/Ersatzrad** front/rear/spare wheel; **wechseln** change; **die Radkappe** [-n] hub-cap; **die Nabe** [-n] hub)

der Reifen [-] tyre (**der Reifenschaden** [≈]; *colloq* **der Platte** *adj n*
puncture; **platt** flat; **platzen** burst; **der Schlauch** [≈e] inner tube;
der Reifendruck tyre pressure; **prüfen** check; **das Reifenprofil**
tread)

das Rücklicht [-er] rear-light

der Rücksitz [-e] back seat

der Rückspiegel [-] rear mirror

der Schalthebel [-] gear-lever

der Scheinwerfer [-] headlight (**der Nebelscheinwerfer** fog-light;
der Rückfahrscheinwerfer reversing light)

das Schiebedach [≈er] sliding roof

das Schloß [≈sser] lock (**die Zentralverriegelung** central locking)

der Schmutzfänger [-] mud-flap

die Schneekette [-n] snow-chain

der Sicherheitsgurt [-e] seat-belt

die Sicherung [-en] fuse (***durch|brennen** blow)

der Sitz [-e] seat (**der Vorder-/Hintersitz** front/rear seat)

das Standlicht [-er] sidelight(s) (**mit Standlicht *fahren** drive on
sidelights)

der Stoßdämpfer [-] shock absorber

die Stoßstange [-n] bumper

der/das Tachometer; der Geschwindigkeitsmesser speedometer

der Tank [*pl* -s or -e] tank (**das Benzin** petrol; **es ist mir
ausgegangen** I've run out)

der Tankanzeiger [-] fuel gauge

der Tankverschluß [≈e] petrol-cap

die Tür [-en] door

das Ventil [-e] valve

das Verdeck [-e] hood (**mit offenem Verdeck *fahren** drive with
the top down)

der Vergaser [-] carburettor

der Verteiler [-] distributor

der Vorderradantrieb front-wheel drive (**der Hinterradantrieb**
rear-wheel drive)

der Wagenheber [-] jack

der Warnblinker hazard warning lights

das Warndreieck [-e] hazard warning triangle

die **Warnlampe** [-n] warning light
die **Windschutzscheibe** [-n] windscreen (der **Scheibenwischer** [-]
 windscreen-wiper; die **Scheibenwaschanlage** screen wash)
die **Zündkerze** [-n] spark-plug
die **Zündung** ignition (der **Zündschlüssel** [-] ignition key; das
 Zündschloß [⁼sser] ignition lock)
der **Zündverteiler** [-] distributor (der **Kontakt** [-e] point)

DIE TEILE EINES RADES PARTS OF A CYCLE

der **Dynamo** [-s] dynamo
das **Flickzeug** [-e] repair kit
der **Gepäckträger** [-] luggage rack
die **Kette** [-n] chain
die **Klingel** [-n] bell
die **Lampe** [-n] lamp
die **Lenkstange** [-n] (pair of) handlebars
die **Motorradbrille** [-n] (pair of) goggles
das **Pedal** [-e] pedal
die **Pumpe** [-n] pump
das **Rad** [⁼er] cycle; wheel (der **Radkranz** [⁼e] wheel rim)
der **Rahmen** [-] frame
der **Rückstrahler** [-] reflector
der **Sattel** [⁼] saddle (die **Satteltasche** [-n] saddle-bag)
das **Schutzblech** [-e] mudguard
die **Speiche** [-n] spoke
die **Stange** [-n] crossbar
das **Vorderlicht** [-er] front light (das **Rücklicht** rear light)
der **Zweitaktmotor** [G -s *pl* -en]; der **Zweitakter** [-] two-stroke
 (engine)

AUF DER STRASSE ON THE ROAD

der **Abschleppwagen** [-] breakdown vehicle
der **Abstand** [⁼e] distance (**Abstand *halten** keep one's distance)
die **Abzweigung** [-en] fork; turning
die **Ampel/Verkehrsampel)**[-n] traffic light (das **Rot-/Gelb-/
 Grünlicht** [⁼er] red/amber/green light; ***über'fahren** shoot; go

through; **bei Rot** on red; **die Bedarfsampel** pedestrian-controlled light)

der Anlieger [-] local resident (**Anlieger frei** access only)

die Autobahn [-en] motorway (**das Autobahnkreuz [-e]** motorway intersection; **die Anschlußstelle [-n]** junction; **die Ein-/Ausfahrt [-en]** entrance/exit)

die Auto-/Straßenkarte [-n] road map

die Autoschlange [-n] queue of cars

der Bahnübergang [ᵂe] level crossing

das Bankett [-e]; die Bankette [-n] verge; shoulder (**Bankette nicht befahrbar** keep off verge)

die Bundesstraße [-n] = A road (**die Landstraße** = B road)

der Bürgersteig [-e] pavement

die Einbahnstraße [-n] one-way street

die Fahrschule [-n] driving school

die Fahrzeugpapiere *n pl* vehicle documents

der Führerschein [-e] driving-licence (**vor|zeigen** show)

der Fußgängerüberweg [-e] pedestrian crossing

die Garage [-n] garage (**die Tiefgarage** underground car-park)

die Gebühr/Straßengebühr [-en]; die Maut [-en] toll

die Geschwindigkeit [-en] speed (**das Tempolimit [-s]; die Geschwindigkeitsbeschränkung [-en]** speed limit; ***über'schreiten** exceed; break)

das Glatteis black ice

das Halteschild [-er] stop sign

die Hauptverkehrs-/Stoßzeit rush-hour

die Kreuzung [-en] crossroads

die Kurve [-n]; die Biegung [-en]; die Windung [-en] bend

der Mittelstreifen [-] central reservation

die Notbremsung [-en] emergency stop

die Notrufsäule [-n] emergency telephone point

die Panne [-n] breakdown (**die Reifenpanne** puncture; **eine Panne *haben** break down)

das Parkhaus [ᵂer]; die Hochgarage [-n] multi-storey car-park

der Parkplatz [ᵂe] car-park; parking-space

das Parkverbot ban on parking (**das Halteverbot** ban on stopping; **im Parkverbot *stehen** be parked illegally; **das Park-/**

Halteverbotsschild [-er] no-parking/no-stopping sign; **die Parkscheibe** [-n] parking-disc; **die Parkuhr** [-en] parking-meter)

die Querstraße [-n] junction; turning

der Rasthof [⁼e] service area with motel

der Rastplatz [⁼e] lay-by; rest area

die Raststätte [-n] service area

die Reiseroute [-n] route

die Reparaturwerkstatt [⁼en] service garage (**der/die Mechaniker/in** [-/-nen] mechanic; **reparieren** repair)

die Ringstraße [-n] ring road

der Scheinwerfer [-] headlight (**ab|blenden** dip; **auf|blenden** switch to full beam; **mit Abblendlicht *fahren** drive on dipped headlights)

das Schlagloch [⁼er] pot-hole

die Sichtweite visibility

die Spur [-en] lane (**die Stand-/Kriechspur** hard shoulder/crawler lane)

der Stau [*pl* -s or -e] traffic jam

die Steuerplakette [-n] tax disc

das Stoppschild [-er] stop sign

der Strafzettel [-] parking-/speeding-ticket

die Straße [-n] street; road (**die Hauptstraße** main road; **die Seiten-/Nebenstraße** side road)

die Straßenbauarbeiten *f pl*; [on sign] **Baustelle** *f sing* road-works

die Straßenkarte [-n] road-map

das Straßenschild [-er] road sign

die Straßenverkehrsordnung highway code

die Straßenwachthilfe recovery service

die Tankstelle [-n] petrol station (**der Tankwart** [-e] petrol pump attendant; **die (Zapf)säule** [-n] pump; **SB** [= **die Selbstbedienung**] self-service; **der Kraftstoff** fuel; **das Benzin** petrol; **das Super** four-star; **bleifrei** unleaded; **der Diesel** diesel; **das Öl** [-e] oil; **der Ölwechsel** oil-change; **die (Druck)luft** (compressed) air; **das Kühlwasser** radiator water; **das Gefrierschutz-/Frostschutzmittel** antifreeze; **kontrollieren** check)

die Überführung [-en]; **der Fly-over** [-s] fly-over

die Umgehungsstraße [-n] bypass

die Umleitung [-en] diversion
der Umweg [-e] detour
der Verkehr traffic (**der Durchgangs-/Gegenverkehr** through/
  oncoming traffic; **der Verkehrsunfall [∺e]** traffic/road accident)
der Verkehrskreisel [-] roundabout
das Verkehrszeichen [-] road sign
die Vorfahrt *no pl* priority (**Vorfahrt *lassen** + D/***haben** give
  way to/have right of way; **Vorfahrt beachten!** give way!)
die Waschanlage [-n]; die Waschstraße [-n] car-wash
der Weg [-e] road; way (**unterwegs** on the way)
der Wegweiser [-] signpost
die Wende [-n] (um 180°) U-turn
die Zufahrtsstraße [-n] access road

erlaubt; gestattet permitted
gefährlich dangerous
gesperrt closed (**gesperrte Straße** road closed)
langsam slow
obligatorisch compulsory
verboten; untersagt prohibited

DIE LEUTE, DENEN MAN BEGEGNET
THE PEOPLE YOU MEET
der/die Anhalter/in [-/-nen]; der/die Tramper/in [-/-nen] hitch-
  hiker
der/die Autofahrer/in [-/-nen] motorist (**der/die Fahrer/in** driver)
der/die Chauffeur/in [-e/-nen] driver; chauffeur
der/die Fahrlehrer/in [-/-nen] driving instructor (**der/die
  Fahrschüler/in [-/-nen]** learner-driver)
der/die Fußgänger/in [-/-nen] pedestrian
der/die Kilometerfresser/in [-/-nen]; der Verkehrsrowdy [-s] road-
  hog
der/die Lkw-Fahrer/in [-/-nen] lorry driver
der Mechaniker [-] mechanic
der/die Mitfahrer/in [-/-nen] passenger
der/die Motorradfahrer/in [-/-nen] motor-cyclist

die Politesse [-n] traffic warden
der/die Polizist/in [-en/-nen] policeman/woman
der/die Radfahrer/in [-/-nen] cyclist
der/die Reisende *adj n* traveller
der/die Sonntagsfahrer/in [-/-nen] Sunday driver
der/die Verkehrspolizist/in [-en/-nen] traffic policeman/-woman

WAS MAN TUT WHAT YOU DO

*ab|biegen turn off
*ab|schließen lock
an|schalten switch on (**ab|schalten** switch off)
*an|schieben give a push
sich an|schnallen put on your seat belt
*an|springen start [of engine]
sich auf den Weg machen set off
*auf|fahren auf + A drive into the back of
auf|prallen auf + A collide with
be'schleunigen accelerate
bremsen brake
eine Panne *haben break down
sich ein|ordnen get in lane
*fahren in + A crash into
Gas *n* ***geben** put your foot down
*halten; *an|halten stop
*heiß|laufen run hot
hupen sound the horn
in Ordnung *f* ***bringen** fix
krachen crash
langsamer *fahren slow down
mieten hire
mit X Stundenkilometern *fahren drive at X kilometres an hour
motorisieren motorize
parken park
reparieren repair
rückwärts *fahren (in + A) reverse (into)
schalten change gear

schleppen; ab|schleppen tow
schleudern; schlittern skid
starten start (up); start the engine
***stehen|bleiben** stall
stoppen stop
trampen; per Anhalter *fahren hitch-hike
über'holen overtake
über'prüfen check
über'queren cross
sich ver'irren get lost
voll|tanken fill up
warten service
wenden do a U-turn
***zusammen|fahren mit** + D collide with

Andere Verkehrsmittel
Other means of transport

EISENBAHNEN RAILWAYS
die Abfahrt [-en] departure
die Ankunft [⸗e] arrival
der Anschluß [⸗sse] connection
die Anzeigetafel [-n] train indicator
die Auskunft information (office)
die Bahn railway; tram (**mit der Bahn** by rail; by tram)
der Bahndamm [⸗e] (railway) embankment
der Bahnhof [⸗e] station (**auf dem Bahnhof** at the station)
die Bahnhofsgaststätte [-n] station buffet
die Bahnhofshalle [-n] station concourse
der/die Bahnhofsvorsteher/in [-/-nen] station-master; station
  supervisor
der Bahnsteig [-e] platform (**die Bahnsteigkarte [-n]** platform
  ticket)
der Bahnübergang [⸗e] level crossing
der Bahnwärter [-] signalman; level-crossing keeper (**das
  Stellwerk [-e]** signal-box)

die Brücke [-n] bridge
die Bundesbahn German Railways
der Einschnitt [-e] cutting
die Eisenbahn [-en] railway
der Eisenbahner [-] railwayman
die Fahrkarte [-n]; **der Fahrschein** [-e] ticket (**die einfache
Fahrkarte** single; **die Rückfahrkarte** return; **die Wochen-/
Monatskarte** [-n] weekly/monthly season; **lösen** buy [ticket];
zweimal einfach nach + D two singles to . . . ; **nach** + D (**hin**)
und zurück return to . . . ; **(un)gültig** (not) valid; **der Zuschlag**
[ː e] supplement; **zuschlagpflichtig** supplement payable; **zum
halben Preis** half price)
der Fahrkartenautomat [-en] ticket machine
der/die Fahrkartenkontrolleur/in [-e/-nen] ticket collector; ticket
inspector
der Fahrkartenschalter [-] ticket office
der Fahrplan [ː e] timetable (**werktags** Monday to Saturday;
Sonn- und Feiertage Sundays and public holidays; **über** + A
via)
der Fahrpreis [-e] [price]; **das Fahrgeld** [money] fare (**der
ermäßigte Fahrpreis** reduced rate)
der Fernverkehr main-line services (**der Vorortsverkehr** suburban
services; **der Fern-/Vorortsbahnhof** main-line/suburban station)
das Fundbüro [-s] lost-property office
das Gepäck luggage (**die Gepäckaufbewahrung** left-luggage; **das
Schließfach** [ː er] left-luggage locker; **die Gepäckannahme**
baggage check-in; **die Gepäckausgabe** baggage reclaim)
das Gleis [-e] track (**die Weiche** [-n] (set of) points; **die Schwelle** [-n]
sleeper)
die Haltestelle [-n] stop
der Kofferkuli [-s] luggage trolley
die Reservierung [-en] reservation (**die Platzreservierung** seat-
reservation (office))
die Richtung [-en] (**nach** + D) direction (of)
der Schaffner [-] guard; ticket inspector
der Schalter [-] ticket window
die Schiene [-n] rail

die Seilbahn/Drahtseilbahn [-en]; die Schwebebahn [-en] cable railway **(die Sesselbahn** chair-lift)

das Signal [-e] signal **(halt** red; **freie Fahrt** green)

die Sperre [-n] [on station]; **die Schranke** [of level crossing] barrier

die Strecke [-n] line; track **(das Streckennetz [-e]** network)

der Träger/Gepäckträger [-] porter

der Tunnel [-] tunnel

die Unterführung [-en] subway

die Verbindung [-en] connection

das/der Viadukt [-e] viaduct

der Wartesaal [-säle] waiting-room

der Zeitungsstand [¨e] news-stand

*ab|fahren depart [train]

*an|kommen arrive

*aus|steigen (aus + D) get out (of)

den Zug *nehmen take the train

einen Speisewagen führen have a dining-car

*ein|fahren pull in [to station]

*ein|steigen (in + A) get in(to)

ent'werten cancel; validate [ticket]

er'reichen catch

*halten stop

lochen; knipsen punch

mit dem Zug *fahren travel by train

reservieren *lassen reserve

*um|steigen change (trains)

ver'kehren run [of train etc.]

ver'passen miss [train etc.]

Verspätung *f* ***haben** be late

vom Bahnhof ab|holen meet at the station

zum Bahnhof *bringen take to the station

durchgehend through

planmäßig on schedule

pünktlich on time

verspätet late

LOKOMOTIVEN UND ZÜGE
ENGINES AND TRAINS

der Autoreisezug [¨e] motor-rail (train)
der EuroCity [-s] international fast train
der EuroCity-Express [*pl* **-Expresszüge**] international express
der Güterzug [¨e] goods train (**der Zug im Personenverkehr**
  passenger train)
der InterCity [-s] inter-city fast train
der InterCity-Express [*pl* **-Expresszüge**] inter-city express
die Lok [-s]; **die Lokomotive** [-n] engine (**der Lok(omotiv)führer** [-]
  engine-driver; **die Dampflok** steam engine; **der Dieseltriebwa-**
  gen [-] diesel locomotive)
die Standseilbahn [-en] funicular
der TEE [*pl* - or -s] [= **Trans-Europ-Express**] TEE
der Triebwagen [-] railcar
der Zug [¨e] train (**der Schnellzug** express; **der D-Zug**
  [= **Durchgangszug**] fast train; **der Eilzug** stopping train; **der**
  Nahverkehrs-/Personenzug slow train; local; **der Vorort(s)zug**
  suburban train; **der Zug mit Schiffsanschluß** boat-train)

IM ZUG IN THE TRAIN

das Abteil [-e] compartment (**das Dienstabteil** guard's compartment; **der Gang** [¨e] corridor)
der Dienstwagen [-] guard's van
das Gepäck luggage (**das Gepäcknetz** [-e] luggage rack)
der Güterwagen [-] goods wagon
die Klasse [-n] class (**erster/zweiter Klasse** first/second class)
der Kopf front (of train) (**das Ende** back)
der Kurswagen [-] through carriage
der Liegesitz [-e] couchette
die Notbremse [-n] emergency brake
der Platz [¨e] seat (**der Fensterplatz** window-seat; **reserviert**
  reserved)
der Schlafplatz [¨e] berth (**zurecht|machen** make up)
die Toilette [-n] toilet (**besetzt** occupied; **frei** vacant)

der Wagen carriage (**der (Nicht)raucherwagen** (non-)smoking
carriage; **der Schlaf-/Liege-/Speisewagen** sleeping-/couchette/
dining-car; **der Gepäckwagen** luggage-van)

FLUGZEUGE PLANES

die Abfertigung check-in (**der Abfertigungsschalter** [-] check-in
desk)

der Abflug [≃e] take-off

der Abstieg descent

die Ankunftshalle [-n] arrival lounge (**die Abflughalle** departure
lounge; **die Ankunfts-/Abflugtafel** [-n] arrivals/departure board)

der Aufruf [-e] (boarding) call

die Besatzung [-en] crew

das Bodenpersonal ground staff

die Bordkarte [-n] boarding-card (**an Bord *gehen** board)

das Charterflugzeug [-e] charter aircraft (**chartern** charter)

der Duty-free-Shop [-s] duty-free shop (**zollfrei** duty-free)

das Fahrwerk landing-gear

der Fallschirm [-e] parachute

der Flug [≃e] flight; flying (**der Rück-/Charter-/Linien-/Direktflug**
return/charter/scheduled/direct flight; **die Flugzeit** [-en] flying
time)

der Flügel [-] wing

der Fluggast [≃e] passenger [male or female]

der Flughafen [≃] airport

die Flughöhe [-n] altitude (**in einer Flughöhe von** + D at an
altitude of)

die Flugkarte [-n] ticket (**nicht termingebunden** open)

die Fluglinie [-n]; **die Fluggesellschaft** [-en] airline

der Fluglotse [-n] air-traffic controller (**die Flugsicherung** air
traffic control)

der Flugplatz [≃e] airfield

der Flugpreis [-e] air fare

der Flugsteig [-e]; **das Gate** [-s] (boarding-)gate

das Flugzeug [-e]; **die Maschine** [-n] plane (**das Düsenflugzeug** jet
plane; **der Jumbo-Jet** [-s] jumbo jet)

der Gangplatz [∺e] aisle seat (**der Fensterplatz** window seat)
die Geschwindigkeit [-en] speed
das Gepäck baggage (**das Handgepäck** hand baggage; **die Gepäckausgabe** baggage claim)
der Heißluftballon [-s] hot-air balloon
der Hijacker [-] hijacker
die Höhe [-n] altitude
der Hubschrauber [-] helicopter
die Kabine [-n] cabin
der Kontrollturm [∺e] control tower
die Landung [-en] landing (**zur Landung an|setzen** come in to land; **die Landebahn** [-en] landing runway; **die Landebahnfeuer** *n pl* runway lights; **die Notlandung** emergency landing)
das Luftkissenfahrzeug [-e] hovercraft
die Luftkrankheit airsickness
das Luftloch [∺er] air pocket
der Luftpirat [-en] hijacker
das Luftschiff [-e] airship
die Mannschaft [-en] crew
der Notausstieg [-e] emergency exit
die Paßkontrolle passport check
der/die Pilot/in [-en/-nen] pilot
der Propeller [-] propeller
der Radar radar
die Rakete [-n] rocket (***ab|schießen** launch)
der Raucherplatz [∺e] smoking seat (**der Nichtraucherplatz** no-smoking seat)
das Raumschiff [-e] spaceship
die Rollbahn [-en] taxi-way
der Rumpf [∺e] fuselage
die Schallmauer sound barrier (***durch'brechen** go through)
die Schalttafel *sing* controls
das Segelflugzeug [-e] glider
der Sicherheitsgurt [-e] seat-belt (**an|legen** fasten)
der Start [-s] take-off (**beim Start** at take-off; **die Startbahn** [-en] take-off runway)
der Steward [-s] steward (**die Stewardeß** [-ssen] stewardess)

der/das Terminal/Air-Terminal [-s] air terminal
die Turbulenz turbulence
Überschall- supersonic
das UFO/Ufo [-s] [= unbekanntes fliegendes Objekt] UFO (**die
fliegende Untertasse [-n]** flying saucer)
das Wasserflugzeug [-e] seaplane
der Windsack [ːe] windsock
der Zoll customs; duty (**der Zollbeamte [-n]/die Zollbeamtin [-nen]**
customs officer; **der Paß [ːsse]** passport; **durch'suchen** search;
durch'leuchten X-ray)
die Zwischenlandung [-en]; der Stopover [-s] stopover

ab|drehen turn
*ab|fliegen; starten take off
annulieren; stornieren cancel
sich an|schnallen fasten belts
be'stätigen confirm
ein|checken check in (**ab'fertigen** check [sb] in)
*fliegen fly
im Sturzflug *m* ***hinunter|gehen** nosedive
landen land (**im Bach landen** *colloq* ditch; **der Bach [ːe]**
stream)
*über'fliegen fly over
um|buchen change [flights]
zwischen|landen stopover

SCHIFFE SHIPS
der Anker [-] anchor
der Anlegeplatz [ːe]; die Anlegestelle [-n] embarkation point
das Backbord port (**das Steuerbord** starboard; **nach Back-/
Steuerbord** to port/starboard)
das Beiboot [-e] ship's boat
die Boje [-n] buoy
das Boot [-e] boat
die Boots-/Kreuzfahrt [-en] cruise (**die Flußfahrt** river cruise)
der Bug bow(s)
der Dampfer [-] steamer

das Deck [-s] deck (**an Deck** on deck; **das Bootsdeck** [-e] boat deck)

das Ding(h)i [-s] dinghy (**das Schlauchboot** [-e] inflatable dinghy)

das Dock [-s] dock

die Fähre [-n]; **das Fährboot** [-e] ferry (**die Autofähre** car ferry)

das Fahrgastschiff [-e] water-bus

die Flagge [-n] flag [on ship]

das Floß [ːe] raft

der Flugzeugträger [-] aircraft carrier

der Frachter [-]; **das Frachtschiff** [-e] freighter

die Gangway [-s] gangway

der Hafen [ː] harbour; port (**die Hafenrundfahrt** [-en] trip around the harbour)

das Heck [*pl* -e or -s] stern

das Hovercraft [-s]; **das Luftkissenfahrzeug** [-e] hovercraft

die Jacht [-en] yacht

die Kabine [-n] cabin (**die Doppelkabine** two-berth cabin)

der Kahn; **der Fracht-/Lastkahn** [ːe] barge

der Kai [-s] quay(side)

das Kanu [-s]; **das Paddelboot** [-e] canoe

die Kommandobrücke [-n] bridge

die Landungsbrücke [-n] jetty

der Landungssteg [-e] landing-stage

das Lotsenboot [-e] pilot boat (**der Lotse** [-n] pilot)

der Mast [G -(e)s; *pl* -en or -e] mast

das Motorboot [-e] motor boat (**der Motor** [G -s *pl* -en] engine)

der Ozeandampfer [-]; **das Linienschiff** [-e]; **der (Ozean)liner** [-] liner

die Reling [*pl* -s or -e] rail(ing)

das Rettungsboot [-e] lifeboat (**der Rettungsring** [-e] lifebelt; **das Rettungsfloß** [ːe] life-raft)

das Ruder [-] rudder; helm; oar

das Ruderboot [-e] rowing-boat

das Schiff [-e] ship (**das Motorschiff** power vessel; **das Segelschiff** sailing-ship)

der Schiffsarzt [ːe] ship's doctor

der Schlepper [-] tug

der Schornstein [-e] funnel
die Schwimmweste [-n] life-jacket
der Seemann [pl -leute]; [navy] der Matrose [-n] seaman
das Segelboot [-e] sailing-boat (**das Segel [-]** sail)
der Tanker [-] tanker
das Tragflügelboot [-e] hydrofoil
das Tretboot [-e] pedalo
die Überfahrt [-en] crossing
das U-Boot [= Unterseeboot] [-e] submarine

an Bord *gehen embark (**von Bord gehen** disembark)
an|legen berth
*aus|laufen; in See *gehen put to sea
aus|schiffen put ashore
aus|setzen; zu Wasser *lassen launch
ein|docken dock
eine Bootsfahrt machen go boating
ein|schiffen take on board
gelöscht *werden unload [ship]
*laden load
mit dem Schiff *fahren (nach + D) sail (to)
paddeln canoe
rudern row
segeln sail [a sailing-boat]
über|setzen ferry across
vor Anker m *gehen drop anchor (**den Anker lichten** weigh
  anchor)

BUSSE, STRASSEN- UND U-BAHN
BUSES, TRAMS, AND THE UNDERGROUND

die Bahn colloq/Straßenbahn [-en] tram
der Bus/Autobus [pl -busse] bus (**der Reisebus** coach; **mit dem Bus
  *fahren** go by bus)
der Busbahnhof [ᵉe] bus station
der Busfahrer [-] bus driver (**der Straßenbahnfahrer** tram driver)
die Bushaltestelle [-n] bus-stop (**die Straßenbahnhaltestelle** tram-
  stop; **die Bedarfshaltestelle** request stop)

die Dauer-/Zeitkarte [-n] season ticket (**die Monats-/Wochen-karte** monthly/weekly season; **die Netz-/Streifenkarte** rover/ multiple ticket)
der Einstieg [-e] entrance (**der Ausstieg** exit)
die Endstation [-en] terminus
der Fahrgast [¨e] passenger [male or female]
der Fahrschein [-e] ticket (**gültig bis** + A valid as far as/until; **der Nachtzuschlag [¨e]** night-time supplement; **die Zone [-n]** zone)
der Fahrscheinautomat [-en] ticket machine
das Fahrscheinheft [-e] book of tickets
die Häufigkeit frequency
der/die Kontrolleur/in [-e/-nen] inspector
die Linie [-n] line (**die Richtung [-en]** direction; **in Richtung Flughafen** to the airport)
die Rolltreppe [-n] escalator
die S-Bahn [-en] [= Stadt-Bahn] local train/network
der/die Schaffner/in [-/-nen] conductor; inspector
der/die Schwarzfahrer/in [-/-nen] fare-dodger
der Sitzplatz [¨e] seat (**der Stehplatz** standing place)
der Tarif [-e] (scale of) fares (**die Ermäßigung [-en]** reduction)
die Teilstrecke [-n]; die Zahlgrenze [-n] fare-stage
der Tunnel [*pl* - or -s] tunnel
die U-Bahn [-en] [= Untergrundbahn] underground; under-ground train
die U-Bahnstation [-en] underground station
die Verbindung [-en] connection
das Wartehäuschen [-] bus-shelter

*an|halten stop
ent'werten cancel; validate [ticket, in machine]
*schwarz|fahren travel without paying
ver'passen miss
vorne/hinten *sitzen sit at the front/back

TAXIS TAXIS
die Droschke [-n] cab (**die Pferdedroschke** horse-drawn cab)
der Fahrpreis [-e] fare

das Taxi [-s]; die Taxe [-n] taxi (**mit dem Taxi** by taxi)
der/die Taxifahrer/in [-/-nen] taxi-driver
die Taxifahrt [-en] taxi ride
der Taxistand [ːe] taxi-rank
das Trinkgeld [-er] tip

*bringen zu + D take (sb) to
frei *sein be free (**besetzt *sein** be taken)
*nehmen take
*rufen call
warten wait

SEE ALSO: **Accidents; Directions; Holidays; Towns; War, Peace, and the Armed Services**

55. War, Peace, and the Armed Services
Krieg, Frieden und die Streitkräfte

Krieg War

der Abzug [⁼e] evacuation; withdrawal
der Angriff [-e] attack (**durch|führen** launch; **der Gegenangriff** counter-attack; **der Bombenangriff** bombing raid)
die Anwerbung enlistment
die Aufklärung; die Erkundung reconnaissance
die Belagerung [-en] siege
die Besatzung occupation
der Beschuß bombardment
die Blockade [-n] blockade
die Bombardierung [-en] bombing
die Burg [-en] castle (**die Zinne** [-n] battlement)
der Deserteur [-e]; **der/die Fahnenflüchtige** *adj n* deserter
die Disziplin discipline
die Ehre honour
die Eroberung [-en] conquest
die Fahne [-n] flag
der/die Feind/in [-e/-nen] enemy
der Feldzug [⁼e] campaign
die Festung [-en] fortress
der Flüchtling [-e] refugee
die Folter [-n] torture
die Front [-en] front (**an die Front schicken** send to the front; **die Ostfront** the Eastern Front; **der Rücken** the rear)
das Gas [-e] gas (**das Tränen-/Giftgas** tear-/poison gas; **die Gasmaske** [-n] gas-mask)

der/die Gefangene *adj n* prisoner (**der/die Kriegsgefangene**
prisoner of war; **das Gefangenenlager** [-] prisoner of war camp)

die Geisel [-n] [*always f*] hostage (***nehmen** take; **das Lösegeld**
ransom)

die Grausamkeit cruelty

der/die Held/in [-en/-nen] hero (**das Heldentum** heroism; **die
Heldentat** [-en] exploit)

die Invasion [-en] invasion

der Kampf [=e] combat; fight (**der Zweikampf** duel)

die Kapitulation capitulation; surrender

das Kommando [-s] command; commando

das Konzentrationslager [-]; **das KZ** [*pl* - or -s] concentration
camp

der Krieg [-e] war (**der erste/zweite Weltkrieg** the First/Second
World War; **Krieg führen/er'klären** make/declare war)

das Kriegsgericht [-e] court martial

das Kriegsmaterial munitions

der Luftangriff [-e] air raid

der Luftschutz air-raid precautions (**der Luftschutzwart** [-e] air-
raid warden; **der Luftschutzbunker** [-]; **der Luftschutzraum** [=e]
air-raid shelter; **der Atombunker** [-] nuclear shelter)

der Marsch [=e] march (**der Vorbeimarsch** march-past)

das Massaker [-] massacre

der Militärdienst military service (**ab|leisten** do)

die Mobilmachung mobilization

die Moral morale (**gut** high; **schlecht** low)

die Munition ammunition (**die Muni** ammo)

der Nachschub supplies

die NATO NATO

die Niederlage [-n] defeat

der Niederschlag [=e] fall-out (**radioaktiv** radioactive)

die Offensive [-n] offensive

das Opfer [-] victim; sacrifice

die Plünderung pillage

der Rückzug [=e] retreat (**den Rückzug *an|treten** beat a retreat)

der Ruhm fame; glory

das Scheitern failure

das Schießen; die Schießerei fire; firing (**unter Beschuß** *m*
  *ge'raten come under fire)
die Schlacht [-en] (bei/von + D) battle (of)
das Schlachtfeld [-er] battlefield
die Schußweite range (**in/außer Schußweite** within/out of range)
der Schützengraben [ˀ] trench
der Sieg [-e] (den Sieg *davon|tragen be victorious; **der/
  die Sieger/in [-/-nen]** victor; **die Besiegten** *pl adj n* the
  conquered)
der/die Spion/in [-e/-nen] spy
der Stacheldraht barbed wire
die Strategie [-n] strategy
die Taktik [-en] tactic(s)
die Tarnung camouflage
der Tod [-e] death
der/die Verbündete *adj n* ally (**die Alliierten** the Allies)
das Verhör [-e] interrogation (**beim Verhör** under interrogation)
der/die Verräter/in [-/-nen] traitor (**das Exekutionskommando [-s]**
  firing-squad)
die Verstärkung *sing* reinforcements
der Wachtposten [-]; [group] die Wache [-n] guard (**Wache
  *haben** be on guard; **die Wache [-n]** [also] sentry)
der Widerstand resistance (**Widerstand leisten** resist)
die Wunde [-n] wound (**die Verwundeten** *pl adj n* the wounded)
der Zivilist [-en] civilian (**Zivil-** civilian *adj*)

*ab|schießen [plane]; ***nieder|schießen** [person] shoot down
*an|greifen attack
be'festigen fortify
be'waffnen arm
blockieren blockade
desertieren desert
Dienst *m* ***haben** be on duty
*ein|fallen in + A invade
*ein|nehmen [town]; ***fest|nehmen** [person] capture
*er'schießen shoot (dead)
er'sticken suffocate

explodieren explode
flüchten flee
kämpfen fight; give battle
kapitulieren capitulate; surrender
*laden load
*leiden suffer
marschieren march
massakrieren massacre
mobil machen mobilize
plündern pillage; plunder
scheitern fail
*schießen shoot
*schlagen beat
schützen protect
sprengen blow up
tarnen camouflage
torpedieren torpedo
töten kill
um'ringen surround
*ver'brennen burn
ver'folgen pursue
ver'gasen gas [kill by gassing] (**mit Gas vergiftet** gassed [on
    battlefield])
ver'sorgen mit + D provide with
ver'stärken reinforce
ver'teidigen defend
ver'wüsten lay waste
zer'stören destroy
zielen/an|legen auf + A aim at (**richten/anlegen/zielen auf** + A
    aim [weapon] at)
sich *zurück|ziehen retreat

blutig bloody
heroisch heroic
kriegerisch warlike
tödlich deadly
tot dead

unversehrt unscathed
vermißt missing
verwundet wounded
wehrlos defenceless

Frieden Peace

die Abrüstung disarmament (**die Atomabrüstung** nuclear disarmament)
die Durchsetzung enforcement
die Freiheit freedom
der Frieden [-] peace; peace settlement (**Frieden *schließen** make peace)
die Konferenz [-en] conference
die Menschenrechte *n pl* human rights
die Neutralität neutrality
der Pakt [-e] pact (***(ab|)schließen** make; conclude)
der Pazifismus pacifism
die Reparationen *f pl* reparations
die Verhandlung [-en] negotiation
der Vertrag [¨-e] treaty (**der Friedensvertrag** peace treaty)
die Waffenruhe [-n] (short) truce
der Waffenstillstand [¨-e] truce; armistice

sich einigen über + A agree about
er'setzen compensate for
garantieren guarantee
ge'währen grant
ratifizieren ratify
***unter'schreiben** sign

Die Wehrmacht und die Luftwaffe
The army and the air force

Achtung! attention! (***still|-/stramm|stehen** stand to attention)
die Armee [-n] army; the armed forces (**die Bundeswehr** Federal Armed Forces; **die reguläre Armee** regular army)

die Artillerie artillery

die Beförderung promotion (**zum . . . befördert *werden** be promoted to the rank of . . .)

der Dienstgrad [-e]; **der Rang** [ⁿe] rank

das Feldlager [-] camp

der Feldposten [-] picket

das Hauptquartier [-e] headquarters

die Infanterie infantry

die Kantine [-n] mess; canteen (**das Kasino** [-s] officers' mess)

die Kaserne [-n] barracks (**der Kasernenhof** [ⁿe] barrack square)

die Kavallerie cavalry

das Kommando [-s] command; order (**der Befehl** [-e] written order; **be'fehligen** be in command of)

die Luftwaffe [-n] air force

der Luftwaffenstützpunkt [ⁿe] air base

das Manöver [-] manœuvre (**im Manöver *sein** be on manœuvres)

die Militärakademie [-n] military academy

die Militärkapelle [-n] military band

die motorisierten Streitkräfte motorized troops

die Patrouille [-n] patrol

der Pionier [-e] engineer (**die Pioniere** the engineers)

die Truppe [-n]; **die Einheit** [-en] unit (**die Truppen** the troops; **das Trüppchen** [-] detachment)

der Urlaub leave

die volle Stärke full strength

die Wachtstube [-n] guardroom

das Wecksignal [-e] reveille

ANGEHÖRIGE PERSONNEL

der Befehlshaber [-] commander (**der Oberbefehlshaber** Commander-in-Chief)

der/die Berufssoldat/in [-en/-nen] regular

der Brigadegeneral [*pl* -e or ⁿe]; **der Brigadier** [-s] brigadier/air commodore

der/die Einberufene *adj n* conscript

der Feldmarschall [ⁿe] field marshal/marshal of the air force

der Feldwebel [-] sergeant
der Gefreite *adj n* lance-corporal/aircraftman first class
der General [*pl* -e or ∹e] general/air chief marshal
der Generalleutnant [-s] lieutenant-general/air marshal
der Generalmajor [-e] major-general/air vice-marshal
der Hauptfeldwebel [-] staff sergeant/flight sergeant
der Hauptgefreite *adj n* corporal/leading aircraftman
der Hauptmann [*pl* -leute] captain/flight lieutenant
der Kaplan [∹e] chaplain
der Kommandant [-en] commandant
der Leutnant [-s] second lieutenant/pilot officer
der Oberleutnant [-s] lieutenant/flying officer
der Oberst [G -en or -s; *pl* -en or -e] colonel/group captain
der Oberstleutnant [-s] lieutenant-colonel/wing commander
der Offizier [-e] officer
der Major [-e] major/squadron leader
der Rekrut [-en] recruit
der/die Soldat/in [-en/-nen] soldier (**der einfache Soldat** private/
  aircraftman second class; **Soldat Schmidt** Private Schmidt/
  AC 2 Schmidt; **der Unbekannte Soldat** the Unknown Soldier)
der Träger [-] stretcher-bearer
der Unteroffizier [-e] non-commissioned officer; corporal

EINHEITEN UNITS

das Bataillon [-e] battalion
die Brigade [-n] brigade
die Division [-en] division
die Gruppe [-n] squadron (**die Schwadron** [-en] cavalry squadron)
die Kompanie [-n] company
das Korps [-] corps
das Regiment [*pl* -e or -er] regiment
die Staffel [-n] flight
der Trupp [-s] squad; detachment

KRIEGSGERÄT ARMAMENTS

das Bajonett [-e] bayonet (**auf|pflanzen** fix)

die Bombe [-n] bomb (**die Atom-/Brand-/Napalmbombe** atom/incendiary/napalm bomb; **die H-Bombe** H-bomb; ***ab|werfen** drop)

der Bomber [-] bomber (**das Ziel** [-e] target; ***treffen** hit)

die Flugabwehr anti-aircraft defence (**die Flak** [-] [= **Flugabwehrkanone**] anti-aircraft gun)

das Flugzeug [-e] aircraft (**das Kampf-/Aufklärungsflugzeug** combat/reconnaissance aircraft)

das Gewehr [-e] gun; rifle

die Granate [-n] shell (**die Handgranate** hand-grenade)

die Haubitze [-n] howitzer

der Jäger [-] fighter (**der Jagdflieger** [-] fighter pilot; **der Abfangjäger** interceptor aircraft)

der Kampfhubschrauber [-] helicopter gunship

die Kanone [-n] cannon

die Kugel [-n] bullet (**die Patrone** [-n] cartridge)

die Landmine [-n] land-mine

das Maschinengewehr [-e]; **das MG** [-s] machine-gun

der Minenwerfer [-]; **der Mörser** [-] mortar

der Panzer [-] tank (**der Panzerwagen** [-] armoured car; **die Panzerfahrzeuge** *n pl* armour)

die Pistole [-n] pistol (**die Maschinenpistole** sub-machine-gun)

das/der Radar radar

die Rakete [-n]; **das Missile** [-s] rocket; missile

der Revolver [-] revolver

das Schwert [-er] sword (***ziehen** draw; **die Scheide** [-n] scabbard)

die Waffe [-n] weapon (**die Schnellfeuerwaffe** automatic weapon)

Die Kriegsmarine The navy

das Boot [-e] boat

der Geschützturm [⸚e] gun turret

die Hängematte [-n] hammock

der Kompaß [-e] compass

die Marine [-n]; **die Flotte** [-n] fleet (**die Kriegsmarine** navy; **der Flottenstützpunkt** [-e] naval base; **die Marineschule** [-n] naval academy; **die Marineuniform** [-en] naval uniform)

die Offiziersmesse [-n] wardroom
das Schiff [-e] ship (**das Kriegsschiff** warship)
der Torpedo [-s] torpedo
die Wache watch **[-n]** (**der wachhabende Offizier [-e]** officer of
the watch)

ANGEHÖRIGE PERSONNEL

der Admiral [*pl* -e or ⸚e] admiral (**der Konter-/Vize-/Großadmiral**
rear-admiral/vice-admiral/admiral of the fleet)
der Gefreite *adj n* able seaman
der Kapitän [-e] captain (**der Korvettenkapitän; der Kapitän-**
leutnant [-s] lieutenant-commander)
der Leutnant zur See sub-lieutenant
der Maat [G -s; *pl* -e or -en] mate; petty officer (**der Obermaat**
chief petty officer)
der Marineflieger [-] naval airman
der Marineoffizier [-e] naval officer
der Marinesoldat [-en] marine
der Matrose [-n] seaman (**der Leichtmatrose** ordinary seaman)
der Oberleutnant zur See lieutenant
der Seeoffiziersanwärter [-] naval cadet

SCHIFFE SHIPS

das Flaggschiff [-e] flagship
der Flugzeugträger [-] aircraft-carrier
die Fregatte [-n] frigate
das Kanonenboot [-e] gunboat
die Korvette [-n] corvette
der Kreuzer [-] cruiser
der Minenleger [-] minelayer (**das Minensuchboot [-e]** mine-
sweeper; **die Mine [-n]** mine)
das Patrouillenboot [-e] patrol boat
das Schlachtschiff [-e] battleship
das U-boot [= Unterseeboot] [-e] submarine
der Zerstörer [-] destroyer

SEE ALSO: **Accidents; History; Politics; Science; Transport**

56. The Weather Das Wetter

die **Änderung** [-en] change
die **Atmosphäre** atmosphere
das **Barometer** [-] barometer
die **Besserung** [-en] improvement
die **Dürre** [-n] drought (die **Dürreperiode** [-n] period of drought)
die **Feuchtigkeit** humidity (die **Luftfeuchtigkeit** atmospheric
  humidity)
der **Himmel** [-] sky (am **Himmel** in the sky)
die **Kälte** cold (**bitter** bitter)
das **Klima** [*pl* -s or **Klimate**] climate
die **Luft** [¨e] air (in der **Luft** in the air; der **Luftdruck** air pressure;
  der **Luftzug** [¨e] draught)
die **Meteorologie** meteorology
die **Sichtweite** visibility
die **Temperatur** [-en] temperature (die **Höchst-/Tiefsttemperatur**
  maximum/minimum temperature; das **Thermometer** [-] thermometer; der **Grad** [-e] degree; **zwanzig Grad** twenty degrees)
die **Wärme**; die **Hitze** heat
das **Wetter** weather (der **Wetterbericht** [-e] weather report; die
  Wettervorhersage [-n] weather forecast; **laut Wettervorhersage**
  according to the forecast)

Wie ist das Wetter? What's the weather like?

es ist . . .
  angenehm pleasant
  drückend oppressive
  eisig icy
  feucht damp
  frostig frosty
  gut good
  heiß hot
  heiter bright; fine

kalt cold
kühl cool
mies foul
mild mild
neb(e)lig foggy; misty
rauh harsh; raw
regnerisch rainy; wet
scheußlich ghastly
schlecht bad
schön nice; fine
schrecklich; furchtbar dreadful; terrible
schwül close
sonnig sunny
stickig stifling
stürmisch stormy
trocken dry
ungünstig heavy
veränderlich changeable
warm warm
windig windy
winterlich wintry

der Himmel ist . . .
  bedeckt overcast
  bewölkt; wolkig cloudy
  dunkel dark
  klar clear
  trüb dull

sich ändern change
sich auf|hellen brighten up
auf|hören stop
auf|klaren clear (up)
***aus|sehen nach** + D look like (**es sieht nach Sturm aus** it looks
  stormy)
sich bessern improve
blitzen flash [lightning]
donnern thunder

drohen threaten
dunkeln grow dark
*frieren freeze (**es wird Frost geben** it'll freeze)
*gießen pour
hageln hail
sich legen die down; blow over
nieseln drizzle
prasseln pelt down
regnen rain (**stark/Bindfäden** *m pl* **regnen** rain hard/cats and
   dogs [literally: *strings*]; **schütten/in Strömen** *m pl* ***gießen** pour
   with rain)
*scheinen shine
*schmelzen melt
schneien snow
stürmen blow a gale
tauen [get warmer]; **auf|tauen** [melt] thaw
sich ver'schlechtern get worse
vorher|sagen forecast
wehen blow [wind]

bei gutem/schlechten Wetter in good/bad weather
bei Regen/Schnee/Kälte in the rain/in snow/in cold weather
im Schatten *m* in the shade
in der Sonne in the sun
in der Wärme in the warm

Wettererscheinungen Weather phenomena

die Aufheiterung [-en] bright period/interval
der Blitz [-e] (flash of) lightning (***(ein|)schlagen in** + A strike;
   der Blitzableiter [-] lightning-conductor)
die Bö(e) [*pl* Böen] squall
die Brise [-n] breeze
die Dämmerung; das Zwielicht twilight (**die Morgendämmerung**
   dawn; **die Abenddämmerung** dusk)
der Donner thunder (**der Donnerschlag [ᵉe]** clap of thunder)
der Dunst haze
das Eis ice (**das Glatteis** black ice; **der Eiszapfen [-]** icicle)

das Erdbeben [-] earthquake
die Flutwelle [-n] tidal wave
der Frost [¨-e] frost (**hart**; **streng** hard)
das Gewitter [-] thunderstorm
der Hagel hail (**das Hagelkorn** [¨-er] hailstone)
die Hitzwelle [-n] heatwave (**die Hundetage** *m pl* dog days)
die Lawine [-n] avalanche
das Mondlicht; **der Mondschein** moonlight (**der Mond** [-e] moon)
der Nebel fog; mist
der Niederschlag [¨-e] precipitation; shower
der Orkan [-e] hurricane
der Regen rain (**der Regentropfen** [-] raindrop; **der Platz-/Schnee-/Niesel-/Dauerregen** cloudburst/sleet/drizzle/continuous rain; **der Regenbogen** [-] rainbow; **der Regenguß** [¨-sse] downpour)
der Reif/Rauhreif hoar frost (**bereift** frost-covered)
der Schatten [-] shade; shadow (**die Finsternis** darkness)
der Schauer [-] shower
der Schnee snow (**die Schneeflocke** [-n] snowflake; **der Schneefall** [¨-e] snowfall; **der Schneesturm** [¨-e] snowstorm; blizzard **das (Schnee)gestöber** [-]; **der Schneeschauer** [-] snow flurry; wintry shower; **der Papp-/Pulverschnee** sticky/powdery snow; **die Schneewehe** [-n] snowdrift; **der Schneematsch** slush; **der Schneeball** [¨-e] snowball; **der Schneemann** [¨-er] snowman)
der Smog smog
die Sonne [-n] sun (**der Sonnenschein** sunshine; **der Sonnenstrahl** [G -(e)s *pl* -en] ray of sunshine; sunbeam)
der Sonnenaufgang [¨-e] sunrise (**der Sonnenuntergang** sunset; **bei Sonnenaufgang/Sonnenuntergang** at sunrise/sunset; ***auf|-/*unter|gehen** rise/set)
der Staub dust (**die Staubwolke** [-n] cloud of dust)
das Sternenlicht starlight (**der Stern** [-e] star)
der Sturm [¨-e] storm; gale
der Tagesanbruch daybreak (**bei Tagesanbruch** at daybreak)
der Tau dew
das Tauwetter thaw
der Tornado [-s] tornado

die Überschwemmung [-en] flood
das Unwetter [-] violent storm; tempest
der Wind [-e] wind (**der Windstoß [ӟe]** gust of wind; **der Nord-/
Süd-/Ost-/Westwind** north/south/east/west wind)
der Wirbelwind [-e] whirlwind (**der Wirbelsturm [ӟe]** cyclone)
die Wolke [-n] cloud (**die Wolkenschicht [-en]** cloud layer; **der
Wolkenbruch [ӟe]** cloudburst; downpour)

SEE ALSO: **Accidents; Clothing; Disasters; Holidays; Nature**